MW00795291

DANGER!

A TRUE HISTORY OF
A GREAT CITY'S WILES
AND TEMPTATIONS

By

WILLIAM F. HOWE

and

ABRAHAM H. HUMMEL

WITH THE
INTRODUCTORY CHAPTER
*The Pleasant Fiction of the
Presumption of Innocence*

First published in 1886

Read & Co.

Copyright © 2020 Read & Co. History

This edition is published by Read & Co. History,
an imprint of Read & Co.

This book is copyright and may not be reproduced or copied in any
way without the express permission of the publisher in writing.

British Library Cataloguing-in-Publication Data
A catalogue record for this book is available
from the British Library.

Read & Co. is part of Read Books Ltd.
For more information visit
www.readandcobooks.co.uk

CONTENTS

THE PLEASANT FICTION OF
THE PRESUMPTION OF INNOCENCE
By Arthur Train.......................................5

PREFACE 21

AUTOBIOGRAPHICAL 25

CHAPTER I
ANCIENT AND MODERN PRISONS 31

CHAPTER II
CRIMINALS AND THEIR HAUNTS.................35

CHAPTER III
STREET ARABS OF BOTH SEXES...................43

CHAPTER IV
STORE GIRLS 56

CHAPTER V
THE PRETTY WAITER GIRL 64

CHAPTER VI
SHOP-LIFTERS....................................76

CHAPTER VII
KLEPTOMANIA....................................86

CHAPTER VIII
PANEL HOUSES AND PANEL THIEVES.............91

CHAPTER IX
A THEATRICAL ROMANCE 99

CHAPTER X
A MARINER'S WOOING...........................119

CHAPTER XI
THE BARON AND "BARONESS".....................131

CHAPTER XII
THE DEMI-MONDE 139

CHAPTER XIII
PASSION'S SLAVES AND VICTIMS 146

CHAPTER XIV
PROCURESSES AND THEIR VICTIMS..............153

CHAPTER XV
QUACKS AND QUACKERY 156

CHAPTER XVI
ABORTION AND THE ABORTIONISTS............167

CHAPTER XVII
DIVORCE..177

CHAPTER XVIII
BLACK-MAIL 186

CHAPTER XIX
ABOUT DETECTIVES 194

CHAPTER XX
GAMBLING AND GAMBLERS.....................207

CHAPTER XXI
GAMBLING MADE EASY 217

CHAPTER XXII
SLUMMING......................................221

CHAPTER XXIII
OUR WASTE BASKET —
CONTEMPORANEOUS RECORDS AND
MEMORANDA OF INTERESTING CASES..........228

THE
PLEASANT FICTION
OF THE PRESUMPTION
OF INNOCENCE

By Arthur Train

There was a great to-do some years ago in the city of New York over an ill-omened young person, Duffy by name, who, falling into the bad graces of the police, was most incontinently dragged to headquarters and "mugged" without so much as "By your leave, sir," on the part of the authorities. Having been photographed and measured (in most humiliating fashion) he was turned loose with a gratuitous warning to behave himself in the future and see to it that he did nothing which might gain him even more invidious treatment.

Now, although many thousands of equally harmless persons had been similarly treated, this particular outrage was made the occasion of a vehement protest to the mayor of the city by a certain member of the judiciary, who pointed out that such things in a civilized community were shocking beyond measure, and called upon the mayor to remove the commissioner of police and all his staff of deputy commissioners for openly violating the law which they were sworn to uphold. But, the commissioner of police, who had sometimes enforced the penal statutes in a way to make him unpopular with machine politicians, saw nothing wrong in what he had done, and, what was more, said so most outspokenly. The judge said, "You did," and the commissioner said, "I didn't." Specifically, the judge was complaining of what had been done to Duffy, but more generally he was charging the police with despotism and oppression and with systematically disregarding the sacred liberties of the citizens which it was their duty to protect.

Accordingly the mayor decided to look into the matter for himself, and after a lengthy investigation came to the alleged conclusion that the "mugging" of Duffy was a most reprehensible thing and that all those who were guilty of having any part therein should be instantly removed from office. He, therefore, issued a pronunciamento to the commissioner demanding the official heads of several of his subordinates, which order the commissioner politely declined to obey. The mayor thereupon removed him and appointed a successor, ostensibly for the purpose of having in the office a man who should conduct the police business of the city with more regard for the liberties of the inhabitants thereof. The judge who had started the rumpus expressed himself as very much pleased and declared that now at last a new era had dawned wherein the government was to be administered with a due regard for law.

Now, curiously enough, although the judge had demanded the removal of the commissioner on the ground that he had violated the law and been guilty of tyrannous and despotic conduct, the mayor had ousted him not for pursuing an illegal course in arresting and "mugging" a presumptively innocent man (for illegal it most undoubtedly was), but for inefficiency and maladministration in his department.

Said the mayor in his written opinion:

"After thinking over this matter with the greatest care, I am led to the conclusion that as mayor of the city of New York I should not order the police to stop taking photographs of people arrested and accused of crime or who have been indicted by grand juries. That grave injustice may occur the Duffy case has demonstrated, but I feel that it is not the taking of the photograph that has given cause to the injustice, but the inefficiency and maladministration of the police department, etc."

In other words, the mayor set the seal of his official

6

approval upon the very practice which caused the injustice to Duffy. "Mugging" was all right, so long as you "mugged" the right persons.

The situation thus outlined was one of more than passing interest. A sensitive point in our governmental nervous system had been touched and a condition uncovered that sooner or later must be diagnosed and cured.

For the police have no right to arrest and photograph a citizen unconvicted of crime, since it is contrary to law. And it is ridiculous to assert that the very guardians of the law may violate it so long as they do so judiciously and do not molest the Duffys. The trouble goes deeper than that. The truth is that we are up against that most delicate of situations, the concrete adjustment of a theoretical individual right to a practical necessity. The same difficulty has always existed and will always continue to exist whenever emergencies requiring prompt and decisive action arise or conditions obtain that must be handled effectively without too much discussion. It is easy while sitting on the piazza with your cigar to recognize the rights of your fellow-men, you may assert most vigorously the right of the citizen to immunity from arrest without legal cause, but if you saw a seedy character sneaking down a side street at three o'clock in the morning, his pockets bulging with jewelry and silver! Would you have the policeman on post insist on the fact that a burglary had been committed being established beyond peradventure before arresting the suspect, who in the meantime would undoubtedly escape? Of course, the worthy officer sometimes does this, but his conduct in that case becomes the subject of an investigation on the part of his superiors. In fact, the rules of the New York police department require him to arrest all persons carrying bags in the small hours who cannot give a satisfactory account of themselves. Yet there is no such thing under the laws of the State as a right "to arrest on suspicion." No citizen may be arrested under the statutes unless a crime has actually been committed. Thus, the police regulations deliberately compel every officer either to violate the law or to be made the subject of charges for dereliction of duty. A confusing state of things, truly, to a man who wants to do his duty by himself and by his fellow-citizens!

The present author once wrote a book dealing with the practical administration of criminal justice, in which the unlawfulness of arrest on mere "suspicion" was discussed at length and given a prominent place. But when the time came for publication that portion of it was omitted at the earnest solicitation of certain of the authorities on the ground that as such arrests were absolutely necessary for the enforcement of the criminal law a public exposition of their illegality would do infinite harm. Now, as it seems, the time has come when the facts, for one reason or another, should be faced. The difficulty does not end, however, with "arrest on suspicion," "the third degree," "mugging," or their allied abuses. It really goes to the root of our whole theory of the administration of the criminal law. Is it possible that on final analysis we may find that our enthusiastic insistence upon certain of the supposedly fundamental liberties of the individual has led us into a condition of legal hypocrisy vastly less desirable than the frank attitude of our continental neighbors toward such subjects?

The Massachusetts Constitution of 1785 concludes with the now famous words: "To the end that this may be a government of laws and not of men." That is the essence of the spirit of American government. Our forefathers had arisen and thrown off the yoke of England and her intolerable system of penal government, in which an accused had no right to testify in his own behalf and under which he could be hung for stealing a sheep. "Liberty!" "Liberty or death!" That was the note ringing in the minds and mouths of the signers of the Declaration and framers of the Constitution. That is the popular note to-day of the Fourth of July orator and of the Memorial Day address. This liberty was to be guaranteed by laws in such a way that it was never to be curtailed or violated. No mere man was to be given an opportunity to tamper with it. The individual was to be protected at all costs. No king, or sheriff, or judge, or officer was to lay his finger on a free man save at his peril. If he did, the free man might immediately have his "law"—"have the law on him," as the good old expression was—for no king or sheriff was above the law. In fact, we were so energetic in providing safeguards for the individual, even when a wrong-doer, that we paid very little attention to the effectiveness of kings or sheriffs or what we had substituted for them. And so it is to-day. What candidate for office, what silver-tongued orator or senator, what demagogue or preacher could hold his audience or capture a vote if, when it came to a question of liberty, he should lift up his voice in behalf of the rights of the majority as against the individual?

Accordingly in devising our laws We have provided in every possible way for the freedom of the citizen from all interference on the part of the authorities. No one may be stopped, interrogated, examined, or arrested unless a crime has been committed. Every one is presumed to be innocent until shown to be guilty by the verdict of a jury. No one's premises may be entered or searched without a warrant which the law renders it difficult to obtain. Every accused has the right to testify in his own behalf, like any other witness. The fact that he has been held for a crime by a magistrate and indicted by a grand jury places him at not the slightest disadvantage so far as defending himself against the charge is concerned, for he must be proven guilty beyond any reasonable doubt. These illustrations of the jealousy of the law for the rights of citizens might be multiplied to no inconsiderable extent. Further, our law allows a defendant convicted of crime to appeal to the highest courts, whereas if he be acquitted the people or State of New York have no right of appeal at all.

Without dwelling further on the matter it is enough to say that in general the State constitutions, their general laws, or penal statutes provide that a person who is accused or suspected of crime must be presumed innocent and treated accordingly until his guilt has been affirmatively established in a jury trial; that meantime he must not be confined or detained unless a crime has in fact been committed and there is at least reasonable cause to believe that he has committed it; and, further, that if arrested he must be given an immediate opportunity to secure bail, to have the advice of counsel, and must in no way be compelled to give any evidence against himself. So much for the law. It is as plain as a pikestaff. It is printed in the books in words of one syllable. So far as the law is concerned we have done our best to perpetuate the theories of those who, fearing that they might be arrested without a hearing, transported for trial, and convicted in a king's court before a king's judge for a crime they knew nothing of, insisted on "liberty or death." They had had enough of kings and their ways. Hereafter they were to have "a government of laws and not of men."

But the unfortunate fact remains that all laws, however perfect, must in the end be administered by imperfect men. There is, alas! no such thing as a government of laws and not of men. You may have a government more of laws and less of men, or vice versa, but you cannot have an auto-administration of the Golden Rule. Sooner or later you come to a man—in the White House, or on a wool sack, or at a desk in an office, or in a blue coat and brass buttons—and then, to a very considerable extent, the question of how far ours is to be a government of laws or of men depends upon him. Generally, so far as he is concerned, it is going to be of man, for every official finds that the letter of the law works an injustice many times out of a hundred. If he is worth his salary he will try to temper justice with mercy. If he is human he will endeavor to accomplish justice as he sees it so long as the law can be stretched to accommodate the case. Thus, inevitably there is a conflict between the law and its application. It is the human element in the administration of the law that enables lawyers to get a living. It is usually not difficult to tell what the law is; the puzzle is how it is going to be applied in any individual case. How it is going to be applied depends very largely upon the practical side of the matter and the exigencies of existing conditions.

It is pretty hard to apply inflexibly laws over a hundred years old. It is equally hard to police a city of a million or so polyglot inhabitants with a due regard to their theoretic constitutional rights. But suppose in addition that these theoretic rights are entirely theoretic and fly in the face of the laws of nature, experience, and common sense? What then? What is a police commissioner to do who has either got to make an illegal arrest or let a crook get away, who must violate the rights of men illegally detained by outrageously "mugging" them or egregiously fail to have a record of the professional criminals in his bailiwick? He does just what all of us do under similar conditions—he "takes a chance." But in the case of the police the thing is so necessary that there ceases practically to be any "chance" about it. They have got to prevent crime and arrest criminals. If they fail they are out of a job, and others more capable or less scrupulous take their places. The fundamental law qualifying all systems is that of necessity. You can't let professional crooks carry off a voter's silverware simply because the voter, being asleep, is unable instantly to demonstrate beyond a reasonable doubt that his silver has been stolen. You can't permit burglars to drag sacks of loot through the streets of the city at 4 A.M. simply because they are presumed to be innocent until proven guilty. And if "arrest on suspicion" were not permitted, demanded by the public, and required by the police ordinances, away would go the crooks and off would go the silverware, the town would be full of "leather snatchers" and "strong-arm men," respectable citizens would be afraid to go out o' nights, and liberty would degenerate into license. That is the point. We Americans, or at least some of the newer ones of us, have an idea that "liberty" means the right to steal apples from our neighbor's orchard without interference. Now, somewhere or other, there has got to be a switch and a strong arm to keep us in order, and the switch and arm must not wait until the apples are stolen and eaten before getting busy. If we come climbing over the fence sweating apples at every pore, is Farmer Jones to go and count his apples before grabbing us?

The most presumptuous of all presumptions is this "presumption of innocence." It really doesn't exist, save in the mouths of judges and in the pages of the law books. Yet as much to-do is made about it as if it were a living legal principle. Every judge in a criminal case is required to charge the jury in form or substance somewhat as follows: "The defendant is presumed to be innocent until that presumption is removed by competent evidence"... "This presumption is his property, remaining with him throughout the trial and until rebutted by the verdict of the jury."... "The jury has no right to consider the fact that the defendant stands at the bar accused of a crime by an indictment found by the grand jury." Shades of Sir Henry Hawkins! Does the judge expect that they are actually to swallow that? Here is a jury sworn "to a true verdict find" in the case of an ugly looking customer at the bar who is charged with knocking down an old man and stealing his watch. The old man—an apostolic looking octogenarian—is sitting right over there where the jury can see him. One look at the plaintiff and one at the accused and the jury may be heard to mutter, "He's guilty,—all right!"

"Presumed to be innocent?" Why, may I ask? Do not the jury and everybody else know that this good old man would never, save by mistake, accuse anybody falsely of crime? Innocence! Why, the natural and inevitable presumption is that the defendant is guilty! The human mind works intuitively by comparison and experience. We assume or presume with considerable confidence that parents love their children, that all college presidents are great and good men, and that wild bulls are dangerous animals. We may be wrong. But it is up to the other fellow to show us the contrary.

Now, if out of a clear sky Jones accuses Robinson of being a thief we know by experience that the chances are largely in favor of Jones's accusation being well founded. People as a rule don't go rushing around charging each other with being crooks unless they have some reason for it. Thus, at the very beginning the law flies in the face of probabilities when it tells us that a man accused of crime must be presumed to be innocent. In point of fact, whatever presumption there is (and this varies with the circumstances) is all the other way, greater or less depending upon the particular attitude of mind and experience of the individual.

This natural presumption of guilt from the mere fact of the charge is rendered all the more likely by reason of the uncharitable readiness with which we believe evil of our fellows. How unctuously we repeat some hearsay bit of scandal. "I suppose you have heard the report that Deacon Smith has stolen the church funds?" we say to our friends with a sententious sigh—the outward sign of an invisible satisfaction. Deacon Smith after the money-bag? Ha! ha! Of course, he's guilty! These deacons are always guilty! And in a few minutes Deacon Smith is ruined forever, although the fact of the matter may well have been that he was but counting the money in the collection-plate. This willingness to believe the worst of others is a matter of common knowledge and of historical and literary record. "The evil that men do lives after them—" It might well have been put, "The evil men are said to have done lives forever." However unfair, this is a psychologic condition which plays an important part in rendering the presumption of innocence a gross absurdity.

But let us press the history of Jones and Robinson a step further. The next event in the latter's criminal history is his appearance in court before a magistrate. Jones produces his evidence and calls his witnesses. Robinson, through his learned counsel, cross-examines them and then summons his own witnesses to prove his innocence. The proceeding may take several days or perhaps weeks. Briefs are submitted. The magistrate considers the testimony and finally decides that he believes Robinson guilty and must hold him for the action of the grand jury. You might now, it would perhaps seem, have

13

some reason for suspecting that Robinson was not all that he should be. But no! He is still presumed in the eyes of the law, and theoretically in the eyes of his fellows, to be as innocent as a babe unborn. And now the grand jury take up and sift the evidence that has already been gone over by the police judge. They, too, call witnesses and take additional testimony. They likewise are convinced of Robinson's guilt and straightway hand down an indictment accusing him of the crime. A bench warrant issues. The defendant is run to earth and ignominiously haled to court. But he is still presumed to be innocent! Does not the law say so? And is not this a "government of laws"? Finally, the district attorney, who is not looking for any more work than is absolutely necessary, investigates the case, decides that it must be tried and begins to prepare it for trial. As the facts develop themselves Robinson's guilt becomes more and more clear. The unfortunate defendant is given any opportunity he may desire to explain away the charge, but to no purpose.

The district attorney knows Robinson is guilty, and so does everybody else, including Robinson. At last this presumably innocent man is brought to the bar for trial. The jury scan his hang-dog countenance upon which guilt is plainly written. They contrast his appearance with that of the honest Jones. They know he has been accused, held by a magistrate, indicted by a grand jury, and that his case, after careful scrutiny, has been pressed for trial by the public prosecutor. Do they really presume him innocent? Of course not. They presume him guilty. "So soon as I see him come through dot leetle door in the back of the room, then I know he's guilty!" as the foreman said in the old story. What good does the presumption of innocence, so called, do for the miserable Robinson? None whatever—save perhaps to console him in the long days pending his trial. But such a legal hypocrisy could never have deceived anybody. How much better it would be to cast aside all such cant and frankly admit that the attitude of the continental law toward the man under arrest is founded upon common sense and the experience of mankind.

14

If he is the wrong man it should not be difficult for him to demonstrate the fact. At any rate circumstances are against him, and he should be anxious to explain them away if he can.

The fact of the matter is, that in dealing with practical conditions, police methods differ very little in different countries. The authorities may perhaps keep considerably more detailed "tabs" on people in Europe than in the United States, but if they are once caught in a compromising position they experience about the same treatment wherever they happen to be. In France (and how the apostles of liberty condemn the iniquity of the administration of criminal justice in that country!) the suspect or undesirable receives a polite official call or note, in which he is invited to leave the locality as soon as convenient. In New York he is arrested by a plainclothes man, yanked down to Mulberry Street for the night, and next afternoon is thrust down the gangplank of a just departing Fall River liner. Many an inspector has earned unstinted praise (even from the New York Evening Post) by "clearing New York of crooks" or having a sort of "round-up" of suspicious characters whom, after proper identification, he has ejected from the city by the shortest and quickest possible route. Yet in the case of every person thus arrested and driven out of the town he has undoubtedly violated constitutional rights and taken the law into his own hands.

What redress can a penniless tramp secure against a stout inspector of police able and willing to spend a considerable sum of money in his own defence, and with the entire force ready and eager to get at the tramp and put him out of business? He swallows his pride, if he has any, and ruefully slinks out of town for a period of enforced abstinence from the joys of metropolitan existence. Yet who shall say that, in spite of the fact that it is a theoretic outrage upon liberty, this cleaning out of the city is not highly desirable? One or two comparatively innocent men may be caught in the ruck, but they generally manage to intimate to the police that the latter have "got them wrong" and duly make their escape. The others resume their tramp from city to city, clothed in the presumption of their innocence.

Since the days of the Doges or of the Spanish Inquisition there has never been anything like the morning inspection or "line up" of arrested suspects at the New York police head-quarters.* (*Now abolished.) One by one the unfortunate persons arrested during the previous night (although not charged with any crime) are pointed out to the assembled detective force, who scan them from beneath black velvet masks in order that they themselves may not be recognized when they meet again on Broadway or the darker side streets of the city. Each prisoner is described and his character and past performances are rehearsed by the inspector or head of the bureau. He is then measured, "mugged," and, if lucky, turned loose. What does his liberty amount to or his much-vaunted legal rights if the city is to be made safe? Yet why does not some apostle of liberty raise his voice and cry aloud concerning the wrong that has been done? Are not the rights of a beggar as sacred as those of a bishop?

One of the most sacred rights guaranteed under the law is that of not being compelled to give evidence against ourselves or to testify to anything which might degrade or incriminate us. Now, this is all very fine for the chap who has his lawyer at his elbow or has had some similar previous experience. He may wisely shut up like a clam and set at defiance the tortures of the third degree. But how about the poor fellow arrested on suspicion of having committed a murder, who has never heard of the legal provision in question, or, if he has, is cajoled or threatened into "answering one or two questions"? Few police officers take the trouble to warn those whom they arrest that what they say may be used against them. What is the use? Of course, when they testify later at the trial they inevitably begin their testimony with the stereotyped phrase, "I first warned the defendant that anything which he said might be used against him." If they did warn him they probably whispered it or mumbled it so that he didn't hear what they said, or, in any event, whether they said it or not, half a dozen of them probably took him into a back room

16

and, having set him with his back against the wall, threatened and swore at him until he told them what he knew, or thought he knew, and perhaps confessed his crime. When the case comes to trial the police give the impression that the accused quietly summoned them to his cell to make a voluntary statement. The defendant denies this, of course, but the evidence goes in and the harm has been done. No doubt the methods of the inquisition are in vogue the world over under similar conditions. Everybody knows that a statement by the accused immediately upon his arrest is usually the most important evidence that can be secured in any case. It is a police officer's duty to secure one if he can do so by legitimate means. It is his custom to secure one by any means in his power. As his oath, that such a statement was voluntary, makes it ipso facto admissible as evidence, the statutes providing that a defendant cannot be compelled to give evidence against himself are practically nullified.

In the more important cases the accused is usually put through some sort of an inquisitorial process by the captain at the station-house. If he is not very successful at getting anything out of the prisoner the latter is turned over to the sergeant and a couple of officers who can use methods of a more urgent character. If the prisoner is arrested by headquarters detectives, various efficient devices to compel him to "give up what he knows" may be used—such as depriving him of food and sleep, placing him in a cell with a "stool pigeon" who will try to worm a confession out of him, and the usual moral suasion of a heart-to-heart talk in the back room with the inspector.

This is the darker side of the picture of practical government. It is needless to say that the police do not always suggest the various safeguards and privileges which the law accords to defendants thus arrested, but the writer is free to confess that, save in exceptional cases, he believes the rigors of the so-called third degree to be greatly exaggerated. Frequently in dealing with rough men rough methods are used, but considering the multitude of offenders, and the thousands of police officers, none of whom have been trained in a school of gentleness, it is surprising that severer treatment is not generally met with on the part of those who run afoul of the criminal law. The ordinary "cop" tries to do his duty as effectively as he can. With the average citizen gruffness and roughness go a long way in the assertion of authority. In the task of policing a big city, the rights of the individual must indubitably suffer to a certain extent if the rights of the multitude are to be properly protected. We can make too much of small injustices and petty incivilities. Police business is not gentle business. The officers are trying to prevent you and me from being knocked on the head some dark night or from being chloroformed in our beds. Ten thousand men are trying to do a thirty-thousand-man job. The struggle to keep the peace and put down crime is a hard one anywhere. It requires a strong arm that cannot show too punctilious a regard for theoretical rights when prompt decisions have to be made and equally prompt action taken. The thieves and gun men have got to be driven out. Suspicious characters have got to be locked up. Somehow or other a record must be kept of professional criminals and persons likely to be active in law-breaking. These are necessities in every civilized country. They are necessities here. Society employs the same methods of self-protection the world over. No one presumes a person charged with crime to be innocent, either in Delhi, Pekin, Moscow, or New York. Under proper circumstances we believe him guilty. When he comes to be tried the jury consider the evidence, and if they are reasonably sure he is guilty they convict him. The doctrine of reasonable doubt is almost as much of a fiction as that of the presumption of innocence. From the time a man is arrested until arraignment he is quizzed with a view to inducing him to admit his offence or give some evidence that may help convict him. Logically, why should not a person charged with a crime be obliged to give what explanation he can of the affair? Why should he have the privilege of silence? Doesn't he owe a duty to the public the same as any other witness? If he is innocent he has nothing to fear; if he is guilty—away with him! The French have no false ideas about such things and at the same time they have a high regard for liberty. We merely cheat ourselves into thinking that our liberty is something different from French liberty because we have a lot of laws upon our statute books that are there only to be disregarded and would have to be repealed instantly if enforced.

Take, for instance, the celebrated provision of the penal laws that the failure of an accused to testify in his own behalf shall not be taken against him. Such a doctrine flies in the face of human nature. If a man sits silent when witnesses under oath accuse him of a crime it is an inevitable inference that he has nothing to say—that no explanation of his would explain. The records show that the vast majority of accused persons who do not avail themselves of the opportunity to testify are convicted. Thus, the law which permits a defendant to testify in reality compels him to testify, and a much-invoked safeguard of liberty turns out to be a privilege in name only. In France or America alike a man accused of crime sooner or later has to tell what he knows—or take his medicine. It makes little difference whether he does so under the legalized interrogation of a "juge d'instruction" in Paris or under the quasi-voluntary examination of an assistant district attorney or police inspector in New York. It is six of one and half a dozen of the other if at his trial in France he remains mute under examination or in America refrains from availing himself of the privilege of testifying in his own behalf.

Thus, we are reluctantly forced to the conclusion that all human institutions have their limitations, and that, however theoretically perfect a government of laws may be, it must be administered by men whose chief regard will not be the idealization of a theory of liberty so much as an immediate solution of some concrete problem.

Not that the matter, after all, is particularly important to most of us, but laws which exist only to be broken create a disrespect and disregard for law which may ultimately be dangerous. It would be perfectly simple for the legislature to say that a citizen might be arrested under circumstances tending to create a reasonable suspicion, even if he had not committed a crime, and it would be quite easy to pass a statute providing that the commissioner of police might "mug" and measure all criminals immediately after conviction. As it is, the prison authorities won't let him, so he has to do it while he has the opportunity.

It must be admitted that this is rather hard on the innocent, but they now have to suffer with the guilty for the sins of an indolent and uninterested legislature. Moreover, if such a right of arrest were proposed, some wiseacre or politician would probably rise up and denounce the suggestion as the first step in the direction of a military dictatorship. Thus, we shall undoubtedly fare happily on in the blissful belief that our personal liberties are the subject of the most solicitous and zealous care on the part of the authorities, guaranteed to us under a government which is not of men but of laws, until one of us happens to be arrested (by mistake, of course) and learns by sad experience the practical methods of the police in dealing with criminals and the agreeable but deceptive character of the pleasant fiction of the presumption of innocence.

A CHAPTER FROM
Courts and Criminals, 1912

PREFACE

It may not be amiss to remark, in explanation of the startling and sensational title chosen for this production, that logic has not yet succeeded in framing a title-page which shall clearly indicate the nature of a book. The greatest adepts have frequently taken refuge in some fortuitous word, which has served their purpose better than the best results of their analysis. So it was in the present case. "Danger!" is a thrilling and warning word, suggestive of the locomotive headlight, and especially applicable to the subject matter of the following pages, in which the crimes of a great city are dissected and exposed from the arcanum or confessional of what we may be pardoned for designating the best-known criminal law offices in America.

So much for the title. A few words as to the *motif* of the publication. Despite the efficiency of our police and the activity of our many admirable reforming and reclaiming systems, crime still abounds, while the great tide of social impurity continues to roll on with unabated velocity. Optimists and philanthropic dreamers in every age have pictured in glowing colors the gradual but sure approach of the millennium, yet we are, apparently, still as far from that elysium of purity and unselfishness as ever. Whenever the wolf and the lamb lie down together, the innocent bleater is invariably inside the other's ravenous maw. There may be—and we have reason to know that there is—a marked diminution in certain forms of crime, but there are others in which surprising fertility of resource and ingenuity of method but too plainly evince that the latest developments of science and skill are being successfully pressed into the service of the modern criminal. Increase of education and scientific skill not only confers superior facilities for the successful perpetration of crime, but also for its concealment. The revelations of the newspapers, from week to week, but too plainly indicate an undercurrent of vice and iniquity, whose depth and foulness defy all computation.

We are not in accord with those pessimists who speak of New York as a boiling caldron of crime, without any redeeming features or hopeful elements. But our practice in the courts and our association with criminals of every kind, and the knowledge consequently gained of their history and antecedents, have demonstrated that, in a great city like New York, the germs of evil in human life are developed into the rankest maturity. As the eloquent Dr. Guthrie, in his great work, "The City, its Sins and its Sorrows," remarks: "Great cities many have found to be great curses. It had been well for many an honest lad and unsuspecting country girl that hopes of higher wages and opportunities of fortune, that the gay attire and gilded story of some acquaintance, had never turned their steps cityward, nor turned them from the simplicity and safety of their country home. Many a foot that once lightly pressed the heather or brushed the dewy grass has wearily trodden in darkness, guilt and remorse, on these city pavements. Happy had it been for many had they never exchanged the starry skies for the lamps of the town, nor had left their quiet villages for the throng and roar of the big city's streets. Weil for them had they heard no roar but the river's, whose winter flood it had been safer to breast; no roar but ocean's, whose stormiest waves it had been safer to ride, than encounter the flood of city temptations, which has wrecked their virtue and swept them into ruin."

By hoisting the Danger signal at the mast-head, as it were, we have attempted to warn young men and young women— the future fathers and mothers of America—against the snares and pitfalls of the crime and the vice that await the unwary in New York. Our own long and extensive practice at the bar has furnished most of the facts; some, again, are on file in our criminal courts of record; and some, as has already been hinted, have been derived from the confidential revelations of our private office. With the desire that this book shall prove a useful warning and potent monitor to those for whose benefit and instruction it has been designed, and in the earnest hope that, by its influence, some few may be saved from prison, penitentiary, lunatic asylum, or suicides' purgatory, it is now submitted to the intelligent readers of America,

By the public's obedient servants,

HOWE & HUMMEL

William F. Howe

AUTOBIOGRAPHICAL

It is to be presumed that the readers of this book will expect a few words on a subject "on which," as Lord Byron somewhere remarks, "all men are supposed to be fluent and none agreeable—self." However much the inclination and, I might add, temptation may run in the direction of fluency and diffuseness in this case, my utterance shall be as brief as possible. I, William F. Howe, founder of the law firm of Howe & Hummel, was born in Shawmut street, in Boston, Mass., on the seventh day of July, 1828. My father was the Rev. Samuel Howe, M. A., a rather well-known and popular Episcopal clergyman at the Hub in those days. Our family removed to England when I was yet very young, and consequently my earliest recollections are of London. I remember going to school, where I speedily developed a genius for mischief and for getting into scrapes. I received a liberal allowance of the floggings then fashionable, and I can recall the *hwhish* of the implement of torture to this day. We are all young but once, and when memory calls up the lively pitched battles, and the pummelings I got and gave at school, I am young again—only my waist is a good deal more expansive, my step is not so elastic or my sight so clear. I could recall the names of some of those boys with whom I fought in those happy school days, and tell how one now adorns the British bench, how another holds a cabinet portfolio, how another fell bravely fighting in Africa, and how several, striving neither for name or fame,

> "Along the cool, sequestered vale of life
> Pursue the noiseless tenor of their way";

25

but it would be useless, as would also my experiences at church, listening to my good father's sermons, and falling constantly asleep.

My youthful reminiscences of events which happened, and of which I heard or read in my youth, are mostly chaotic and incongruous; but it is otherwise with the murders. I remember with what thrilling interest I read the story of Greenacre, who cut up the body of his victim, carrying the head wrapped up in a handkerchief, on his knees in the omnibus, and who was supposed to have nearly fainted with fright when, on asking the conductor the fare, received the answer, "Sixpence a *head!*" Then there was the horrible Daniel Good, the coachman at Roehampton, and the monster Courvoisier, the Swiss valet, who murdered his master, Lord William Russell. These atrocities and the trials at Old Bailey, no doubt, gave my mind the bent for the criminal law, not that I was in any sense conscious of the possession of superior powers. It was merely the selective tendency of a fresh and buoyant mind, rather vigorous than contemplative, and in which the desire for a special field of action is but the symptom of health.

At the age of twenty, I entered King's College, London, with the son of the great American statesman and historian, Edward Everett, and succeeded in graduating with some distinction. Soon after, I entered the office of Mr. George Waugh, a noted barrister. 1 had the good fortune to meet the commendation of Mr. Waugh, and I was consequently placed at the head of his corps of assistants, and frequently appeared in the English courts in place of my employer. My connection with this office lasted about eight years, and then, in pursuance of an intention long prior formed and never relinquished, I returned to the country of my birth. My earliest essays at the American bar have been fairly and impartially told by another pen, and, as the autobiographical form of narrative has its limitations as well as its advantages, the reader will pardon me if in this place I drop the "ego" and quote:

"On arriving here, Mr. Howe entered the office of E. H. Seeley, Esq., one of our oldest legal practitioners. Here he remained one year, studying American law and practice with persistent assiduity, and frequently appearing in our courts, 'by grace,' until he was fully licensed. And it may be here stated that out of a list of over one hundred candidates for admission to the bar only eighteen passed, and in that number was included the young lawyer from London.

"His first case of importance in this city was one of extreme delicacy, being a test question as to whether Col. Walter W. Price, a wealthy brewer, was entitled to the position of Colonel of the First Cavalry Regiment, N. G. S. N. Y., he having received the *second* highest number of votes. Mr. Howe took the ground that his client was entitled to the office, being a resident of this city, while his competitor, Smith, the founder of the great umbrella house, who had received the largest number of ballots, resided in Brooklyn. This question was argued before the Brigade Court, and, its decision being adverse, Mr. Howe carried the case to the Court of Appeals, where a favorable decision was rendered, and Mr. Price duly installed in the position. This was the young lawyer's first technical victory of note, and it brought him almost at once into considerable prominence.

"He soon after opened an office at the corner of Chambers and Centre streets, devoted his entire time and energy to civil matters, was highly successful, and soon achieved a considerable share of popularity. In 1859, finding himself crowded with business, he removed to his present large suite of offices on the corner of Centre and Leonard streets, which had formerly been occupied by the late Judge Russell, and from that time down to the present he has made criminal matters a specialty.

"Mr. Howe's first appearance in the New York courts as a criminal lawyer was in 1859. A man, by the name of Devine, had been tried and convicted in the Court of Special Sessions on a charge of larceny. He took Devine's case to the General Term of the Supreme Court, contending that the conviction was illegal, inasmuch as the statute provides that *three* justices should sit, whereas at the trial of Devine but *two* had attended. Many members of the bar laughed at him, declaring his position untenable. In this he was opposed by Assistant District Attorney, the present Chief Justice, Sedgwick. The Court decided the point well taken and ordered the discharge of the prisoner, Devine.

"In defending a German named Jacob Weiler, indicted for the murder of his wife, by shooting, in 1862, Mr. Howe took the ground that the deceased shot herself, a discharged pistol being found by her side. This case was very thoroughly canvassed by the entire press of the city, and occasioned the greatest excitement among the German population. The trial lasted eight days, and resulted in a disagreement of the jury. At this stage of the proceedings, owing to a misunderstanding (which it would hardly be in good taste to explain at this late day), Mr. Howe withdrew from the defense. Other counsel were substituted, when the case was re-tried, and the prisoner was convicted and sentenced to state prison for life.

"Mr. Howe has tried more capital cases than any six lawyers in America combined. There has not been a murder case of note for the past twenty-five years in which he has not appeared as counsel. The records of the Courts of Oyer and Terminer and General Sessions show that he has tried more than three hundred homicide cases since the year 1860. Mr. Howe, as a specialist in diseases of the brain, is regarded by physicians as the peer of the most eminent alienists in practice."

The circumstances under which Mr. A. H. Hummel became associated with me, first as an office boy, in 1863, at a salary of two dollars per week, and subsequently, in May, 1869, as my partner, have been told more than once in the public press. Mr. Hummel was born in Boston, July 27, 1849; came, with his parents, to this city at an early age; attended Public School No. 15, on East Fifth street, and made my acquaintance on a January morning before he was fourteen years old. I have at hand a newspaper clipping, taken from the Rochester, N. Y., *Democrat*

28

and Chronicle of March 25, 1877, in which is printed an elaborate notice of the law firm of Howe & Hummel, in which the junior partner is thus characterized:

"Soon after Mr. Howe opened his office, a bright lad, conversant with foreign languages, applied on a cold January morning, in the year 1863, for employment, and was accepted. His duties as office boy were to answer questions, make fires, do errands, and do copying and translations. Such was his winning address, his ready tact, his quick perceptions, his prudence and discretion, that he not only performed his duties to perfection but, in his few spare moments, learned law. While he grew but little in stature, he made great progress in his chosen profession. As he had fluent command of the German language—a useful adjunct to the practice of a criminal lawyer in New York—and gave promise of attaining a high rank as an advocate, Mr. Howe made him his partner before he was admitted to the bar. To-day, in stature, he is probably the smallest professional man in America; but size is not 'the standard of the man,' and if Abe's stature were in proportion to his merit he would be a veritable giant indeed."

With this sentiment I most cordially coincide, and at the same time bring these somewhat rambling and discursive reminiscences to an end.

WILLIAM F. HOWE

DANGER!

CHAPTER I

ANCIENT AND MODERN PRISONS

From old Dutch and Knickerbocker records it appears that as far back as the year 1600 there existed a place for the confinement of malefactors in the City of New York. At that early date in its history the town must certainly have been restricted to a half dozen or so of narrow, crooked streets, in the immediate vicinity of what is now known as the Bowling Green. The population did not, probably, number more than a few thousands; but, nevertheless, we find from these same records that, even in that small community, criminals were so numerous and crime so rife that a jail or Bridewell had already been established for the safe-keeping and punishment of evildoers, and a system of citizen-police inaugurated for the preservation of the local peace.

It was not, however, until some years later, 1642, that the "Staat Huys" was built, a municipal building, with a portion of it erected especially for the housing of dangerous criminals. Thus it would seem that for upwards of two centuries crime and criminals have had their haunts in this city, and, it is safe to say, while the more ancient cities of Europe have, unquestionably, originated more felons of every grade, there are few places that can rival New York in the number of actual crimes committed

31

during its comparatively brief existence on the earth's map.

During the earlier history of the embryo city, the nature of the offenses perpetrated on the then small community, and the type of men who boldly executed the crimes, were undoubtedly of the same pattern as those which obtain among us to-day, but with this difference, that with the onward march of Improvement, hand-in-hand with the progress of Science and Civilization, have also grimly stalked fashionably-clothed and modernly-equipped Crime and the scientifically-perfected law-breaker, with his modern and improved methods. Man's villainies, like his other passions, remain the same to-day as when the murderous club of Cain crushed the skull of his brother Abel, and the maiden earth was crimsoned with the first blood that appealed for vengeance. They differ only in the manner of commission, and the commission would appear to be assisted by modern invention and appliances.

To expect large civilized communities dwelling together to be free from crime would be to imagine an elysium on earth, for where poverty exists crime will assuredly be found, and poverty will never be divorced from civilization. It would also appear that, in accordance with the growth and expansion of the young city in other respects, vice and crime kept pace, while youthful depravity early began to trouble the good people then as it worries the same class of persons to-day, for in 1824 we find that a House of Refuge, for the reformation of juvenile delinquents, was built, ostensibly superseding the old "Society for the Prevention of Pauperism." To follow in detail the history of crime in this city, from so early a date, would be of very little service here, but a simple chronicle, referring to the periods at which prisons were found to be necessary, may be briefly touched upon as tending to show how crime increased and criminals multiplied, as the city grew in wealth and population.

The new "Staat Huys," before alluded to, was erected on the corner of Pearl street and Coenties Slip, a locality then considered the most central in the infant town, and as offering the best facilities for securely keeping prisoners. It served its double purposes of jail and city hall until 1698, when it was decided by the authorities to build another—a larger and more commodious structure; while, in the meantime, the old military block-house in the immediate neighborhood of the Governor's residence was conscripted and made use of, additionally to the "Staat Huys," for the accommodation of the constantly-increasing number of culprits.

The new building—City Hall—was erected on Broad street, on the ground now covered by the sub-treasury building, and was finished in 1699, but was not used as a jail until five years subsequent. In the winter of 1704 the sheriff was required to have the city jail prepared for the reception of felons. Crime, however, would appear to have become a monster of terrible mien in those days, far exceeding all the efforts of the authorities to restrict or even to limit the number of malefactors, aside from the apparent impossibility of diminishing them, for again, in 1758, another new jail was found absolutely necessary to the needs of the inhabitants, and was erected on what was then known as "The Fields," now City Hall Park, and where, tradition has it, the prisoners were most barbarously treated. This new place of confinement, together with those previously in use, served their purpose very well until 1775, when the new Bridewell was erected, when all were converted into military prisons during the occupancy of the city by the British. The frightful cruelties that were then practiced upon the patriot soldiers, unfortunate enough to be inmates of those prisons, are too familiar to every one to need mention here.

Shortly after the Revolution, the Penitentiary was established at Bellevue. In 1816, a portion of the almshouse was set apart for the punishment of felons, by the institution of the treadmill. This was on Twenty-sixth street, near First avenue, the present site of Bellevue Hospital, and its part occupancy as a prison somewhat relieved the overcrowded condition of the jail. The city jail still continued in City Hall Park, and was used as a debtors' prison, remaining so until 1832, when it was entirely converted into the Register's Office, the present Hall of Records, and is such to this day. It stands opposite the *Staats Zeitung* building in old Tryon Row.

The Penitentiary was soon found to be too small for the keeping of the greatly-increased number of prisoners, and so, in 1836, the buildings on Blackwell's Island were constructed, and two years later, again, the Tombs, the sombre, miasmatic, Egyptian edifice on Centre street, was completed; which latter had been in course of construction for some years.

In addition to the prisons previously alluded to, there was begun, in 1796, a state prison, which was erected in the Village of Greenwich, about West Tenth street, near the North River, and which is still in existence to-day (1886), being occupied by, and known as, the Empire Brewery. It was used as a state prison until the completion of the present extensive buildings at Sing Sing, on the Hudson.

Such is, briefly, a history of the establishment of the prisons of this city, but of the unfortunate class of criminals that have, from time to time, occupied them, much remains to be said, and will be found in the succeeding pages.

CHAPTER II

CRIMINALS AND THEIR HAUNTS

New York, from being the largest city on the western hemisphere; in almost hourly communication with every part of the known world; the vast wealth of its merchants; elegant storehouses crowded with the choicest and most costly goods, manufactured fabrics, and every kind of valuable representing money; with its great banks, whose vaults and safes contain more bullion than could be transported by the largest ship afloat; its colossal establishments teeming with diamonds, jewelry and precious stones gathered from all parts of the known and uncivilized portions of the globe; with all this countless wealth, these boundless riches, in some cases insecurely guarded, in all temptingly displayed, is it any wonder, then, that this city should always have proved the paradise of thieves? The fact of its being the chief city of the New World, alone caused it to be the principal magnet of attraction for all the expert criminals of the Old World, in addition to those who were "to the manner born."

What trouble they proved to the police of some years ago, and the frequency with which crimes of every kind were committed, is best evidenced by referring to the records of that time, when jails and prisons were crowded and courts and judges were kept busy trying offenders against the laws, while the entire police and detective force was unable and inadequate to successfully reduce the occurrence of the one or diminish the number of the other. It was at that time appropriately styled the "Thieves' Paradise," for even after some daring and expert felon had been captured by the authorities and securely lodged in jail, the meshes of the law, as it then existed, were so large, and the manner of administering justice (?) so loose, that the higher class of criminal, possessed of political influence, or, better still, of money, invariably escaped the punishment his crime deserved. The very police themselves were, in many cases, in league with the thieves and shared in the "swag" of the successful burglar, expert counterfeiter, adroit pickpocket, villainous sneak and panel thief, or daring and accomplished forger; hence crime, from being in a measure "protected," increased, criminals multiplied and prisons were made necessarily larger.

But this was years ago, and under a far different police system than that now in vogue, the merits and efficacy of which it will be both a duty and a pleasure hereafter to fully mention. The collusion between the police and the criminals, at the times of which we speak, became a very serious matter, in which the public early began to exhibit its temper. So late as the year 1850 it was an anxious question whether the authorities or the lawless classes should secure the upper hand and possess the city, and this condition of affairs, this triangular strife of supposed law and order on one side, protection to law-breakers on the other, and the protests of an indignant, outraged and long-suffering people on the third, prevailed until the year that Bill Poole was murdered by Lew Baker on Broadway, which notable event marked an epoch in the city's history, and to some extent improved the then existing state of affairs, as it occasioned the dispersal of a notorious gang of swell roughs, whose power was felt in local politics, and directed the attention of every lover of peace and justice to the enactment of better laws and a sterner method of executing them.

About the year 1855, two classes of "toughs," or, as they were dubbed in those days, "rowdies," appear to have had and maintained some control of the city, overawing the regularly constituted authorities, intimidating the police by their numbers, and carrying things with a high hand generally. One class consisted of the individuals comprehended in the title of

"Bowery Boy"—a term which included that certain, or rather uncertain, element of New Yorker residing in the streets running into the Bowery and adjacent to it, below Canal street, and the other, a rival gang, called "Dead Rabbits," which unsavory distinction was adopted by an equally questionable portion of humanity dwelling in the Fourth and Sixth wards and streets in the vicinity of Catherine and Roosevelt. There were among these two gangs of the city's representative "toughs," materials of a far different kind from the actual felon, but who were none the less dangerous, and among them may be classed many leaders of ward politics and volunteer fire companies, and from which Lew Baker and his victim, Bill Poole, "The Paudeen," "Reddy, the Blacksmith," and numerous others were afterwards developed; but they were oftener far more guilty than the real criminals, for they aided and abetted, and in cases of arrest befriended them, causing their subsequent escape from the penalties justly due for their crimes.

As a type of the veritable "Bowery Boy" may be taken the leader of that gang of notorious "toughs," one who, from his well-earned reputation as a bar-room and street rough-and-tumble fighter, has become a historical personage, under the sobriquet of "Mose." His faithful lieutenant, "Syksey," of "hold de butt" fame, will not soon be forgotten either, as both figured prominently in the terrible pitched battles the two rival gangs frequently indulged in, to the terror and consternation of all New York. Of the rival mob, known as "Dead Rabbits," Kit Burns, Tommy Hedden and "Shang" Allen are names long to be remembered by the terror-stricken citizens who lived in the days when the fights between these notorious aspirants for pugilistic and bloody honors were often of the deadliest and most sanguinary character, lasting for days at a time; when entire streets were blockaded and barricaded, and the mobs were armed with pistols and rifles. Even cannons were sometimes used, and the police, even when aided by the military, were powerless to suppress these battles until many were killed and wounded on both sides. In these desperate conflicts it was no unusual sight to see women, side by side with men, fighting as valiantly as their husbands, sons or fathers, and the records of the courts and prisons of those days tell dreadful stories of murders, robberies and other crimes done under cover of these periodical street fights.

At this time the locality known as the "Five Points" was probably the worst spot on the face of the civilized globe. In and around it centered, perhaps, the most villainous and desperate set of savage human beings ever known to the criminal annals of a great city. To pass through it in daylight was attended by considerable danger, even when accompanied by several officers of the law. Woe to the unfortunate individual who chanced to stray into this neighborhood after dark. A knock on the head, a quick rifling of pockets, a stab if the victim breathed, a push down some dark cellar, were frequently the skeleton outlines of many a dreadful tragedy, of which the victim was never afterwards heard. The name "Five Points," was given to that particular spot formed by the junction or crossing of Worth, Baxter and Park streets, but nearly embraced all the neighborhood comprised in the locality bounded by Centre, Chatham, Pearl and Canal streets in the Sixth ward, and was frequently afterwards mentioned as the "Bloody Sixth," from the many daily conflicts eventuating there.

The "Five Points," from being the hiding-place and residence of the most bloodthirsty set of criminals, vagabonds and cut-throats, has, through the influence of the Five Points Mission House and the gradual encroachments of business houses, become quite respectable, and while now sheltering a large number of the foreign element, has ceased, to a great extent, to longer excite terror in the community. Still, it has not entirely lost its former well-merited title of "Thieves' Nest." It is comparatively a safe thoroughfare in daylight, and after dark, if one is on constant guard, he may safely pass unharmed.

In the Fourth ward, just beyond the locality written about,

was another terrible rendezvous for an equally desperate set of men. It was known as Slaughter-house Point, and a criminal here was, for a time, safe from the police, as its many intricate streets and tumble-down houses offered a safe hiding-place for every kind of outlaw, even up to very recent years. Here the terrible garroter dwelt for a long time; aye, and throve, too, until our criminal judges began sentencing every one of them convicted before them to the extreme penalty of twenty years in Sing Sing, which largely suppressed that class of criminals in this city.

The methods of the garroter were quick, sure and silent. At Slaughter-house Point and its environs many a returned East India sea captain, whose vessel was moored to one of the docks at the foot of a contiguous street, has either strayed or been beguiled into this neighborhood, drugged and robbed. Others, whose business or chance brought them within the reach of this set of desperadoes, have fared similarly. Sad has been the fate of many an individual unfortunately falling into the clutches of these murderous villains. A stealthy step, an arm thrown under the chin of the unsuspecting victim, a bear-like clasp, and total unconsciousness. To rifle the pockets of the unlucky man— sometimes stripping him and throwing him off the dock— and escape into one of the many dark and dismal passages abounding in the neighborhood, was but a few minutes' work, and nothing remained to tell how the drama, perhaps tragedy, was enacted.

Another class of dangerous criminals haunted the precincts of Water and Cherry streets, and that immediate locality. They were all frequenters of the well-known establishments presided over by such eminent lights of the profession as Kit Burns, Jerry McAuley, Johnny Allen, etc., but all three of whom afterwards forswore their evil ways and died in the odor of piety.

These various gangs inhabiting the portions of the city already indicated were eventually succeeded by others in widely separated localities. The succeeding gangs were quite as numerous, but not quite as ferocious or formidable, so far as numbers were concerned, but more dangerous and daring individually; for while the former type lived in communities by themselves, and dwelt in certain well-known streets and houses, using their bloodthirsty propensities occasionally against themselves in their street fights, the latter at all times waged an indiscriminate and perpetual war on the respectable element of society. To the latter and more modern gangs, which were really worse, so far as the higher classes of crimes were concerned, belonged such men as "Reddy, the Blacksmith," "Dutch Heinrich." Chauncey Johnson, "Johnny, the Mick," and their favorite places were "Murderers' Row," and other notorious localities on Broadway, Houston, Crosby and adjacent streets.

The war did much to bring these latter into prominence. They made money when money was in the hands of every one, when bounty-jumpers were as thick as berries on the bushes, and the leading streets of the city were a blaze of light at night, from the myriads of colored lamps displayed by the pretty waiter-girl saloons and other notorious and questionable dives. When the war ceased these and kindred gangs of "toughs" were again superseded by those at present to be found in various parts of the metropolis, but which, thanks to an excellent system of police, are all or nearly all under complete espionage of the local authorities.

It now becomes our duty, as faithful chroniclers, to point out the localities at present occupied by that class of the population, and tell the secret of their lives and how they exist. The region which most engrosses the attention of the police is that conspicuously known as "Mackerelville," which for some years past has borne rather an unsavory reputation. While there are many deserving and worthy persons dwelling in the locality, quite a different type of humanity also makes its home there. The neighborhood in question is comprised in Eleventh, Twelfth and Thirteenth streets, and First avenue, and Avenues A, B and C. It harbors a wild gang of lawbreakers, ready and willing to commit any kind of lawless act, in which the chances of escape are many and detection slight. Notwithstanding the decimation of its ranks by frequent and well-deserved trips to the penitentiary of its members, for every crime from murder down, it appears to survive, to the terror of the respectable poor living in the neighborhood and the constant dread of the police officer. It is a locality and a gang much dreaded at night, but not nearly so much now as formerly, for when a member commits a crime of any importance now he is invariably ferreted out, arrested and punished.

The Tenth Avenue gang is a chance affair, owing its existence to the successful and bold express robbery occurring some years ago, but which is still fresh in the minds of most people from the skillful manner in which it was executed, and from the number of prominent rascals participating in it. The robbery referred to, at the time of its occurrence, was current talk, and continued a subject of conversation for many weeks afterwards. A number of ingenious, daring and highly-cultured train robbers, under the leadership of the notorious Ike Marsh, among whom was one who has since attained celebrity as an actor, boarded a train on the Hudson River Railroad, near Spuyten Duyvil, the spot immortalized by Washington Irving, and, entering the express car, bound and gagged the messenger in charge, threw the safe off and jumped after it. The iron box contained a large amount of greenbacks and government bonds, which the thieves succeeded in appropriating. Some of these daring robbers were subsequently arrested and lodged in the White Plains jail, but on the day set for the trial, the sheriff discovered that his prisoners of the night before, whom he imagined quite secure, had left, without waiting to say good-bye. Some friends and confederates came to their assistance, released them and drove them down to the city, from whence they finally reached our sister Kingdom, recently made famous as the abode of the fashionable defaulter.

The successful perpetration of this bold robbery suggested to a number of idle men the idea of robbing the freight cars as they remained apparently unguarded on the tracks in the vicinity of the West Thirtieth street station, and led to the formation of the notorious Tenth Avenue gang. The cars arriving from the west and other points loaded with valuable goods and merchandise, offered facilities of a most tempting kind to the members of this gang, and large quantities nightly disappeared until, week after week, the goods stolen aggregated thousands of dollars loss to the railroad company. The proximity of the river aided the operations of this gang very materially, for much of the goods were spirited away with the assistance of the river thieves and their boats, both sets of thieves acting, of course, in collusion.

It is a very difficult thing to map out just the precise localities where criminals reside now, owing, in a great measure, to the efficiency of the present police, who keep evil-doers under constant surveillance, preventing them remaining long in any one place. Of course, such streets as are contained in wards of the city where the poorest people dwell will invariably have their quota of questionable characters; but the days when gangs of roughs, "toughs" or thieves can flourish in one particular section, it is to be hoped, are matters of the past.

It is a matter of surprise to other nations, and of congratulation to ourselves, that at the present such crimes against persons and property as burglary, pocket-picking and highway robbery are much rarer in proportion than in any other cosmopolitan city in the world.

CHAPTER III

STREET ARABS OF BOTH SEXES

To the wealthy resident of Fifth avenue and other noted fashionable thoroughfares, the incidents of actual every-day life that are here revealed will read like a revelation. To the merchant and the business man they may probably read like romance. To the thrifty mechanic, however, who occupies a vastly different social sphere, who hurries to his work in the morning, and with equal haste seeks to reach his home at night, this chapter may, perhaps, cause a tear to glisten in his manly eye when the facts, here written for the first time, meet his gaze, and, may be, are associated with some young male or female relation or friend who has "gone wrong." But to the officers of the Society for the Suppression of Vice, and other kindred useful societies, newspaper men, the police, and others whose daily vocations happen to keep them out late o' nights, the truths here unfolded are of too frequent occurrence and are too familiar sights to need any other corroborative evidence than is supplied by their own experience and the exercise of their own observation.

Youthful vice and depravity, of all grades, is, unfortunately, the natural result of that civilization which finds its outgrowth in large and necessarily closely-packed communities. Where ground is dear, poor people must seek rooms in dwellings where the rent is cheap, and these dwellings are, for the most part, erected in cheap neighborhoods—and cheap neighborhoods mean questionable companionships and associations, and bad associations beget a familiarity with immorality of all kinds. No one can question the truth of this. For instance, the honest

43

and industrious mechanic, receiving fair wages for his work, must hire lodgings or rooms in some tenement; he goes to work during the day, leaving his wife, if he happens to have one, at home to perform those hard household duties which fall to the lot of her class; the children—and there are generally several, for one of the chief luxuries within the reach of the poor is children—are allowed to take care of themselves as best they can between times; they naturally go to the streets to play; they have no gardens, with shady graveled walks running between beds of bright flowers; no nursery, no governesses, no nurses with French caps, and, shame be it said, hardly any public parks; there are not even trees in this great city to cast a shade for these little creatures in summer nor to help break the force of the wind in winter—but they play in the streets just the same, and are under no restraint whatever, and therein lies their temptation. What wonder that they afterwards people the gilded palaces of vice "up-town," or fill the prisons of the city and state?

They may be approached by any one, and they are led away by many. Sometimes the ever-watchful and lynx-eyed Chinaman singles out some pretty little girl, on the pretense that he has some curious things to show her in his laundry. Sometimes an old, eminently respectable gentleman (?) has a package of candy for the little girls. Sometimes, again, bright-eyed young girls are attracted, like butterflies to bright flowers, to the gaudy signs of the Bowery museums. Sometimes there are other inducements, in the way of store windows, or a chance acquaintance (and they are always around, too, these obliging acquaintances), and the purchase of some trinkets, then a hotel, a room, and our little friend has eaten of the apple. But this is premature.

The unconstrained freedom of the street, therefore, is undoubtedly one great source of danger to the young but there are many others which, in varying degrees, conspire to ensnare and corrupt them. So that the wonder is that so many escape rather than that so many are contaminated.

The manner in which poor people—the very poor—live in this

44

city is, of itself, fearfully demoralizing in its effects upon their children. Oftener than otherwise, a family, in some cases six or seven in number, will occupy but *two* rooms; one, a kitchen, the other, a *sleeping* apartment. In the latter room are sometimes the father, mother, one or two daughters, say ten, twelve or fifteen years of age, and as many sons, younger or older, as the case may be. Just think of it! think of the tender age at which these children are familiarized with what should be as a sealed book. Think of—what frequently happens—a drunken father reeling to the marriage bed in such a room! Think of brothers and sisters of such ages lying side by side, and think of the mistakes that might occur when—which is possible—the whole family may have taken liquor and the floor is one common bed. There are hundreds of families living in this big, charitable city in this degrading manner. Is it any surprise that children here are bad and criminally vicious at five years of age and upwards?

It not infrequently happens that the parents of families so circumstanced are sent to the "Island," in which case the children are then, indeed, upon the streets. Yet they are so precocious and resourceful that they generally are able to take care of themselves, and so become flower girls, news girls, wharf rats, etc.

There are yet other causes which go to affect the lives of the children of the poor. It sometimes happens that the happy and virtuous home of a comparatively well-to-do mechanic is broken up by unforeseen circumstances, against which no provident provision, except a life insurance policy, could guard. The head of the family meets with some serious accident, incapacitating him for labor, and straightway, instead of being the breadwinner and family support, he becomes a care and a burden. The poor wife is thrown upon her resources, and she naturally invokes the assistance of her children in the desperate endeavor of maintaining a roof over their heads. In this way the ranks of the flower and news girls are frequently recruited.

Through the cursed effects of drink, the heads of many

families are frequently sent to the "Island" for from ten days to six months, and when the sheltering arms of some beneficent society, or the kindly offices of some good Samaritan, are not directed to the forlorn and destitute condition of the children, the unfortunate young creatures are forced upon the streets to beg, steal, sell papers, flowers, etc., and also visit the offices of bankers and brokers, doing anything, in short, to get the means to live. They live in the streets, sleep in hallways, alleyways, anywhere, a prey to the first evil-disposed man that meets them. It is a common sight to see children on the streets in all parts of the metropolis—boys and girls—aged from five to fifteen years, selling papers, shoplifting, stealing, and,—worse. Have they parents? Who knows, who inquires, who cares? Some of them are very pretty girls, too. All the worse for them.

The same causes which conspire to throw girls upon their own resources to gain a livelihood, operate with the brothers; but the latter are more fertile in means of accomplishing that end. Girls can only sell papers, flowers or themselves, but boys can black boots, sell papers, run errands, carry bundles, sweep out saloons, steal what is left around loose everywhere, and gradually perfect themselves for a more advanced stage and higher grade of crimes, finally developing into fully-fledged and first-class criminals.

So much for the causes which help to create this class of street Arabs, whom it is almost a labor of supererogation to describe, especially to those who daily hear the familiar cries, "Telegram!" "News!" "Telegram!" "New-es!" "Mail 'n' Express!" uttered chiefly by young girls, all over the town. Pretty girls they are, too, many of them, with large, lustrous eyes, long, well-oiled hair, nice shoes upon their feet, short dresses, disclosing evidences of graceful forms, ruddy complexions, and armed with many winsome little actions calculated to conciliate patronage. They are to be seen on Park Row, the Bowery, Chatham street, around the post-office, hotels, elevated railroad stations, the ferries leading to Brooklyn, Jersey City and Staten Island—everywhere, in fact, where there is a chance of disposing of the afternoon newspaper.

The larger number of these little girls emerge from their hiding-places about eleven o'clock in the morning. Their hiding-places may have been a hotel, an assignation house, their parents' homes, some hallway, the News Girls' Lodging House, resorts in North William, Bayard, Hester, New Bowery, or any other street in which cheap rooms can be obtained. It is not to be presumed that all news-girls are bad; on the contrary, many are very good, respectable little things, but a few only remain so, for their associations are bad, and many men who purchase papers from them are constantly tempting them, so that it is very difficult for any of them to remain good for any length of time.

Be that as it may, however, the news girl in this case arrives down-town about noon. She strolls down among the brokers and bankers, and in many cases is winked at, conversed with and asked to visit different offices, which invitation is generally accepted, for a little money is to be made by the call, with which the afternoon papers are purchased. Sometimes the selling of papers is merely a pretext under which a better opportunity is afforded of conversing with men. The papers are hawked in saloons, upon the streets, in cars, and other places. If any one should chance to buy a paper and offers a nickel, the girl invariably has no change; when the purchaser, nine times out of ten, tells her to keep the change. They are extremely shrewd, smart, intelligent and wide awake.

Their papers all sold, about nine or ten o'clock at night they saunter up Chatham street, the Bowery and other thoroughfares; or, if it is the summer season, they will be found in the City Hall park, playing, sitting on the benches, or accosting passing pedestrians. The Battery, too, has its frequenters, and the piers and docks at night are crowded with them. This life they pursue until they engage regularly in a life of shame, by becoming regular boarders in some one of the many dives in the cellars of Chatham street, the houses of prostitution in Forsyth, Hester, Canal, Bayard and other streets. Or, again, they may be found

47

in the various pretty-waiter-girl saloons of the Bowery, or such notorious resorts as Hilly McGlory's, Owney Geoghegan's, and so on. The public parks, however, are favorite places, and they may be found even in Union Square and Madison Square, and sometimes in Central Park. They enjoy themselves, too, for they are often seen on picnics in summer and at balls during the winter. They have their favorites among the opposite sex, too, just as have more favored and aristocratic females. For the love of one of these little girls—Mary Maguire—a member of the notorious Mackerelville gang met a tragic end, at the hands of a jealous rival in City Hall park, by being stabbed to death. Little Mary was only fourteen years of age. She was afterwards sent to the House of the Good Shepherd.

Newsboys are largely responsible for leading girls of this class into the tempting paths of vice. In purchasing their papers at the newspaper offices, generally in cellars, they are subjected to many indignities and familiarities, which, at first resented, are gradually accepted as a matter of course. Once the descent is begun, the journey is completed by outsiders, until the girls become corrupt and unscrupulous, with a knowledge of the ways of the world that would surprise many a matronly head.

In many cases, girls of five and six years are sent out as decoys by the larger ones to "rope in" customers; for detectives and agents of the various societies, on the lookout for depraved girls, teach those young Messalinas caution. When one of these smaller girls has secured a customer she pilots the way to the place where the larger ones are to be found. In one instance this was a cellar, under ground, not fifty feet from the corner of Chatham and William streets; outwardly an oyster saloon, but a door opened in a wooden partition, through which one entered another room, and in which, at one time, there were actually no less than nine small girls, ranging in age from ten to sixteen years.

There are a few places where these girls resort in the day-time and remain all day, and where they are visited by regular frequenters of the houses. Here, also, may be found those young girls who, leaving home in the morning and telling their parents they are going to work, remain all day; returning home again in the evening with, perhaps, a couple of dollars in their pockets, and at the end of the week hand their parents what the old people innocently suppose is the week's wages of their daughters, honestly obtained.

There are old-time procuresses, who, having once been news-girls themselves, know just how to proceed to capture recruits for Hester street boarding-houses, and they obtain them, too, from the ranks mentioned. Parents that drive their children in the streets to get money, and beat them if they fail to fetch it home, are generally sure to either make prostitutes of their little ones or have them run away entirely, particularly when a tempting offer is made them by male or female. There are thousands of men in this city, as well as there are in London, who employ procuresses, whose efforts and operations, unfortunately, are not confined to news-girls, but include the pretty daughters of well-to-do mechanics and trades people.

Many of these girls become closely identified with the lives of Chinamen, and it is astonishing how fond some of these girls become of their almond-eyed protectors.

Should any observant individual pass through Elizabeth, Bleecker, Canal, Hester, Bayard, Dover, Pell, Mott, Baxter, Rose, Chambers streets, and the other localities mentioned, at night, he will see what becomes of the pretty news-girls. But there are instances in which they have obtained work in various factories and wholesale houses and remained respectable.

Thus far, the news-girl. Of the pretty flower girl—she with the engaging manner, and interesting face above a tray of flowers— not much remains to be said, for she has almost become an institution of the past. Thrown upon her own resources, from like causes affecting others of her sex, she was once to be met with in the lobby of every theatre in town, every resort where gentlemen were supposed to frequent, club-houses, drinking saloons, omnibuses, cars, and the streets. Even houses of ill fame found her gently and firmly looking for trade. Wherever there was a chance to intercept a gentleman, there was she, and her importunities to purchase were redoubled when a lady accompanied a gentleman. They did a thriving business in the pretty-waiter-girl saloons, for men could hardly escape them, and nearly all bought bouquets for their favorites in those places.

It is safe to say that very few of the flower girls were virtuous. They remained out until all hours of the night and plied a double trade, selling both their flowers and themselves. There was one well-known house in Thirteenth street which these little girls made a headquarters. It was between Broadway and University place. The proprietress had no other "ladies" but flower girls, as she found them more profitable, charged them higher prices for accommodations, whether by the day or week, and as but few places would assume the risk of harboring the waifs, they were compelled to pay her extortionate rates.

Some time since a man could hardly pass along Fourteenth street or Union Square, at night, without his being accosted by one of these girls, who, instead of asking him to purchase flowers, would invariably remark, "Give me a penny, mister?" by which term, afterwards, all these girls of loose character were known to ply their trade. Many of these girls were so exceedingly handsome as to be taken by gentlemen of means and well cared for, and one instance is known where a flower girl married a very wealthy man of middle age.

As a class, they were excessively immoral. They purchased their flowers, out and out, from the florists and made handsome profits, amounting to as much as two and three dollars a night when the weather was fine; but their habits and immoralities became so patent that the societies put a stop to their selling, by sending some to the House of the Good Shepherd, and arresting others for soliciting and other unlawful acts; so that to-day it is very much to be doubted if there are more than half a dozen in the city.

"Wharf rats," street gamins, Arabs, and other euphonious terms are applied to that class of boys, who, having no homes, make one for themselves in the streets. They black boots—some of them—in the day-time, sell newspapers in the afternoons, lie in wait for incoming travelers from the trains to carry satchels, etc., and make a little money from all sources to supply themselves with food and raiment. The balance, if any is left, they spend in going to the gallery of some theatre, visiting some museum, or adjourning to their favorite haunt—which frequently is a low beer-dive in some obscure street, play pool or cards or dice for drinks, and otherwise contrive to kill time, until their "business" of the next day begins.

It used to be a familiar sight to see the saloons of Baxter, Mott and Mulberry streets filled with these boys. It was only a few years ago that they had their own theatre, yclept "The Grand Duke's Theatre," at 21 Baxter street, in the cellar under a stale beer dive, where really clever performances were given of an imitative character, by a company of boys; and which, by the way, was the only theatre which for years defied the efforts of the authorities to collect the license. The admission fee was ten cents, and curiosity seekers came from all parts of the city to witness the really laughable and, in many cases, meritorious character-sketches given within its damp walls. It was subsequently broken up by the police.

Boys and girls appear to be alike in one respect—the streets of the city are full of them at all hours of the day and night. The water, however, would appear to act like a magnet upon the needle, having peculiar attractions for them at all times, and to which vicinity, at night in summer, they naturally gravitate. On the piers which jut out into the rivers on all sides of the city, any one can see troupes of gamins every warm, pleasant day. Some are fishing, others are pitching pennies, others, again, playing various apparently harmless games, but all with eyes for the main chance—an opportunity to steal anything come-at-able. To the policeman who, from curiosity or to get a sniff of sea breeze, chances to stroll upon the pier, he finds them all engaged as described. Ships are unloading cargoes of assorted merchandise, which is being placed upon the dock. Bags of coffee are in one place, chests of tea in another, hogsheads of molasses and sugar, and various other kinds of goods are distributed all over the place. Some boys are playing "tag," and they run around and over the bags of coffee, behind the hogsheads of sugar, ostensibly in play, but all the while keeping a sharp eye on the watchmen, police and people employed there. A favorable chance occurring, a boy drops behind one of the bags of coffee and quickly and expeditiously rips it open with a sharp knife and bounds away. The coffee thus loosened freely discharges itself upon the dock in a little heap. In like manner a knot in the wood forming a head in a barrel of sugar is knocked out, leaving a round hole, into which the Arab thrusts a long, thin stick and, dexterously withdrawing it, contrives to pull out considerable sugar. The bung of a molasses barrel is burst in, a stick inserted, which, when pulled out, has some of the contents thickly adhering to it. Thus much accomplished, every boy provides himself with an old tomato or other can, and it would surprise anyone not familiar with these things, to see how rapidly and ingeniously these dock rats will fill those cans to overflowing with all kinds of goods, from the openings thus made in the vessel containing them.

These same tactics are employed by the street gamins in front of those grocery stores where barrels, boxes and cases are placed upon the sidewalk, and it is almost an impossibility for any one but the sharpest to catch them thus stealing, so clever and adroit are they. One of their very neat tricks is for a boy to place himself in view of the proprietor of a store, who, knowing the youth is after some of the goods outside, keeps a sharp eye on him. Suddenly, the boy makes a dash for some oranges and flies up the street, the proprietor in full chase. At the distance of, perhaps, half a block, the boy stops, allowing himself to be caught, when the irate shopkeeper roughly clutches him and, looking for the oranges stolen, is considerably chopfallen to find the boy has taken nothing. Upon being asked why he run away, the boy says he "thought he saw his brother and ran after him to speak to him." It seems plain enough, and the grocery man returns to find that, in his absence, twenty boys have plenteously helped themselves to everything within reach. It is now too late to re-catch the boy that he first ran after. It is a piece of strategic cleverness that rarely fails to succeed; and if any one underrates the *finesse* of the street Arabs of New York, he will stand a very good chance some day of being a sufferer from them.

The operations of these embryo professionals are not confined to any one kind of theft. They are adepts in all the ways of petty thieving. Sometimes, a drunken sailor or 'longshoreman will stagger out of a saloon and, unsteadily navigating along, will fall, or seat himself on a door-step and, either falling asleep or into a semi-conscious condition, will be surrounded by a gang of these playful boys, while one, the leader, probably, will sneak up to the unlucky man and relieve him of all he has about him, when they will scamper off.

These boys are often taken in hand by professional burglars, who use them to keep watch, posting one of them as a sentry, perhaps employing another to squeeze through some small aperture and open the doors of the place to be burglarized, for the fact of their whole lives being passed upon the streets their education is of that character which tends to make them quick, bright, smart and skillful in all things, and, when added to natural gifts of intelligence, render them very dangerous as thieves or thieves' assistants. Readers of Charles Dickens will recall, in this connection, the use to which burglar Bill Sykes applied little Oliver Twist.

Many of these gamins have houses under the docks. The floor is laid just above high-water mark. It is boarded in on all sides with lumber stolen, day by day, from adjoining yards. Here they pass their leisure time in comparative safety and quiet, and considerable comfort, as the whole gang contribute to furnishing up the club-rooms. Stoves, chairs, tables, benches, and other evidences of taste, are to be found there, and an occasional cheap picture, circus bill or flash theatrical poster ornaments the sides of this not uncomfortable place. Here the members play cards, dice and other games, drink beer, smoke and otherwise enjoy themselves. These houses sometimes exist for years unknown to the police, and many a boy, detected in the commission of some petty theft, has run along the pier, pursued by the policeman, when, suddenly scrambling over the pier, he has disappeared, leaving the wondering officer to guess what had become of him.

In some portions of the town, garrets are made use of as club-rooms and places of rendezvous, and are exceedingly well arranged. These places are used as storehouses, too, for the safe-keeping of stolen articles of all kinds.

An instance of the daring and ingenuity of these "wharf rats," as well as an illustration of some of their methods, is furnished in the following: Procuring a boat—loaned frequently with the owner's knowledge of what it is to be used for—these boys will row, with muffled oars, under some dock having valuable goods upon it. The only sound that disturbs the silence of the night is the dull splash, splash and swish of the waters against the dock or some vessel moored there. Everything is quiet, while the night watchman slowly paces along his narrow beat, at the one end of which are the dancing, moonlit waters and at the other the sleeping city. A favorable chance offering, the heads of the boys appear above the string-piece, and a bag or sack is hurriedly lowered into the boat. Other goods follow until, sufficient having been taken, the boat moves off as silently as it appeared. Sometimes, a boat is rowed under the pier where barrels of whisky or other spirits lie, and, by inserting an auger between the planks of the dock, a hole is bored in the barrel, when the liquor which escapes is guided into a barrel. In this way many goods are stolen right under the noses, apparently, of the watchmen and guardians.

Sometimes these wharf rats are captured in the act, when

fierce fights ensue. They know there is no escaping punishment, and they fight desperately. Having no homes or parents there is no escape for them, for, even if not convicted of the theft, they must go to the House of Refuge.

After all, but little blame can be attached to these unfortunate boys and girls, for they are just precisely what their associations have made them. They learn to swear, smoke, chew, steal, before they can walk, and grow up to be what they are. The House of Refuge only serves to confirm them in their viciousness and evil propensities by herding them with other criminals; so that, by the time they are released they are ready and willing to take greater chances in securing larger results, when the end invariably is the State prison—probably for life.

CHAPTER IV

STORE GIRLS

Since the time when Mary Rogers, the beautiful cigar girl of Broadway, met her sad fate over in Hoboken, the pretty shop girls of New York have contributed more than their full quota to the city's contemporaneous history. They have figured in connection with many of its social romances and domestic infelicities, as well as with its scandals and its crimes—secret and revealed. In Gotham's grave and gay aspects—in its comedy, its tragedy, and its melo-drama, we are perpetually running across the charming face, graceful form, and easy, gay demeanor of the pretty shop girl.

As a rule, the temptress of the store is pretty—frequently quite beautiful, and almost invariably handsomer than those fortunate daughters of Mammon whom she is called upon to serve, and who often treat her with such top-lofty hauteur. And how stylish she frequently is, and how difficult it is to describe this incommunicable quality of *style*, which those artful setters of baits—the dealers in ready-made fabrics—understand so well! Who has not noticed how the tall, slender-framed girls, with their graceful movements and flexible spines, their long, smooth throats and curved waists, are drafted off to stand as veritable decoy-ducks? Who has not observed the grace and ease with which they wear risky patterns and unusual *façons,* and so delude the arrogant but ungraceful customer into buying, in the belief that she will look just as well as the pretty model? The average well-to-do woman, with some pretensions to good looks, sees a beautiful young creature with Junoesque air parading before her in bold color-combinations and doubtful harmonies, and she imagines she can venture the same thing with like effect. But alas! what a travesty the experiment frequently is!

Many of the New Yorkers who read this page will recall the Original Dollar Store on Broadway and its fascinating young salesladies. Some of these were perfect sirens with their loveliness of feature and delicacy of color; their luxuriant hair, made amenable to the discipline of the prevailing fashion; the gown stylish and perfect, and frequently not at all reticent in its revelations of form; the countenance calm, watchful and intelligent—frequently mischievous; the walk something akin to the serene consciousness of power which we are told that Phryne exemplified before her judges, and accompanied with that grace which is the birthright of beauty in every age and under any circumstances.

For many reasons the tone of morality, in some instances, among store girls in this city is not high. A variety of obvious causes contribute to this result, among which may be mentioned their generally poor salaries: their natural levity, and the example of their companions; their love of dress and display, coupled with a natural desire for masculine attentions; long hours in close, impure air; sensational literature; frequent absence of healthy or adequate home influence; and the many temptations which beset an attractive girl in such a position.

Many of them enter stores as mere children in the capacity of cash girls. They are the children of poor parents, and as they grow up to young maidenhood, they acquire a sort of superficial polish in the store, and are brightened without being educated. Some grow up and take their places as full-blown salesladies, and begin to sigh for the gayety of the streets, for freedom from restraint, and for amusements that are not within their reach. Naturally *au fait* in style, with taste and clever fingers, they dress in an attractive manner, with the hope of beguiling the ideal hero they have constructed from the pages of the trashy story paper. It is a sort of voluntary species of sacrifice on their part—a kind of suicidal decking with flowers, and making preparation for immolation. Full of pernicious sentimentality, they are open to the first promising flirtation. They see elegantly-dressed and diamonded ladies, and their imagination is fed from the fountains of vulgar literature until they dream that they, too, are destined to be won by some splendid cavalier of fabulous wealth. Learning from the wishy-washy literature that their face is their fortune, and so, reading what happened to others, and how perfectly lovely and romantic it all was, they are ready for the wiles of the first gay deceiver. Waiting in vain for their god-like ideal, they are finally content to look a little lower, and favorably receive the immodest addresses of some clerk in their own store, or succeed in making a street "mash."

Sometimes the pretty girl rushes impetuously into marriage, repents and separates from her husband. She is still good looking, and her marital experience has given her an air of easy assurance, and she readily finds employment as a saleslady. Her influence afterwards, among girls comparatively innocent and without her experience, cannot but be pernicious, and at the same time must exert a certain formative and shaping process in determing the peculiar character of the whole class of girls in the store.

Very frequently she does not attain even to the questionable dignity of a marriage ceremony. Flattered by the attentions of some swell, the pretty shop girl will be induced to accompany him to the theatre and to supper in a concert saloon. Her vanity is kindled by his appearance. She rejoices in the style of his clothes, in the magnificence of his jewelry, and she thinks her mission in life is to walk beside the splendid swell, amid rose gardens, theatres and supper rooms, for the remainder of her life. Finally she yields to his soft solicitations, and her prospects are forever blighted. She becomes an incorrigible flirt, meets her "fellows" on the corner of the street near the store, spends a certain number of evenings and nights with them at hotels where no course of catechism takes place at the clerk's desk. She goes to Coney Island or local beer gardens on Sundays, manifesting a vivid animal pleasure in her enjoyment, with little manifestation of gratitude towards her escort who is supplying the money.

Sometimes, again, an exceptionally pretty girl will fall a victim to the proprietor, the manager or some of the superintendents of the store; and there have been cases of this kind heard in the courts, in one of which the proprietor not only seduced the girl, but married her, afterwards obtaining a divorce because of her incontinence. Sometimes the lapse of these girls from the paths of virtue is accompanied with exceptional hardships. The young lady is beautiful as well as good perhaps, and the pride of her idolizing parents, who have taught her that she is fit to be the wife of a duke. She attracts the eye of a man about town, and the process of courting and flattery—of sapping and mining—begins, with the result that he has had in view since the inception of the acquaintance. He is not a bad fellow as the world goes; but providence and society have made it very hard for single men to show kindness to single women in any way but one. He is sorry at her situation; but she is hardly the person for him to marry, even with her blooming, flower-like face. In such a situation—and such situations are far too common with the class—Byron's lines, slightly altered, seem peculiarly applicable to the pretty shop girl:

> "'Twas thine own beauty gave the fatal blow,
> And help'd to plant the wound that laid thee low."

Sometimes it happens that the pretty girl, wearied of waiting for her knightly deliverer, comes across the advertisement of a gifted seeress—the seventh daughter of a seventh daughter, perchance, or "the only English prophetess who has the genuine Roman and Arabian talismans for love, good luck, and all business affairs;" or the wonderful clairvoyant who can be "consulted on absent friends, love, courtship and marriage." Not infrequently she falls into the toils of those advertising frauds, who frequently combine the vile trade of procuress with the ostensible trade of fortune-telling. When the girl is drawn to this den, the trump card offered her is, of course, the young gentleman, rich as Crœsus and handsome as Adonis, with whom she is to fall in love. He is generally described with considerable minuteness, and the time and place of meeting foretold. This may be fictitious, and it is fortunate for her if it is so. Rut the seeress too frequently needs no powers of clairvoyance or ratiocination to make these disclosures, for some *roue;* who has exhausted the ordinary rounds of dissipation, or some fast young fellow seeking a change, has made a bargain with the prophetess for a new and innocent victim—the amount of the fee to depend on the means and liberality of the libertine and the attractiveness of the victim. The vain, silly girl is dazzled with the wily woman's story, and readily promises to call again. At her next visit the man inspects her from some place of concealment, and if she meets his views, either an introduction takes place or a rendezvous is perfected. Thus the acquaintance begins, with the result which every intelligent reader can see for himself. Sometimes the picture of the scamp is shown, but in every case there is but one end in view on the part of the seeress, and that end is almost invariably achieved. The girl thus becomes clandestinely "gay," and spreads the influence of her evil example and impure associations among her shopmates. Pope has told us in four immortal lines the effects of a constant contact with vice. In the second epistle of his Essay on Man, he writes:

"Vice is a monster of so frightful mien,
As, to be hated, needs but to be seen;
Yet seen too oft, familiar with her face,
We first endure, then pity, then embrace."

In the case of the class of young girls under consideration this truth is peculiarly applicable. In consequence of their associations they hear and see things whose influence is almost wholly bad and pernicious. Those disguised advertisements in the newspapers called "Personals" are of this evil character. To young girls, with minds imperfectly disciplined, there is a fatal fascination in the mystery of surreptitious appointments and meetings. Mystery is so suggestive and romantic, and the young girl who, from piqued curiosity, is tempted to dally with a "Matrimonial" or a "Personal," is an object of commiseration. From dallying and reading and wondering, the step is easy to answer such notices. She believes that she has a chance of getting a rich and handsome husband, who will take her to Europe, and, in other respects, make her life a sort of earthly paradise. The men who write such advertisements know this besetting female weakness and bait their trap accordingly. And so a young girl, too frequently, walks alone and unadvised into the meshes of an acquaintanceship which leads to her ruin. It is perhaps as useless to ask the men who are base enough to conceive these things to refrain from publishing them, as it is to urge the mercenary proprietors of certain newspapers to refrain from printing them in their columns. Yet it must be perfectly clear to all right-thinking minds, that it is in vain for parents to warn, parsons to preach, friends to advise, for the good to deplore, and the ignorant to wonder, at the increasing deterioration of our metropolitan morals, while these tempting lures to feminine destruction are so alluringly displayed.

It would be doing very imperfect justice to this theme did we fail to record our conviction that some of the salesladies and shop girls of the city are thoroughly good, virtuous, honest and respectable. Many of them, amid unhealthy influences and corroding associations, preserve the white flower of a blameless life, and become the honored wives of respectable citizens. But these are a small minority. At the same time it is useless to disguise the fact that there are others whose character needs stronger colors for proper delineation than have hitherto been employed. There are those among pretty shop girls who simply give up their leisure time to surreptitious appointments. This is the worst and most dangerous form in which this prevalent vice stalks abroad, and it more clearly stamps the character of a community than does its more open and brazen manifestations. Many causes may lead to a woman's becoming a professional harlot, but if a girl "goes wrong" without any very cogent reason for so doing, there must be something radically unsound in her composition and inherently bad in her nature to lead her to abandon her person to the other sex, who are at all times ready to take advantage of a woman's weakness and a woman's love. Seduction and clandestine prostitution have made enormous strides in New York, and especially among the young women and girls connected with stores, within the last decade.

Not long ago a woman, who then occupied a prominent position in a Sixth avenue store, was met up-town in the evening. She is very good looking—strong and lithe and tall, with a cloud of handsome hair that glistens like bronze; large dreamy eyes that flash and scintillate witchingly; a handsome, pouting, ruddy mouth; while her neck, white and statuesque, crowns the full bosom of a goddess. She said that she came out evenings occasionally to make money, not for the purpose of subsistence, but to meet debts that her extravagance had caused her to contract. She said in substance: "You see my appetite is fastidious, and I like good eating and drinking. I have the most expensive suppers sometimes. I am engaged to be married to a young fellow who works on a daily newspaper and who is busy at night. We shall be married some day, I suppose. He does, not suspect me to be 'fast,' and you don't suppose I am going to take the trouble to undeceive him. This is not a frequent practice of mine; I only come out when I want money, and I always have an appointment before I come out. I always dress well of course, and can pick up a gentleman anywhere when I like. Yes, I know I have good feet, and I know how to use them. I have hooked many a fifty dollars by showing a couple of inches of my ankle. Of course, I hate being in the store, but my fellow is rather jealous, and I keep going there as a blind. Will I reform when I am married? Perhaps so—if he gives me heaps of money. I am no worse than thousands of girls, single and married, who put on airs of purity and church-going. I know plenty of ladies who pay five hundred dollars at the store for silks and finery, which they persuade their husbands they bought for one-fourth of the price. And, for my part, I am going to eat well, dress well, and enjoy myself as long as ever I can get the money, by hook or by crook."

CHAPTER V

THE PRETTY WAITER GIRL

Readers of the works of Le Sage will recall the polite devil which the ingenious novelist releases from his captivity in a vial, for the purpose of disclosing to the world the true inwardness of society in Spain. Something of the role of this communicative imp we purpose to enact in this chapter, the subject matter of which, we may safely venture to assert, is new to at least nine-tenths of the residents of this great city. And if people, to the manner born, are unacquainted with the form and manifestations of this particular phase of crime, how much more ignorant must be those casual visitors, who only, at long intervals, are called by business, or impelled by anticipations of pleasure, to visit the Empire City?

The mode of life of the merchant or business man does not bring him in contact with crime or the haunts of criminals. He may pass down Sixth avenue, or Third avenue and the Bowery, on the Elevated railroad; or through Greene, Wooster, and Bleecker streets, the Bowery, Fourth avenue, Forsythe, Canal, Thirty-fourth, Houston, Twenty-third and Chatham streets, and other thoroughfares, in a street car, knowing nothing about the inmates of the houses lining either side of those same streets, or their manner of life, or anything about those inhabiting the basement beneath. It is only when the startling head-lines in his favorite morning paper call his attention to some frightful crime committed, that he learns either of its character, or location, or the causes which produced it. To this lack of knowledge on the part of the respectable portion of the community of the location of questionable places and the haunts of felons, is to be attributed many of the robberies which, from time to time, are chronicled in the newspapers. In the case of "the stranger within our gates" the danger of straying into the sloughs of vice and consequent victimization, is of course greatly increased. And just here it is worthy of remark that there appears to be some mysterious fatality by which strangers, greenhorns and "innocents," generally, contrive to wander by unerring though devious ways, straight into the talons of vigilant night-hawks.

Concert saloons and pretty waiter girls are treacherous things to meddle with. Neither can be depended upon and generally both have unsavory reputations. The only thing pretty about the girls is a pretty bad record.

During the war for the Union, when enlistments for the army were lively, and bounty jumpers flourished, and money was nearly as plentiful as salt, concert saloon proprietors made enormous fortunes. They were then a new sensation in this country; indeed, it may be said the war brought them into being. Broadway, from Fourteenth street to the Battery was literally lined on both sides with them, and when at night the lamps in front of these places were lighted, it rendered the street almost as bright as day. Then, as now, they were principally confined to the basements or cellars of buildings, but while some of them were known to be the rendezvous of thieves and other criminals, there were a few which enjoyed a better reputation, and were frequented by people of comparative respectability.

The pretty waiter girl, of course, was the principal magnet used to draw customers to these saloons. She was and is to-day, in fact, the only attraction. Music of a coarse description is used to attract the passer-by, who, glancing at the place from whence it proceeds, sees flaring lights, gaudy and brilliant signs— generally the figure of some female in tights—and is allured in by the unusual appearance, and the picture his imagination forms of a jolly time to be had within. Still, the girl is the feature. It is a safe conclusion, that no waiter girl in a concert saloon is virtuous, nor was there ever a really good girl engaged in any such saloon. They are there to be bought by any one fancying them, and therein lies the charm—if charm it can be called—of these places. A stranger has nothing to do but walk down the steps, enter the saloon, seat himself at a table, and he will immediately be besieged by a crowd of girls—if that be what he is seeking. As the stranger knows not the locality of other places of entertainment, he accommodates himself to circumstances and takes what he sees before him. Hence concert saloons thrive—but chiefly upon out-of-town people—countrymen, in fact.

There are various causes which conspire to make pretty waiter girls. They belong to three classes: First, the young girl who, but recently fallen into sin, is placed there by "her friend," which appellation more frequently than otherwise stands for "her seducer"; second, the young female who naturally seeks a position as waitress, because it pays her best, the proprietors of some saloons paying a weekly salary, in others a percentage upon the drinks sold; and third, an older kind of female who, having run the gauntlet of nearly all forms of feminine degradation, and losing most of the charms belonging to her sex, sees a chance, upon the percentages allowed by the "boss," and the overcharge squeezed from frequenters, of making a living, with a prospect of once in a while finding a man so drunk as not to have any choice in a companion for the night. To this sort of individual, all females are beautiful and the ancient and faded siren has as good a chance for patronage as her younger and more favored rival. Hence the concert saloon has its advantages for all kinds of women, as well as its uses for all kinds of men. The price of drinks in these places varies according to the tact of the pretty waiter girl, the sobriety of the customer, or the "rules of the house." In all cases, however, drinks are higher than at ordinary bars, for the musicians have to be paid, the girls to receive a percentage, as well as the proprietor to reap his harvest. Besides, the smiles of lovely women must be reckoned at something. In the Chatham street and Bowery dives, the worst and cheapest of liquors and beers are dispensed to customers. In many of these concert saloons "private rooms" have been arranged, where anyone so disposed may choose his female companion and retire to quaff a bottle of wine (?) at five dollars a bottle—a customer who indulges in such a luxury as wine being too important and consequential to associate with the common visitors. Money here as elsewhere has its worshipers.

With this preface we shall now introduce the reader to the inside of one of these concert saloons, and show him the pretty waiter girl as his fancy pictures her, and as she really is: Chancing to walk along the street, the ears are assailed by the clash of music emanating from some basement, down perhaps a half a dozen steps. A number of red globes, surrounding as many gas jets, serve to show the entrance, on either side of which are full length paintings of women in short skirts. The door is of green leather or oil-cloth. Pushing this open, we enter and seat ourselves at one of the many round tables with which the place is plentifully supplied. In a second—not longer—several girls are beside us, and some sit down at our table. One—perhaps two at once—will immediately ask if we are not going to treat, and, in response, drinks are ordered. While one of the girls proceeds to supply the order, and before the drinks are brought, we glance around the saloon. On one side is the bar, at which several persons are standing, drinking with some of the sweet-voiced houris. The barkeeper and proprietor, both in their shirt sleeves, are behind it. On one side of the bar is a slightly-raised platform, upon which is a piano-player, a violinist and a shrill fifer. This is the music that charms and attracts. Around the room are men of all kinds, sailors, laboring men, seedy individuals, lovers, thieves, a few poor gamblers, fellows in hard luck and waiting for "something to turn up." Sprinkled over the place, talking, laughing, joking and striving to induce them to buy drinks, are a number of the waiter girls. The floor is plentifully and generously covered with plain sawdust, which answers the double purpose of effectually hiding the large cracks, and of absorbing the expectorations and spilled beer. The time is yet early and business is not very brisk, so we chat with the prettiest and youngest of the girls for a second only, when we are again importuned to drink by another of the fair ones, even before the first round is brought, for it must be understood that only the girl ordering the drinks gets any percentage. The drinks brought, the price is asked and the amount paid, as follows: Two beers, two lemonades with a stick in it for two girls, and two brandies for two others; total, one dollar and forty cents. Now the girls don't drink brandy, they have a little colored water, but they charge for brandy all the same, and pay the proprietor in pasteboard tickets, which are supplied by him to the girls in packages of five dollars worth and upwards. For that which she charged one dollar and forty cents she pays in checks forty cents, thus making a clear one dollar—five cents each for two beers, ten cents each for lemonades, and five cents each for the colored water. The customer pays ten cents for each glass of beer, twenty cents each for lemonade and forty cents each for brandy. When the customer fails to call for drinks fast enough to suit the girls, they will leave for some other table where they may be more liberally patronized. It is getting later, and as we are about to leave, an unsteady and heavy foot is heard descending the steps outside, the doors are pushed violently open and a big, burly man reels into the place. He is not entirely intoxicated, but just enough so not to care for anything or anybody, and as he shuffles independently along he is approached by a couple of girls, who, taking an arm each, affectionately guide him to a chair. Being seated, he smiles benignly upon his fair captors and asks them to drink. He is evidently, from his dress, a successful butcher or saloon-keeper and has plenty of money about him. The drinks brought, he takes a roll of money from his pocket, and, thinking it is a five-dollar bill, gives a fifty-dollar bill to the girl. She immediately leaves and in a few seconds returns, giving him change for a five, saying quite pleasantly, "Here's your change," and, as he is about to place it in his pocket, asks him for "a quarter for luck." Several girls now gather around the man, and by smiles, caresses, and other affectionate and flattering demonstrations, finally persuade him into one of the private rooms, when he is lost to our sight, but we distinctly hear the order, "bottle of wine."

Soon another man enters very drunk, and, seating himself, is soon similarly surrounded. In about a minute one of the girls leaves and whispers to the proprietor, who, emerging from behind his rampart, catches the unlucky visitor by the collar, and with the aid of a club compels him to ascend the steps again to the street. The man not having any money was an unwelcome guest, and they had no use for him.

Several others now enter, many of whom are personally known to the girls, and mutual glances of recognition pass between them. These pass on down to the further and privileged part of the place and are lost to view. The den is now pretty full and business is brisk. The bartender and proprietor are hurriedly passing out ordered drinks. The girls are flying around, executing orders and pocketing change. The piano-player bangs and thumps his hideously-wiry instrument. Glasses are clinking, chairs and tables moving, and altogether there is a discordant tumult well calculated to bewilder the coolest kind of a head.

Suddenly there is a scream—a piercing scream. Everybody starts and looks towards the spot from whence it proceeded. One of the girls quickly says, "Oh, it's nothing, Jimmy is only licking Hattie." The lover has only beaten the poor creature who is supporting him, and, strange as it may appear, she will think all the more of him for this brutality. It is a pretty generally known fact, so far as females of this class are concerned, that if a man occasionally severely beats his mistress, she regards it as a proof that he entertains for her an ardent affection. It is now getting late, and several of the girls are leaving for home with their new-made male friends, and indications point towards the place being closed for the night. The butcher comes forth from his "private room," followed by a number of the girls who have been his companions, and is led to the door and assisted out. We leave also, and as we ascend the steps to the street we discover our butcher in the hands of a policeman who is dragging him off to the station, where we shall leave him for the night.

Now, most of these girls live in what are called furnished rooms, and it is to those that they take their male friends when they leave the saloon, stopping on the way, of course, for "supper." In some cases the girls are panel thieves—but that is rare. In nearly all cases they have lovers and generally provide home comforts for their masters, but in all cases they are for hire. The nature of the business they follow demands their attention at night, so that they sleep nearly all the day. The great majority of them are veritable thieves. To drug a man who carries money, or ply him with liquor until he is unconscious and then rob him of all he has, is a very common proceeding, particularly when afterwards he is put out on the street and left, when the chances are more than a hundred to one that he neither recollects the place where he was nor the girl who stole his money or his valuables. The proprietor, if he can, divides the stolen amount with the girl—with the lover always. Many instances are known of half-intoxicated men leaving valuables with the bar-tender of some of these places, for supposed security, but when requested to be returned were met with a denial that the valuables were ever intrusted to him. With an air of insulted innocence the bartender declares that he never saw the articles or the man before.

We shall now return to our butcher acquaintance, and follow the incident to its ending. So we proceed to the Tombs the next morning, and there in the pen with the other prisoners we find our man. Upon his arraignment in court he tells the following story, which is the truth *verbatim:*

"I was wandering through Chatham street, when my attention became attracted by a bevy of gaudily-dressed girls, who asked me to while away my spare hours in a concert saloon. Smitten with the charms of the tempters I was loth to part with them, and after some preliminary conversation they enticed me to their lair. I had at this time about five hundred dollars in my possession, and after some hours carousal, they robbed and sent me away penniless. This is how it was done: I entered the saloon and was taken to a private room, when I called for some wine, of which we all partook. I may say here that the wine, so called, was really nothing but cider. The girls sat on the sofa in this room with me. We continued to drink and I was the recipient of more caresses than I ever was before in my life. After the lapse of perhaps three hours, some of the girls left me, and when I called for more wine, I found that my money was gone. I was not so drunk at this time that I could not understand that I had been robbed. I asked for the girls that had left, and was told that they had gone home. I paid ninety dollars for wine in this room, but they gave me sometimes cider and whisky mixed, and then when I became really unconsciously intoxicated they put me out, after having taken all my money from my clothes.

"I had made an arrangement to go home with two of the girls, but I suppose when they saw that some of their number had taken all my money, they left me. There was a sofa in this room and one of the girls intimated to me that I had assaulted her and wanted some money. Another said she could not afford to spend her time there unless she was paid. Another induced me to give her money to buy a hat, and then when I lost consciousness they robbed me of all I had, my watch and chain, scarf-pin, ring and the remainder of my money. Many times during the hours I was there, drinks and wine were brought in that I did not order, but the girls would insist that I had ordered it. Once in a while the 'madame' of the place would call in the room, and coming up to me would embrace me and tell me I was a jolly fellow. I could not now recognize any of the girls and do not know which saloon I went into. I live in this city."

As a matter of custom, detectives were placed upon the case after the discharge of the prisoner, but that was the last ever heard of the matter, as he was unable to identify any of the parties arrested.

The foregoing is only a sample of hundreds of similar cases constantly taking place, in some of which the sufferer, if he is a stranger, and has no friends, is oftentimes sent to the Island for ten days for being drunk, while the pretty waiter girl who has drugged, robbed and finally discarded him is never even arrested. There are many other cases, however, in which the pretty waiter girl does not fare so well, and after conviction has to serve out her time, thereby losing her lover and her liberty.

What has been written applies more especially to the concert-saloon waiter girl, and does not in the least pertain to that other class of girls who are found in what are called dance houses, of which latter there are not a few in this city. There are some very peculiar kinds of females to be found in dance houses and not to be met with outside the abodes of Terpsichore. The term, dance house, itself, is susceptible of various interpretations. It may mean anything from Harry Hill's, at Crosby and Houston streets, to an Italian gathering in Mott or Mulberry street. But the performances carried on are precisely alike in all. In the sporting dance house, a series of boxing matches, small theatrical sketches may be acted, a song or two interspersed, and some piano playing, winding up afterwards with a dance, in which all so inclined may indulge, taking either the regular girls employed in the house as partners, or others who have strayed in from the streets.

In the regular dance houses, such as the Haymarket on Sixth avenue, "ladies" are admitted free, but "gentlemen" are charged twenty-five cents admittance, and here regular dancing takes place, such as quadrilles, waltzes, etc. In the French Madame's on Thirty-first street, which is ostensibly a restaurant, the girls come in from the street, and while sipping black coffee, are ready to accept an engagement to dance the *cancan*, which is performed up-stairs in rooms paid for by those desiring to see the questionable performance. It is not infrequently danced by the females in an entirely nude state, with various other concomitants not to be mentioned here, but of such a nature as to horrify any but the most *blasé roué*. There is also the well-known Billy McGlory's, in Hester street, near the Bowery, where general dancing is indulged in until an early hour of the morning, when a universal *cancan* takes place upon the public floor, and where each female boldly exposes just enough of her person to excite desire in the beholder. These girls dance in ordinary street costumes, and in many cases are paid by the proprietor for their services. It is a wild debauch, and needs but to be seen once, to be ever afterward remembered with disgust and loathing.

There are other places, not particularly dance houses nor yet concert saloons, such as the Empire, Star and Garter, Gould's, etc., which are used as general places of resort by all classes of males and Magdalenes. Here may be found the professional prize fighter, men about town, gamblers, merchants, clerks, politicians, bankers, officials of all kinds, and all classes of females, mistresses, *nymphs du pave,* inmates of assignation houses, all intent on fun and dissipation, and a desire to not only see the elephant, but pull it by the tail. Some of the girls-haunting these places have been pretty waiter girls, but find it more profitable to ply their trade as Cyprians. The bars are the chief sources of profit in these as in kindred establishments. Hence females are encouraged to visit them, for when they congregate in force men will follow, and men who enter these places do so for the purpose of finding congenial temporary mates and spending money for drinks.

Of the females who make these places their resort for the best part of the night, and participate in the recklessness and debauchery that has its ending only in an early death and the "Potter's Field," nothing remains to be said, except that they are the same as thousands leading similar lives in other cities of the world. The victims first of man's perfidy, through a too-confiding reliance on his promises, they become so afterwards as a matter of business and livelihood. Each has her lover, of course—what woman of the town has not?—and if she should happen to make a little money in the way of her questionable business, she divides it with him, for generally he has his eyes upon her during the entire course of the evening. Very few of them will leave any of these places with strange men without first notifying their lovers of where they are going and how long they will be away. In return for these services the lover sees to her, helps her to customers, prevents her being imposed upon by others of her sex when in the dance houses or concert saloons, and occasionally acts as her *cavalier servante* to various places for pleasure. There are many girls to be seen in these dance houses who are not over fifteen years of age—and they have lovers, too. In Billy McGlory's, one night, a desperate fight took place there over two rival claimants for the regard of a girl not yet entered on her teens.

It is considered one of the sights of the great city to visit these up-town resorts. Here all the young swells who desire to show country cousins the city, commercial travelers, chaperoned by city salesmen of various business houses, chorus girls from the theaters, and a mixed company generally, are to be found sitting around the various tables, drinking. The atmosphere is foggy with cigar smoke. The saloon is all ablaze with light. On the stage is some fourth-rate performer rendering a popular song. There is a long lunch counter, upon which is placed the materials for manufacturing all kinds of sandwiches. There is the flower girl, with her tray of fresh pansies and roses, casting a reflected bloom upon her otherwise pale face. There are the negro waiters ready to pounce upon the first glass that is half-emptied of its contents, so that its owner seeing no glass before him feels it incumbent to order again. There are crowds of females—girls and women in street costumes—some smoking cigarettes sitting poised on men's knees; others at the tables quaffing stimulants like their male companions. There are voices loud, mingled with the constant succession of orders for drinks shouted out unpleasantly by the waiters. There is the sound of clinking and

74

jingling of glasses, the constant rapping on tables, boisterous laughter, an occasional oath, and once in a while an hysterical scream, as some unfortunate woman succumbs to the influence of rum. Above all this is heard at intervals, the sound of music, as it squeezes itself through the thick and sticky air. Men and women are continuously going and coming, and all this drags on until daylight appears, and the persons in the place, from sheer fatigue and exhaustion, seek some place to sleep until the next night, when the females go through the same scenes, with a new lot of the same kind of men. That is the up-town place as it is to-day. The stories one hears are the same as those told two thousand years ago. Woman's fall, man's perfidy, woman's frailty, man's inhumanity form the themes, with drunkeness, depravity and debauchery thrown in parenthetically.

Most of the proprietors of these up-town resorts are very prosperous and would not countenance theft of any kind, nor permit any woman guilty of it to come into their saloons if they knew them to be thieves. Persons and property are comparatively as safe here as they can reasonably be expected to be; but there are lots of persons who visit these places who are known to be professional thieves and pickpockets, and while apparently in the place for amusement, are really watching for some unfortunate who, under the influence of drink, attempts to find his way home alone. Such an individual is followed, and by one pretext or another is robbed. Danger lurks in all these places for the man who drinks. The temperate man is safe almost anywhere, but the temperate man is not in the habit of visiting such places as have been described, except—once in a while.

CHAPTER VI

SHOP-LIFTERS

Many persons contend that certain kinds of criminals inherit their law-breaking propensities. There are others, less charitably disposed, perhaps, who strenuously insist that all criminals, without exception, are simply born with a natural desire to be bad, and would not be otherwise if they could; that they are prone and susceptible to the worst influences because they incline that way. There are others, again, who as strongly and vigorously urge that felons, of whatever grade, class or character, are made so by circumstances, in which poverty, idleness, inability to obtain work, temptation, and a thousand other things, conspire to be either the direct or indirect causes of the individual falling from the straight path and entering the crooked path of crime. But, from whatever motive, by whatever temptation, whether forced or led, certain it is that both male and female criminals have some peculiar ideas of crime, entertained, perhaps, for reasons only known to themselves. The chances of escape from detection are, no doubt, seriously weighed and carefully considered by the persons bent upon committing felony as a mode of livelihood, and, undoubtedly, some special line is selected, as the particular branch of the profession to be followed, in accordance with the physical and mental fitness of the man or woman to succeed in it.

In other words, they gradually become "specialists," like other professional persons in the respectable walks of life. It may be safely said, however, that a thief in one thing is a thief in all things. He would be callow, indeed, who would predicate that a professional burglar would hesitate to commit highway robbery because his weapon was a jimmy, or that a panel thief would turn up his nose at picking an inviting pocket. It is all in the line of business, and neither professional would lose caste. No doubt both men and women select the peculiar line of crime for which they imagine they are physically and mentally best adapted, and which, in each particular case, seems to offer the most facilities and immunities. For these considerations, shop-lifting has its obvious attractions and temptations for women.

For years past, the newspapers of our large cities almost daily have chronicled the arrests of men and women, in stores, who have been caught in the act of appropriating articles that have been temptingly displayed on the counters. Yet it is very doubtful if there has yet appeared one published account of the exact manner in which such goods have been stolen, or an explanation given of the *finesse* by which, in spite of the Argus eyes of the watchers, clerks, visitors and customers, the thief generally contrives to escape detection. It goes without saying that there are adroit and dexterous shop-lifters of both sexes, while the manner of conducting their operations is as diverse as can well be conceived.

The annual thefts of goods from the retail stores of this city alone aggregate an almost fabulous sum. It is very difficult to reach a reliable approximation of the total amount thus stolen, because store-keepers are naturally averse to having their losses from this source known. As a prominent Sixth-avenue gentleman once remarked, "If I should tell how much I annually lost through thieves, or suffered by shop-lifters, I would have the entire band occasionally paying me visits, thinking I had not provided myself with the usual safe-guards against them." Nevertheless, it can be stated as an absolute fact that not less than half a million dollars' worth of goods yearly disappear from the stores through shop-lifters, embracing all kinds of articles, from diamonds to penny fans.

The professional diamond and jewelry thief, however, is not

to be confounded with the shop-lifter, for the former employs quite a different *modus operandi* in capturing his illicit goods. The diamond thief has been known to display the most fertile ingenuity in devising schemes to rob the unwary though generally alert jeweler. An instance is recorded of a thief entering a jewelry store, leaving his "pal" outside to look in through the window, asking to see some diamond rings. While pretending to examine them with severe criticism, and keeping the salesman engaged, he cleverly attached one end of the string, held by his confederate outside, to several of the most valuable, and quietly dropped them at his feet. His "pal" then quietly pulled them along the floor, out through the door, into the street and decamped. A search of the thief who remained behind disclosed nothing and, as proof was thus wanting, he had to be discharged.

The female shop-lifter is generally a woman well known to the police, as her picture will, in nearly every case, be found in the Rogues' Gallery at Police Headquarters. Usually, when she discovers that her actions are watched and her movements shadowed, she quietly folds her tent and proceeds to some other city where she is comparatively a stranger, and where, unsuspected, she can ply her nefarious occupation with less risk of detection and capture. She is often either the wife of a gambler, professional burglar, forger or other criminal; or she may be the wife of some reputable mechanic whose income is insufficient to supply her with the furbelows her vanity craves; or, again, she is one of those women who, having a natural aversion to labor, seek to support themselves by petty thefts.

The fact is notorious, and easily demonstrated by the records of the police courts, that "a shop-lifter once, a shop-lifter always." It is a lamentable psychological idiosyncrasy that, despite the most earnest and apparently sincere resolutions to lead an honest life, the female shop-lifter, intent on making a legitimate purchase, is incapable of withstanding the temptation offered by a display of fancy articles. She will usually attempt to purloin some trinket or other and be caught again. Perhaps the leniency with which crimes of this character have been treated by the authorities has tended to increase the number of persons engaged in committing them. For, heartless as man is at times, he detests the idea of prosecuting a woman for the commission of a petty theft, when the end, for her, means the penitentiary. In very many, perhaps the majority of, cases he will be satisfied if his goods are recovered, and permit the thief to go unpunished. This is very frequently the case with that class of shop-lifters called, by courtesy, the "kleptomaniac,"—the wealthy lady who steals what she could easily have purchased. This is a phase of female character only accounted for upon the Christian hypothesis that her thieving propensities are a disease, while they are really a manifestation of the same base desires which actuate less fortunate women who expiate their misdemeanor in the penitentiary.

Most of the rich kleptomaniacs are well known to the various store-keepers. A woman of this kind is watched from the moment she enters an establishment until she leaves it. Usually, a trusty employee or detective follows her from counter to counter, unobserved, noting all the articles purloined. When the fair and aristocratic thief enters her carriage and is driven to her palatial residence a bill of the goods so "lifted," addressed to the husband, follows her and, in nearly every case, is paid upon presentation and without questioning. Thus the transaction ends, until another visit from the lady occasions another bill. If the "blue-blooded" thief enters a store, however, where she is not known, and to the proprietor of which her "disease" is unsuspected, she often escapes with her "swag," like the unfortunate female who adopts stealing as a means of subsistence. There should be no distinction made between the wealthy and aristocratic female thief and her less fortunate sister, for the crime is the same in both cases; the only difference being that the latter cannot claim the possession of riches in extenuation of her guilt.

The frequency with which thefts by shop-lifters occur, and the amount of valuable goods stolen, has rendered store-keepers more suspicious and cautious, probably, than any other class of men in the world. Nearly all the large stores on Sixth avenue, Twenty-third street, Broadway, Fourteenth street, and others, where ladies do most of their shopping, and which are perfectly jammed with people nearly all day long, employ either male or female detectives (and in some instances both are used), who are constantly on the alert for the detection of female shop-lifters. Such stores as McCreery's, Lord & Taylor's, O'Neill's, Macy's, Simpson, Crawford & Simpson's, Hearn's, Altman's, Koch's, Kaughran's, Ehrich's, Denning's, Stern's and Le Boutillier's are examples. Some stores have had seats erected near the ceiling, where, secreted among shawls and other pendant goods, the detectives are securely hidden from the sight of all persons, and can thus watch the actions of every woman making a purchase. Other detectives are posted at the different entrances; while still others, having the appearance of buyers, are constantly walking and circulating through the various departments, on the lookout for thieves. During the holidays all these precautions are doubled, and some officers are even posted on the sidewalk, in front of the windows.

Before Christmas these stores carry enormous stocks of every kind of fancy goods, and their lavish display, added to their crowded condition at all times, renders theft easier than usual. So that, try as they may, the proprietors cannot prevent a certain amount of thieving, and thousands of dollars worth of goods are annually lost to each store by the depredations of shop-lifters. Even the small shops of Third and Eighth avenues, and Avenues A and B, are not free from the visits of this class of thieves, and no stores are exempt from the imposition of their tribute.

Before leaving home on a thieving excursion to the stores the female shop-lifter carefully and systematically prepares her clothing, and sees that it is in proper form and ready for business. This she does by first putting on a corset made especially for the purpose, with broad, strong bands which pass over the shoulders. Between her legs she arranges a large bag or receptacle made of some extremely strong cloth, which is suspended from the corset by a stout band running around the waist. Her dress or frock covers this, and in front of the dress is an opening or slit, nicely arranged in the folds so as not to be noticed, which leads into the suspended bag. Over this, in winter, is worn a sealskin sacque, cloth cloak, fur circular, or other garment, according to the means of the wearer. In summer she wears a light shawl, which completely hides the slit in the dress from view. She now takes her muff, which, to the uninitiated eye, has nothing to distinguish it, outwardly, from thousands of other muffs, but which is a master-piece of ingenious contrivance. It is covered with any kind of fur, just as honest muffs are, with the significant exception that, instead of being padded with cotton, the fur rests upon a framework of wire. Between the fur covering and the wire supporting frame, the space usually filled with cotton is left vacant, thus providing accommodation for quite a stock of valuable lace, articles of jewelry, gloves, or anything small and valuable. In the bottom of the muff there is a small slide, on the inside, worked by the hand of the wearer, who, after introducing the stolen article into the muff, presses back this slide and drops the plunder into the cavity between the frame and the fur.

With one of these muffs, shop-lifting is so easy as to be successfully practiced by novices, as not one store-walker in a thousand would suspect that his counters could be worked through a muff worn as these are when in action. Thus equipped, the expert female shop-lifter sallies out. Generally, she dresses rather expensively. Sometimes she uses a carriage, but more frequently walks, stopping to gaze in the store windows as she saunters along; and in no particular can she be distinguished from others of her sex, except, perhaps, that in some cases she is rather more richly and attractively clothed. Upon selecting a store that suits her, she walks boldly in, going at once, and without noticeable hesitation, to the lace or other department, before the counter of which she seats herself, adroitly arranging her dress and the slit. Asking the saleswoman to be shown some kinds of lace, she examines it critically, and, laying it down upon the counter, asks to see another kind, or some feathers, or something else, and so contrives to have several articles just before her, one covering the other, if possible. Having accumulated a number of articles upon the counter in an eligible position, she points to some things high up on a shelf behind the counter, thus getting the saleswoman's back turned towards her for an instant, when, with soft dexterity, she conveys anything that happens to be handily in the way through the slit in her dress into the bag between her legs. The goods examined and priced, "not suiting" her, and other customers coming up, she takes the opportunity of moving to another counter, where the same tactics are repeated, and so on, till she is satisfied with her haul or exhausted her stowage capacity.

The muff is worked in this way: The operator rests her hand, with the muff on it, on the goods which she proposes to sample, and a moment of diverted attention on the part of the salesman or saleswoman is ample for her to transfer to her ingenious warehouse such samples as she can conveniently and quickly pick up with one hand. The movement of concealing the stolen articles is instantaneously executed, and, however well the muff may be stuffed, it cannot be bulged out to attract attention. It is surprising to know the vast quantities of material these bags and muffs will contain. At police headquarters, once, in examining the contents of one of these bags, it was found to actually hold a piece of satin, several cards of lace, a camel's-hair shawl, two large china ornaments, a number of spools of silk, several elegant fans, expensive ostrich plumes, and numberless smaller articles, feathers, artificial flowers and some minor trinkets. Shop-lifters are the terror of the shop-keepers, for the thefts embrace everything of convenient character lying about. With one dexterous sweep they will frequently put out of sight a dozen small articles.

All the articles stolen are carried home, the trade-marks

upon them destroyed, and then subsequently sold to some "fence" for about one-third their value, to finally be resold again over the counter of some other store in another city. It is seldom the female shop-lifter uses a male confederate, but it frequently happens that they travel in couples, one engaging the attention of the seller while the other fills her bag or muff, taking turn about until both have stolen sufficient for the day. Sometimes several trips are made to the same store, but generally one is enough.

It often happens that store-keepers make mistakes and wrongfully accuse respectable ladies of shop-lifting, and in such cases the over-zealous vender suffers greatly, both in loss of custom and, oftentimes, in heavy damages in a court of law. All stores are provided with what are called examination rooms. When a person is suspected of being a thief, some of the attaches of the store, or a detective, as the case may be, taps the person lightly upon the shoulder, and politely invites them into this examination room. Here their bundles and packages are searched and, if warranted, their clothing is personally inspected by some female attendant. Here is where some very curious scenes are enacted. The professional thief will resort to tears, expostulations, explanations, excuses of all kinds, finally begging to be allowed to depart. The discovery of the bag or the muff, however, invariably settles the case and the offender is marched off to jail.

In the case of a mistake, as stated, the store-keeper generally makes the explanations, excuses, and so forth, supplementing them afterwards by payment in a suit for damages.

Men shop-lifters—or, more properly, store thieves—pursue an entirely different method, and confine their operations to a far different kind of store. They go into the thieving business to make it pay, and are not tempted by the display of merely pretty things. They prefer to operate in the wholesale stores, and how ingeniously and systematically they accomplish their object, under the very eyes of people, borders on the marvelous.

It has often been said that the same amount of ingenuity,

thought, care and planning, which is bestowed by criminals upon the perpetration of felony, if directed properly upon some legitimate business would render them successful and rich. Undoubtedly, this is true. What inventive faculties they must have to devise such a convenient contrivance as the shop-lifter's muff, the various burglar's implements, the safe-robber's tools, their delicate files, saws, etc., made from the best of steel, and thousands of other things used in various ways, including the store thief's satchel, must be manifest to the most ordinary comprehension.

As this latter article is used by the class of thief about to be spoken of, a short description of it will not be amiss. To all outward appearance it is a very unpretentious traveling-bag. It looks honest, and does not differ, apparently, from any other bag of its kind. A careful scrutiny hardly discloses any variation from the ordinary valise; but, nevertheless, it has a false side, so ingeniously arranged as to open and close noiselessly, being caught with a well-oiled spring or fastening. The hinges of this false side are made on the iron which, in ordinary satchels, contains the lock, and it opens upwards, when placed in the usual manner upon a table, instead of downwards—just the reverse of the honest one. It is the simplest thing in the world, then, for an expert, carrying a valise of this description by the handle, to place it over a piece of valuable cloth, open the slide, which works with a spring; at the precise moment slip the goods in, and, taking his valise by the handle, walk off undiscovered. To any one who may be watching, the action of the thief is the most natural one in the world, and if the goods themselves are not missed no one would ever suspect they were in the valise carried by the gentleman who merely let it rest for a second on the table. But it is captured all the same, although you cannot see it. It has changed from one place to the other under the magical "presto" of the thief.

The store thief saunters down-town to the dry goods district, watches the wholesale houses, notes the interior of the stores, and carefully makes his selection of some one suitable to his purpose. The next morning, bright and early, he attires himself like a country store-keeper, and, taking his satchel in his hand, he makes haste to reach the store he intends to work, appearing to the quietly-observant porter like an out-of-town buyer, just come off some early incoming train. Asking the porter or clerk, who, probably, about this time, is sweeping out, in expectation of the arrival of some of the salesmen or proprietors, if Mr. Smith, a salesman, is in, he is informed that none of the clerks or salesmen are down yet. Remarking in answer that he will wait a moment or two, as he has just arrived from Schenectady, he deftly places his gripsack upon the counter, over some valuable piece of goods, and saunters around the store, coming back to where his valise is, when, embracing a favorable opportunity, he slips the one, two or three pieces of cloth through the false portion of the valise, and, taking it by the handle in the usual careless manner, "guesses he will go to his hotel and have a wash and return later," and leaves the store not only undetected but entirely unsuspected. Very probably the theft remains undiscovered until the next taking of stock, when it is impossible to tell how the goods were lost, and in many cases some attache of the store is discharged, never knowing for what sin of omission or commission he was suspected. The success of this mode of theft is best shown by the infrequency with which such cases are ever brought to light or its perpetrator ever caught and arrested.

CHAPTER VII

KLEPTOMANIA

In the issue of the New York *World,* bearing date Saturday, May 11, 1867, appeared a long article criticising, exposing, and severely condemning the methods of the city's detective police. "A detective," said the writer, "is presumed to be alike active, capable and honest, and were he such, he would be a public benefactor; but as he is too often either ignorant, indolent, or positively dishonest, he becomes a public pest. That detectives are in league with thieves; that they associate with them publicly and privately on the most intimate terms; that they occasionally 'put up' jobs with them by which the people are alike fleeced and astonished; that although the perpetrators of great robberies are generally known to them, the said perpetrators almost invariably escape punishment; that far more attention is paid to the sharing of the plunder, or the obtaining of a large percentage on the amount of money recovered, than to the furtherance of the ends of justice—all these statements are undeniably true."

Coming to specific charges, the writer said further on: "A handsome female, a Broadway shop-lifter, recently testified that although she had been desirous of reforming her life for a year past, she had been totally prevented from so doing by the extortions of certain members of the detective force, who threatened to reveal her former history unless she 'came down handsomely,' and in order to 'come down,' as they styled it, she was obliged to resort to her old disgraceful business."

The foregoing reference to a concurrent incident was presented to the reader as coldly and curtly as a historic hailstone, striking him but to glance off, and not like a real, breathing story, as it was, appealing strongly to his heart. The following facts, which have been kept inviolate in this office for nearly twenty years, and only brought to light here because those most concerned have passed away, will show what a stirring and pathetic narrative lay beneath the newspaper chronicler's dry words.

Early in the spring of the year above named, an elderly gentleman of undoubted respectability was shown into our private office. He was exceedingly nervous and flurried, and his wan, colorless face looked like an effaced page. In a tortuous, round-about way, he intimated that his married daughter was in great trouble, in consequence of the operation of a great weakness or defect in character which was apparently hereditary. Her mother, his wife, he said, an excellent, kind-hearted, conscientious, truthful woman, had occasionally manifested the kleptomania impulse and had been detected. Happily the crime had been committed under circumstances which obviated exposure; it had been charitably overlooked upon his paying the bill for the purloined goods. Up to the date of her marriage, he had not observed or otherwise become cognizant of the development of the unfortunate trait in his only daughter. Her husband was a noble-minded man who devotedly loved her, and whom she idolized. Two years after her marriage she was caught shop-lifting in an establishment where she was known. By a merciful stroke of fortune, the information and the bill were sent to the father instead of the husband. Great moral and religious influence had been brought to bear on her, and for several years there was cause to believe that she had overcome her weakness. Unfortunately there had been another lapse into temptation. At present she was suffering the tortures of the damned, but in what particular respect she had refused to explain to him. "Father, find me an active, bold and energetic lawyer," she had said in a paroxysm of tears, "and I will tell him what I *cannot* tell you."

The lady came to the office next morning, alone. She was pale as a lily, and she bore on her forehead that shadow of melancholy which tells all the world that a woman is suffering and unhappy. Her eyes were dark and soft as the darkest and softest violet, and she was dressed with the utmost simplicity. She was in a most desponding mood. She said nothing was worth striving for any more. There was no good under the sun for her. The splendor had gone from the grass—the glory from the flower. Life, affection, family ties, love of good name—all these had ceased to appeal to her.

In the *sanctum sanctorum* of a criminal lawyer's office the extremes of mental agony and poignant suffering are sometimes revealed in all their phases; but it would be hard to imagine any one suffering more than this fair, prepossessing woman, as she told how that sleepless and merciless vulture of remorse, aided by the machinations of a licensed fiend in human form, dogged her steps by day and made night horrible. The recital recalled the picture suggested by the lines:

> "Lean abstinence, pole grief and haggard care,
> The dire attendants of forlorn despair."

With pale, quivering lips, she told the story of her humiliation. Primarily, some two years after she became a happy wedded wife, she was impelled by an irresistible impulse to take some article, almost valueless in itself, from the counter of a dry-goods store. She had been making several purchases and had plenty of money in her pocket at the time. Afterwards, as opportunity offered, the wretched larceny was repeated. Then came discovery, and her father's awakening to the realization that his daughter was a thief. He summoned a minister and some worthy Christian women—relatives of his—to talk to her and to urge her to seek strength from that source where it is never withheld when earnestly and penitently invoked. She became a church-member, zealous and earnest in the path of righteousness, partaking regularly of the Sacred Elements, visiting the sick, relieving the distressed, and comforting the afflicted. To use Milton's language,

> "Such a sacred and homefelt delight,
> Such sober certainty of waking bliss,"

she had never felt till then. Under these happy conditions five years passed, and then again during the holiday season, temptation assailed her and was stronger than she. The person who discovered her theft was a detective. He did not arrest and expose her. He did worse. He followed her, obtained an interview and promised to keep her secret if she made it worth his while. She willingly gave him a sum of money, and expected to hear no more of him or of her transgression. But this newer edition of Fagin, who was as vile as the sewers, and who lied like a prospectus, dogged her movements and systematically shadowed her wherever she went, again and again demanding money and threatening her with newspaper publicity. She gave this rapacious vampire all the money she could procure, even borrowing from her father. The pawnbrokers had in safe keeping her diamonds, jewels, and some of her furs and laces. They had been pledged to furnish this licensed black-mailer with money, and still he was insatiate and unappeased. Her husband's suspicions meanwhile had been aroused. She spent so much money in occult ways that he had been impelled to ask her father what he thought L—— was doing with so much money. Fettered thus, with the torments both of Prometheus and Tantalus—the vulture gnawing at her vitals, and the lost joys mocking her out of reach—she had at last in sheer desperation been driven to request her father to procure her the assistance of a fearless lawyer.

It is not expedient to reveal the *modus operandi* used in emancipating this unfortunate lady from her worse than Egyptian bondage. But the reader may rest assured that through the co-operation of the police commissioners the shameless scoundrel was dismissed from the police force. Afterwards, he served a term in a Western state prison, and up to this hour has been heard no more of in New York.

CHAPTER VIII

PANEL HOUSES AND PANEL THIEVES

Some years since respectable New York was startled and horrified by the recitals of criminal life, which, in the fulfillment of a disagreeable public duty, the daily newspapers printed in their news columns. The stirring appeal for the suppression of the evil then made by the press to the moral sentiment of the community, was backed by the judiciary, by the money and influence of wealthy and patriotic citizens, by the various charitable organizations, and by the whole police force. Consequently, the foul Augean stable of vice and iniquity, for the time being, at least, was in a great degree cleansed and purified. The leaders of that foul army of vicious men and women were gradually rooted out and driven away from their noxious haunts. Some found a congenial haven in the State prison, a few reformed, and many died in want. The plague being temporarily stayed, and popular indignation a matter of record, New York, as is its invariable custom, permitted its vigilance to go quietly to sleep, with a fair prospect of it being rudely awakened to find history repeating itself. That this awakening cannot safely be much longer deferred, it is partly the mission of the present chapter to show. For it is useless to deny that we have in this city to-day, a condition of affairs very similar to that which aroused the indignation and called for the severe repressional measures of our immediate predecessors. Up-town, in many instances closely contiguous to the dwellings of people of the highest respectability, there are dens as vile and infamous as ever disgraced any civilized community. Hardly a street, however

91

apparently exclusive and fashionable, can boast that it is free from gambling, prostitution or panel houses.

Some time since, a journalist connected with a prominent morning paper, took great pains to collect statistics concerning houses of prostitution in New York. The article in which the results of his investigation were given, estimates that over $15,000,000 was invested in that business, and that the yearly amount spent in those houses averaged over $10,000,000. In this chapter, however, the reader's attention is more particularly invited to the class of assignation and prostitution bagnios, known as panel houses.

The name "panel house" was originally derived from a false impression prevalent in the community, that the rooms occupied by the inmates were fitted with sliding panels in the walls and partitions, through and by means of which most of the robberies were committed. But, as will be seen hereafter, the term is a misnomer, so far as the fact is concerned. But they had to have some distinctive appellation, and "panel house" is a convenient generic term.

The proprietors of panel houses, in years gone by, were nearly all professional gamblers, a fact which is more or less true to-day, where the real, genuine house of that character exists, but there are hundreds of women who work the "panel game" upon their victims, who hire a simple room in some furnished-room house. If detected the entire house has conferred upon it the name of panel house, and is ever afterwards described and known as such in police and court records.

The real, Simon-pure panel thief is generally a young and pretty female, who has been initiated into the mysteries of the game by either a gambler or a lover, and of whom she is the mistress. It is the conception of a man's brain, needing the assistance of an attractive woman to carry out the scheme, and was probably originally devised by some broken-down gambler to secure enough funds wherewith to resume play. No woman would ever have dreamt of practicing such an intricate and bold robbery, for she could never have carried it out. There are many women engaged in these robberies who are neither young nor handsome, but they are adepts and make up in knowledge and experience what they lack in charms; but the most successful are young and attractive. They succeed better when they are winsome, for reasons which require no explanation.

Strange as it may appear, there are instances on record in which some of the professional females engaged in this panel game have preserved intact their virtue, so far as men generally were concerned, and have remained steadfast and true to their lovers, through all vicissitudes. They have solicited and accompanied men to their rooms, yet still have so contrived and maneuvered, as to have their male companion robbed without indulging in any of the other apparently necessary concomitants to the success of the undertaking. But these women are rare—very rare indeed. The fact of their occasional existence merely proves that the sole object of all women engaged in the nefarious game of panel thieving is robbery—first, last and all the time.

From the well-known dislike of the victims of this game to making their names and losses known by figuring prominently in a court of justice, panel-house thieves escape the punishment they justly deserve and thrive more successfully, perhaps, than other professional robbers. Besides, the game is practiced more particularly upon the most respectable element of the community. Men of families, strangers visiting the city, men of advanced years, and even clergymen are sometimes caught in the net. As may be imagined, people of this class prefer to lose their money rather than have their names made public, and so long as such victims are to be found, panel houses will thrive and thieves become rich. Instances are on record where as much as eight thousand dollars have been secured from a single victim, who, from his prominence in social and business circles, allowed the matter to drop, although he was acquainted with the thief.

A man and a woman are essential to the execution of the panel game. The woman's part consists in "cruising," a term applied to walking the streets to pick up men. The man has two parts to enact, as "runner" and "robber." The first role consists in being on the street watching his female decoy. If he sees a man partially under the influence of liquor, he informs the decoy, who places herself in the way of the obfuscated citizen. Or, in the event of the woman securing a customer herself, the "runner" observes it, and when she and her new-found friend proceed towards the house, the "runner" rapidly goes ahead and unobserved slips in first to make arrangements for the second role in the drama, and which in some cases has ended in a tragedy.

The foregoing more particularly concerns panel thieves, that is, "couples" who adopt the business on their own account. There are regular panel houses, by which is meant houses of ill-fame, with perhaps from ten to twenty girl inmates, where nearly every room in the house is perfectly arranged for systematically pursuing this kind of robbery, and where the moment a girl retires to a room with a gentleman, the proprietor is notified, and when the chance occurs, completely cleans the unconscious victim of every cent he may have about him. These houses, however, are not now as plentiful as they were immediately after the close of the war. The victims of these houses were many, for outwardly they did not differ from ordinary gilded palaces of sin, and, being situated in streets well known to contain respectable seraglios, were frequently visited in the orthodox way by gentlemen in search of the "elephant."

The game, however, is played in precisely the same way in all cases, whether by a "loving couple" on their own account or by one of the many girls in a regular house instituted for the sole purpose. And this is the way it is done: A pretty female, young, with entrancing eyes, an elegant form, richly and fashionably attired, is noticed daintily picking her steps on a street crossing. She is more frequently noticed in the act of crossing a street, as it affords her an opportunity of rendering herself still more attractive and seductive by practicing those apparently aimless little feminine arts that prove so fascinating to the coarser sex. The skirts are just lifted high enough to discover a beautiful foot; perhaps a glimpse of an ankle bewitchingly smothered in lace frills is revealed; while a warm scintillant glance of invitation is thrown at the interested beholder, who, perhaps, follows and engages her in conversation. More than likely he is agreeably surprised to find how lady-like and attractive her manners are, and by his own suggestion or her invitation he readily accompanies her to her home; not, however, without being previously warned that she is married, that her husband is very ugly and jealous, and a big, strong, quarrelsome fellow, to boot.

The room to which she conducts him is apparently an ordinary room, furnished in an ordinary way. It is, however, usually a front room, separated by folding doors from the room in the rear. It is in connection with these folding doors that mystery and danger lurk. These folding doors are a study. Some are so constructed that instead of opening in the center, one of them opens upon hinges which are placed on that portion of the doors where the lock is usually situated, so that it opens at the woodwork on the side. If a chance visitor to one of these rooms should have his suspicions aroused by any act of his companion, and should closely examine the doors, he would find a bolt on the inside securely fastened, but he would not be likely to see that it barely rested in the socket, and thinking everything was all right, his suspicions would be disarmed. As there would be but one other door in the room—that by which he entered—and as he locked that himself, privacy would apparently be insured.

In the folding doors are several minute holes, through which a person behind them can watch all that goes on in the front room. These holes, however, are frequently dispensed with, and a cough or other understood signal by the female gives the thief warning when all is ready for his entrance.

After the lapse of perhaps five minutes the female coughs or makes some understood signal, the door noiselessly opens at the side, a man enters unseen, secures the victims clothing, disappears into the next room, takes the money out of a pocket-book or pocket, replaces the pocket-book in the clothes, takes the watch, the studs out of the shirt, everything, in fact, of any value, and replacing the clothing, softly closes the door again. Now comes the scene: A knock is heard on the other door—that by which the victim entered. With a slight scream the female remarks, that the person knocking is her husband, and with great haste proceeds to dress, all the while telling her now frightened companion that he will kill him if he sees him, hurriedly assists him to dress and half pushing him, forces him out of the room, down the stairs into the street.

Another phase of this trick is when, in the absence of folding doors, the lock or bolt is so arranged that socket and bolt are both upon the door. Another is to fill the socket with some substance, a cork for instance, so that when the bolt is pushed forward, it fails to enter the socket.

An instance is related of an elderly man coming into one of these rooms, and casually remarking to his female friend, "I hope I won't be rapped out of this room by anyone, for I have been in two places to-night and was rapped out of both." That gentleman was robbed in the first house he entered, and must have remarked in the second one that he was "rapped out" of the first, for his companion in this last affair knew what had happened in the other cases, and that he would not have been treated in that manner unless they had secured his money. And so his remark being again overheard, he was unceremoniously "rapped out" of this third and last house. Here is acase from the records which probably illustrates the method as well as any other:

An elderly man, about sixty years of age, entered a panel-room with a dark-haired, flashily-dressed woman, who immediately requested him to bolt the door. This he did, but he might have saved himself the trouble, for the door was no more closed then than it was before. These bolts are very ingenious. The catch on the jamb of the door into which the bolt slides has three false screw-heads in it. In reality it is not attached to the door-casing at all, but is fastened to the body of the bolt by an unseen plate. Consequently, when the door is opened, the catch goes forward with the remainder of the bolt. This, of course, was not noticed by the man, as the gas was not turned up by the woman till after the door was closed. While the man was bolting the door the woman hurried to the dressing-table and hastily laid her hat on one chair and her cloak on the other. This action compelled the man to place his clothes on the couch or on one of the chairs by the folding doors. When all was ready, one of the operators scratched lightly on the door with his finger-nail, to warn the woman he was about to enter the room. The next moment the man boldly opened the door wide, removed the chair out of his way, and glided rapidly to the other chair, on which the man's clothes lay. At this moment the woman redoubled her fascinations, for the purpose of distracting the attention of her companion, in which intent she was eminently successful. The work of going through the man's pockets, and what is technically known as "weeding" his pocket-book, was quickly over, the chair was quietly replaced, the panel-door closed, and the thief appeared with a roll of bills in his hand. The whole thing was done in from twenty to twenty-five seconds. Immediately after the closing of the door the man went outside, and, knocking on the passage-door of the bedroom, said in a loud whisper.

"Jenny, here's Joe; hurry up."

"My God!" exclaimed the girl, jumping up, "you must get away as fast as you can. That's my lover. He's dreadful jealous, and would shoot you as soon as look at you."

It is needless to say that the victim required no urging. He jumped into his clothes as fast as possible, only too glad to get out of the way before the appearance of the terrible imaginary lover, and apparently without the slightest notion that he had been robbed.

The victims of these thefts have really no redress. It is so hard to find the guilty woman afterwards, or even to locate the house, for unless the pleasure hunter suspects some trap he pays no particular attention to the kind of house, its situation, or its number. In the case of a stranger he never seeks the thieves again, but "pockets his loss." If an elderly man, he does likewise. But if he be really an obstinate man, determined upon catching the thieves and prosecuting them, he will invariably be approached and his money and valuables will be returned to him upon condition that he withdraws his complaint. Convictions are very rarely obtained in any case from the difficulty of identifying the parties.

Many of these women never see a penny of the plundered money, the man, in most cases, retaining the whole of the loot. It sometimes happens that a victim discovers that he has been robbed before he leaves, and makes what is called in the vernacular a "kick"; if so, it also sometimes happens that he is unmercifully beaten by the lover and his pals, but it has occurred that when "the kicker" was a man about town, that he has gotten away with his assailant in a manner calculated to make the heart of a Sullivan beat with pleasure.

There is quite a different feature of this panel-game, but which more properly belongs to black-mail, in which, through the peep-holes in the doors, the face of the man or woman in the adjoining room is studied, waited for on the outside, followed to his or her home, and in a few days threatened with exposure, if the sum demanded is not forthcoming.

Couples have been known to ply the panel-game very successfully in some of the most prominent hotels in the city. The lady would make her conquest upon the streets in the ordinary manner and the game would be worked in two rooms of the hotel as already described. This enterprise was carried on successfully by a scoundrel and his wife at one time in one of the best hotels, and although it was generally known, there never was any one to complain against them. It was only by the proprietor specially employing several detectives that they were finally discovered, arrested and punished.

CHAPTER IX

A THEATRICAL ROMANCE

A good many years since, at a fashionable boardinghouse in Philadelphia, a handsome Adonis-shapen young man, well and favorably known by the name of George Hemmings, became acquainted with a member of the fairer sex who had scarcely passed "sweet sixteen," and was accredited with a bountiful supply of beauty, named then Eliza Garrett. An intimacy at once sprung up between the two, which at length ripened into a mutual attachment.

A series of journeys were undertaken by Miss Garrett and Hemmings, and for some time they lived together enjoying all the pleasures and sweets of love; but for some cause the pair separated, and for a number of years saw nothing of each other. Meantime, many changes had occurred in the circumstances of both. Eliza had been transformed into Mrs. Bethune and lived in a fashionable part of Gotham, her reputed husband, John Bethune, Esquire, being a gentleman of wealth and sporting proclivities.

George Hemmings, who, by the way, was very respectably connected, had migrated from the "City of Brotherly Love" to "Gotham," and filled a position as superintendent in a dry-goods establishment.

It was whilst in this city, when "walking down Broadway" one afternoon, Hemmings' attention was attracted by a lady who seemed to have been previously pleased with his acquaintance, and in whom he recognized his former inamorata, Miss Garrett. A grand recapitulation of the pleasantries of by-gone days ensued, and the damsel informed her "once dear George" that she was now Mrs. Bethune, but prevailed upon him to accompany her to her home. Here a hearty welcome was accorded him, and, if his statement be correct, it is said that the intimacy of former times was renewed.

Matters continued in this manner, and Hemmings was induced to leave his former situation and take up his abode at the residence of Mrs. Bethune as general superintendent of that household, inasmuch as Mr. Bethune himself was occasionally absent from the city.

On one occasion, as Mr. Hemmings alleged, the beauteous Mrs. Bethune was violently assaulted by her better-half for some alleged indiscretion, and it was her early lover who played the part of Good Samaritan on the occasion, comforting her as well as he was able himself, and calling in a physician to bind up her wounds. During her sickness, the relationship between Hemmings and the lady seems to have been of the most intimate character. She gave him a pair of diamond ear-rings to pledge for four hundred dollars, which money was a portion of an amount which was to be called into requisition for the necessary engagements and other expenses incurred at the opening of a theatre in Pittsburg, the management to be assumed by Miss Kate Fisher, the well-known "Mazeppa" and equestrienne actress, and George Hemmings. A troupe was thereupon engaged, and the entire company, including Miss Fisher and Hemmings, started for Pennsylvania, where they intended to delight the inhabitants with the drama of the "fiery, untamed steed" order.

Soon after "Cupid George" departed for the West, Mrs. Bethune became a prey to the "green-eyed monster." She realized the temptations that would surely beset George as he basked in the smiles of the alluring and classically modeled equestrienne. Other troubles beset Mrs. Bethune at this juncture. Her husband asked her one day what had become of her diamond ear-rings, and she was seized with confusion and dismay. To disclose the truth would be to incur Bethune's jealousy, natural indignation and too probable violence, and so the convenient idea seems to have occurred to her that by accusing Hemmings of the theft of the jewelry, she would achieve a two-fold success; namely, the one of concealing her own frailty, and the other of snatching her beloved one from a hated supposed rival. Bethune, believing her story, obtained a requisition from Governor Fenton and procured Hemmings' arrest in Pittsburg, and he was accordingly brought to this city. The services of Howe & Hummel were called into requisition, and Hemmings brought into court for trial.

The greatest excitement was aroused amongst theatrical and sporting celebrities, and long before the opening of the court every seat was filled by eager and expectant spectators, and when the prisoner was called to the bar an immense throng surged to and fro to obtain a glimpse at his features, and those of the accusing beauty.

City Judge Russel presided, and the Hon. Robert C. Hutchings, afterwards Surrogate, conducted the prosecution.

Mr. Hutchings opened the case for the people in a fair and temperate speech, stating that he was instructed that he should be enabled to establish a clear case of larceny against the defendant, who then stood indicted for having, on the 19th of October, 1868, at the city of New York, feloniously stolen, taken, and carried away, one pair of diamond ear-rings of the value of $400, the property of one James A. Lynch.

Mr. Hutchings then called Mrs. Eliza Bethune, who, amidst breathless silence, was sworn, and testified that Hemmings was observed by her daughter purloining the ear-rings from her boudoir drawer on the day in question, and that immediately she was informed of the larceny she had sought out Hemmings and ascertained that he had fled to Pittsburgh. On inquiry, she had also traced the missing jewelry to a pawn-office kept by Mr. Barnard, at No. 404 Third avenue, where the articles were pledged by Hemmings. She also went to Pittsburg with Detective Young, and the pawn-ticket of the ear-rings was found on Hemmings, which she took from him. Mrs. Bethune further stated that the officer then handcuffed the prisoner and brought him on to this city.

The witness was then subjected to a rigid cross-examination by Mr. Howe, who propounded questions as follows:

Mr. Howe: Are you married to Mr. Bethune?

Mrs. Bethune (imploringly to Judge Russel): Am I compelled to answer that question?

Judge Russel: Mr. Howe, I have already ruled that these kind of questions are improper.

Mr. Howe (with pertinacity): Your honor, I desire to show that this witness is not the wife of Mr. Bethune; and I contend that, in justice to my client, the question should be answered.

Judge Russel: I rule it out.

Mr. Howe: I take exception to the ruling of the court, and will now put another question, namely:

Is Mr. Bethune your husband? (Sensation in court.)

Judge Russel ruled the question inadmissible, and exception was taken.

Detective John Young, of the Eighteenth Precinct Police, was next called, and deposed: I am connected with the Metropolitan Police of this city; I was sent with a requisition issued by Governor Fenton to Pittsburgh to arrest George Hemmings for grand larceny; I went there with Mr. and Mrs. Bethune; I took Hemmings into custody at the Pittsburgh Theatre; he made a violent resistance, and scuffled with me; I was necessitated to handcuff him in the cars; he became very abusive and threatening; in fact, so much so, that I was compelled to hit him on the head with the butt-end of my pistol; at the time of his arrest he had upon him the ticket of the ear-rings.

Alexander Barnard, a pawnbroker at No. 404 Third avenue, was the next witness, and said: I know the prisoner at the bar; he pledged me with two diamond ear-rings on the 20th of last October, which Mr. Lynch subsequently identified as his property.

Cross-examined by Mr. Howe: Hemmings has frequently

pawned articles of jewelry with me; he pledged them in the name of Mrs. Bethune.

Mr. Howe here requested that the pawnbroker should be directed to produce his book in order that the jury might see the dates, the production of which the counsel insisted would entirely contradict Mrs. Bethune's testimony.

The book was subsequently produced, and Mr. Barnard testified, on further cross-examination by Mr. Howe, that Hemmings had pledged with him a watch belonging to Mrs. Bethune on the 17th of November, being *nearly one month* after the date the ear-rings were pledged.

Mrs. Lynch proved that the ear-rings were her property, and that she had loaned them to Mrs. Bethune.

Mrs. Bethune now took the witness stand, and she was asked by Mr. Howe how long she had known Hemmings, the prisoner at the bar?

Mrs. Bethune: About twelve years.

Mr. Howe: Where did you first become acquainted with him?

Mrs. Bethune: At Philadelphia; I was employed in the United States Mint, and we boarded together in the same house.

Mr. Howe: Did you subsequently come on to New York with him?

Witness (hesitatingly): I did.

Mr. Howe: Were you on terms of peculiar intimacy with him?

Mrs. Bethune: I was not (sensation in the court): we were friends.

Mr. Howe: Was it not at your solicitation that he was taken to live in the same house with yourself and Mr. Bethune?

Mrs. Bethune: Yes, it was; but I merely took him in out of charity, as he was poor and had no clothes (sensation in court).

Mr. Howe: Did you ever stay at the Washington Hotel in this city with him?

Judge Russel here interposed, and informed Mrs. Bethune that she need not answer that question.

Mr. Howe: Did you not visit him when he was employed at A.

DANGER! - A TRUE HISTORY OF A GREAT

T. Stewart's store in this city?

Mrs. Bethune: I did; but I got him employed there.

Mr. Howe (aside): Compassionate woman (laughter). Now, Mrs. Bethune, through whom did you get him employed at that store?

Mrs. Bethune: Through Mr. Griswold, a gentleman of my acquaintance.

Mr. Howe: Did you not know at the time you had Hemmings in your house that he was a married man?

Mrs. Bethune: I did. (Sensation.)

Mr. Howe: Have you not been to the Whitney House with Hemmings?

The court also decided that witness need not answer that question, whereupon counsel took exception.

Mr. Howe: Have you not frequently been to the Chanler House in this city with Mr. Hemmings?

Question overruled.

Mr. Howe: Did you not receive visits from Hemmings in East Fourth street, in this city?

Mrs. Bethune: Am I bound to answer that question?

Judge Russel: I overrule that question, and you need not answer it.

Mr. Howe: Did you ever live in a house in Lombard street, Philadelphia, kept by a Miss Graham, and did you ever meet Hemmings there.

Mrs. Bethune (indignantly): I did not.

Mr. Howe: Did you ever introduce Hemmings to any person at Saratoga as your brother?

Mrs. Bethune (reluctantly): Yes, I have. (Sensation.)

Mr. Howe: How many times have you given Hemmings your jewelry to pledge that he might have money?

Mrs. Bethune: I never gave him permission to pledge any of my jewelry.

Mr. Howe: Do you mean to swear that he has never pledged any of your jewelry prior to the present occasion?

104

Mrs. Bethune: Yes, he has, but not with my consent. (Sensation.)

Mr. Howe: Was that whilst he was living in your house?

Mrs. Bethune: It was.

Mr. Howe: Why did you not have him arrested for so doing?

Mrs. Bethune: Because he cried, and I forgave him. (Sensation.)

Mr. Howe: Yes, you forgave your "BROTHER" (roars of laughter). Now, madam! will you swear that you did not give Hemmings your watch to pledge on the 17th of November last, nearly one month after he pledged the ear-rings?

Mrs. Bethune: I did not; I will swear that I never gave him anything to pledge after he pawned the ear-rings; I did not give him the ear-rings; I paid Kate Fisher the money with which to open the theatre, and not to Hemmings; I did not pay her in the Chanler House, in Hemmings' presence; I paid her on the street, the reason Hemmings went to Saratoga with me, was to take care of Mr. Bethune's horses (immoderate laughter); I will swear that I had not seen Hemmings since he took the ear-rings until I had him arrested; I did not arrest him right away, because I was sick; the ear-rings were not mine, they belonged to Mr. Lynch; I borrowed them from Mrs. Lynch.

Mr. Howe: What was your name when you became acquainted with Hemmings?

Mrs. Bethune: Eliza Garrett.

This closed the case for the prosecution, and Mr. Howe, for the defense, called Dr. J. Kennedy, who testified as follows:

I am a physician, and reside in East Tenth street in this city; I have seen the prisoner before. In October last, I saw him in a house in East Fourth street.

Mr. Howe: What were you doing at that house?

Dr. Kennedy: I was attending a lady there, professionally.

Mr. Howe: Would you know that lady again?

Dr. Kennedy: I should.

Mr. Howe (to Mrs. Bethune): Madam, will you oblige me by

standing up and raising your veil?

The lady complied with Mr. Howe's request, and amidst breathless silence Mr. Howe, addressing Dr. Kennedy, said, "Doctor, is that the lady?"

Dr. Kennedy: It is. (Flutter in the court-room.)

Mr. Howe: How many times did you visit her?

Dr. Kennedy: Eight or ten times.

Mr. Howe: Was Hemmings in the room with her?

Dr. Kennedy: He was. (Sensation.)

Mr. Howe then applied for attachments against two witnesses who had been subpoenaed to prove that Mrs. Bethune had been at the Whitney House and the Washington Hotel with Hemmings, but Judge Russel declined to grant any time, and peremptorily ordered Mr. Howe to proceed with his defense to the jury.

Mr. Howe then arose and addressed the court. He said:

Gentlemen of the Jury: I approach the consideration of this case with some degree of embarrassment, which is necessarily forced upon me, from the fact, that whilst discharging, as I shall endeavor to do, to the best of my ability, my duties as an advocate to the young man accused of this larceny, I regret that I am called upon to animadvert in terms of censure and reproach, upon one who leaves a name which is dear and hallowed to us all—the originator of our being—a name that we all revere and respect when we view it in the beauteous and lovely purity which is thrown around it. But I think, gentlemen, it is not unfair when that name is divested of its purity, and becomes shrouded with that which is base and vile—when the guard which we naturally and intuitively throw around it is dispelled, and, instead of the beauteous statue of monumental alabaster, we see a black, foetid, loathsome thing before us, from which we shrink with indignation and horror, knowing it is that which drags our young men down to degradation, disgrace and death—I say, in entering upon this prisoner's defense, such is the distinction between pure and hallowed and virtuous women (against whom

106

none dare point) and her who forgets herself—forgets the holy ties due to her sex, and her own self-respect: and who assumes the place of wife to a man without that sanction which God has instituted and commanded, and who, entrapping others, comes to court to-day—not the pure being to demand your respect—but one whom we can but contemplate with loathing and disgust, and who has proved herself utterly unworthy of belief. Gentlemen, I simply wish to direct your attention to the proven facts. I have thus ventured to allude to the distinction I have endeavored to draw, not for the purpose of warping your minds, or in any degree throwing an unfair prejudice around this case; but, in view of the solemnity of the oaths you have taken, to do justice between the People of the State of New York and the prisoner at the bar, and to see upon what testimony you are asked to consign an innocent, but foolish young man, for a long term of years to the state prison.

I find in the book before me, gentlemen, to my surprise—and when it will be handed to you I think you will agree with me and share my astonishment—that on the first day of October last Mr. Lynch has sworn that *his* diamond ear-rings were stolen. I find that from the first day of October until the 8th day of December—a long lapse of nearly two months—no steps are taken by those who are alleged to have sustained the loss, and nothing is done until the latter date. I will show you why this demand is made upon the Executive—a novel proceeding altogether, without any indictment being preferred in this office—and a journey is made to Pittsburgh, not by the officers alone, but as we have it on the sworn testimony of the woman in this case, that she, without her protector, without the man Bethune (who is with her now as her husband, and who professed to be so then), proceeded alone to Pittsburgh, and is subsequently followed by Mr. Bethune. That is the first era, the first of October. We next find Mrs. Bethune detailing to you that these ear-rings were taken (how she does not know), but only what she was told by a little girl whom we have not seen. So her story runs. It is pretty for the present; but I hope to destroy the poetry of it very shortly. That this man stole, not on the first of October, but on the 19th of October, and subsequently corrected to-day, by the lady of treacherous memory, to the date of the 20th. At all events, it is perfectly clear, now, according to her last amended allegation, that on the 20th of October she claims a larceny to have been committed. But a Mr. Lynch is supposed to be the owner of the earrings, and not Mrs. Bethune! It transpires that she had merely borrowed them for a while, as she tells you; and then on the 20th of October she learns the loss. Why, gentlemen, did not Mrs. Bethune tell you, that nearly a month after that and in November, she had met this man on the street with Miss Kate Fisher? That they had business transactions, that she knew him—the theatrical manager—that he was to open a theatre—that money was supplied by her for that express purpose? Did not she know within one month after this transaction the same state of facts which she deposes to-day? Why not have had the prisoner arrested on the street then?

No, gentlemen, I will give you my theory of this case; I will render to you what this man has told me, and if it be not a common-sense view of it, no logic—no metaphysics—then discard every word uttered and condemn this man. The pawnbroker throws additional light upon this transaction, and, gentlemen, if you will refer to the date in his book of the 17th of November (a month after his alleged larceny), you will find an important fact which I beseech you to hold, pointedly, in your own estimation. You will remember that she contradicts herself, and stated that she had had no transactions with Hemmings after the alleged larceny. One of the gentlemen on the jury put the very pertinent question (seeing the force of this), whether she had transactions with the prisoner after this alleged stealing. You will remember for yourselves, gentlemen, and I point to it without fear of contradiction, that at first she stated the ear-rings were taken on the 19th of October, but, seeing, with a woman's keen perception, the fatal error she had made in stating that admission, seeing that you, as common-sense men, would have at once said: "Why not have had him arrested then?" she quickly drew back, like a snail when the crashing foot is coming upon it, and drew the horns within the shell which covered it; and, yesterday, corrected the date. She changed the date and put it back from November to October. I congratulate her upon the change! For all the trickery and malice which were embodied in it, only enured to the prisoner's benefit. It was here sworn, to-day, that on the 17th of November last, her watch and chain (her watch and chain, gentlemen) not Mr. Lynch's, but Eliza Bethune's, was pledged in New York at Mr. Barnard's, the identical pawnbroker with whom the earrings were pledged. By whom? By Mrs. Bethune? Oh no! gentlemen! but by Hemmings, the man here. If he accomplished this ubiquitous feat, like the ghost in Hamlet, to be in two places at one time, he is one of the most wonderful performers of the modern day. (Laughter.) He could not be in Barnard's pawn-shop in New York pledging Mrs. Bethune's watch on the 17th of November, a month after the larceny, and be, as she would have you believe, with Kate Fisher performing in Pittsburgh. Why, look at that contradiction! I invoke that book (pointing to the pawnbroker's record), as in other temples I appeal to the Holy one, for my protection. In your hands I place it. Upon your altar do I offer it up; and I believe that you will grant my prayers, that this will be taken as the strongest evidence of the prisoner's innocence. Records cannot lie here. The testimony is that this man had subsequent transactions with Mrs. Bethune, supporting, beyond a doubt, my theory that she gave him the ear-rings to pledge. Now let us see. She tells you (and there are other circumstances of greater peculiarity still around this case)—she tells you that she became acquainted with this man some twelve years since; and although I was prohibited (perhaps properly) by the court from putting other questions, I think I am not saying too much, when I urge that I did elicit from that lady sufficient to justify any one of you in forming an opinion as to the immoral terms of intimacy subsisting between Hemmings and that lady who was upon the witness stand. I can only say that I think there is not one of you composing that jury who would be pleased to have a wife of yours detailing circumstances in any way similar. I think that not only jealousy, but indignation of the strongest character, would be aroused in each of you, and you would unhesitatingly brand her as an adulteress.

Now, gentlemen, we find they have known each other for twelve years, and what besides? Why, she takes him into her house; she gives him an apartment there. Nay, she does more, according to her confession. She saw that he was poor and had no clothes (to use her own expression.) I do not think, gentlemen, that she exactly meant that, when she said it, in its literal signification (laughter), but she certainly said that he had no clothes, and that she clothed him and she "took him in" (loud laughter). She went to A. T. Stewart's (kind-hearted charitable woman!) and saw Mr. Griswold. She interceded with Griswold and got Hemmings a situation in A. T. Stewart's. What relation was Hemmings to her, at this time, to induce her to take this kind and charitable interest in him? I, gentlemen, am not so charitable as she professed to be; neither do I think you will be, gentlemen. I apprehend that the motive which actuated the taking in, the clothing and the obtaining a situation at Stewart's, was another motive altogether (immoderate laughter). What it was, I will leave you to conjecture. Look a little further. Hemmings is no relation to her, and yet we find her taking him to Saratoga! In what capacity? Why, she tells you, to attend Bethune's horses at Saratoga (laughter). Yes, gentlemen, and this hostler, this stable boy, in the same breath, is introduced by this lady as what—a lover! oh, no, she dare not do that—but as a relation—a blood relation! She makes him, for that occasion, her brother at Saratoga! Well, so far, there is no impropriety, you will say; but coupled with several other facts—coupled with the act that that book (the pawnbrokers book) teems with the name of Bethune, as pledging jewelry pledged by Hemmings,

110

and belonging to the lady, you must see the intimacy which unquestionably existed. She admitted to you that time and again he had pledged what? Why, he had pledged her studs, her brooches and God knows what all! What did she? Why not have him arrested then? Oh! well, she says, "he cried—my brother cried." (Loud laughter.) "I did not like to hurt my brother." She forgave him, and I will tell you why.

You know the quotation that "Hell hath no fury like a woman scorned." Mr. Hemmings, who is a fine, healthy, fashionable, well-rounded and vigorous, and, some women might say, good-looking young man, had migrated from the city of New York to spend some time in Pittsburgh, and he was in dangerous proximity to a very enticing and attractive actress, Miss Kate Fisher. (Loud laughter).

Gentlemen, in the play of Othello, which many of you have doubtless seen and read, you will find the episode of the handkerchief, which you will remember belonged to Desdemona; being the gift of her husband, the Moor. You remember Iago (in that case it was a man, however,) instigated his wife to purloin the handkerchief, and to deposit it in the chamber of Cassio, if I am correct; and Cassio, unfortunately, not seeing the little trap that was prepared for him, wound that spotted piece of cambric around his knee to stop the blood flowing from the wound he had received in a drunken brawl. Upon Othello seeing that, he states, that not being jealous, he "was perplexed in the extreme," and the sequel was the murder about which we have so often heard. I say, gentlemen, if ever there was the play of Othello reduced to private life and reacted, it is here. These ear-rings are the handkerchief, and Mrs. Bethune is the Iago. (Laughter.) This young man tells me, that in accordance with ancient usage and time-honored customs existing between this gentleman and lady, she had given him, as she narrated here, money to enable Kate Fisher to open a theatre at Pittsburgh, and that Hemmings was to be the manager. She had given them, from time to time, money obtained from

Barnard's pawn office, through the instrumentality of the unfortunate Hemmings.

That is the history; that is all before you, and it cannot be gainsayed. Then why the arrest this time more than at the others? It explains itself. You have it in testimony that these ear-rings were the property of Mr. Lynch, and that Mrs. Lynch had loaned them to Mrs. Bethune. Hemmings alleges, and I believe with truth, that Mrs. Bethune, whilst riding in a coach with him, and after a "love encounter" (laughter) gave to him these jewels to hypothecate in the place to which he had been a frequent visitor for Mrs. Bethune. He goes to this pawnbroker's not in his own name, but, as the pawnbroker tells you (and I point to that fact as one of the strong points in the defense), that he panned them with him, telling him at the time that they belonged to Mrs. Bethune. Would a thief who stole your property or mine go to a place where he was known, that is if he stole them with the intention of keeping them? There was no larceny here, no dishonest motive about the transaction. Would he go to the pawnbroker to whom he was known and say, "Here is some property; it is not mine, it is Mrs. Bethune's?" On the contrary, you know, gentlemen—you must know—that there are a thousand other pawnbroker's establishments in New York City; and if this had been a felonious taking of these ear-rings, Hemmings could have gone to Simpson's across the way from this court house, or to another place at the Battery, or east, west, north or south, upon any corner in New York to a strange pawnbroker, who did not know him, had there been any felony about the transaction. Another point is, that a felon who steals invariably covers up his crime. The Prosecution brought out this fact, and I appeal to it as their own destruction, why in the name of Heaven did this man, if he intended to appropriate these ear-rings to his own use, carry about him the evidence of his guilt? Why, they told you when they got to Pittsburgh, after the altercation, that he produced the pawn-ticket! Did that look like stealing?

But to revert to the ownership. Mr. Lynch, in a moment of kindness, loaned these ear-rings to his wife. Mrs. Lynch again loaned them to Mrs. Bethune; and, as Hemmings says, whilst riding in a coach, she (Mrs. Bethune) gave him those ear-rings to pledge. He did so pledge them. Mind you, gentlemen, there has been no dispute about that since the commencement; he has never denied the pledging. Having pledged them, as he represents, a request was made to Mrs. Bethune for the return of the ear-rings. She could not produce them, and for the best possible reason; and not until nearly two months after the occurrence is the complaint made before the police magistrate. She wished to hide from Mr. Bethune (the gentleman who sustained the relation of husband to her) what had become of the ear-rings; and, necessarily, she had no resort but to turn round and say: "It is not very pleasant to tell my husband (or the man who stands in that capacity) that I have given those ear-rings to a lover! I cannot, without offending you, tell you the true cause of this affair, but I must, in order to save myself, say, O, this George stole them, and he is in Pittsburgh with Kate Fisher." This is *two months* after the occurrence! And then, on the first of December, a requisition is gotten out, and the more marvelous part of it is, that she goes on alone in the first instance while Mr. Bethune followed subsequently. Now see what occurred in Pittsburgh. She told you she did not know whether he was arrested or not. She "believed" there was a form gone through of getting out some papers. She "believes" she was taken before the mayor; and what became of the case she did not know. But Mr. Bethune, who could not shield himself in this way, very promptly answered that he was arrested at the suit of this man; and Hemmings could not make idle charges there. He was a theatrical manager in Pittsburgh, a public man! and, as they told you, boasted that he was intimate with the members of the press and police force, who were dead-heads at his theatre, and who witnessed the performance gratuitously; so that you perceive he was very well known. Do you believe, will any sane man of common sense credit the statement, that a man who was as well known in Pittsburgh as G. L. Fox is in this city, could afford to arrest a citizen and have the matter made public unless he had reasons to do so?

I say, gentlemen, that the entire case, from the commencement to the end, abounds in doubts suggestive of this man's innocence, especially the fact which cannot be denied, that this lady, *she is not like Cæsar's wife,* above suspicion, shields herself, as no honest woman would, behind that protection which the judge afforded.

Good God, gentlemen, in a court of justice, where jurors are empanelled to decide upon the future prospects and the life of this young man, would your wife or mine refuse to answer such a question? Is it a *shame* for us to acknowledge that the holy bonds of matrimony have united us with a being—the mother of our offspring? Would you deny that you were the husband of a lady, placed upon the witness stand to support a charge against a thief for having stolen your watch? Why, I think, gentlemen, that honor, affection, duty and every obligation known to society, demands, in imperious tones, that instead of denying the wife of your bosom, you stand forward as her champion and say, "Thank God, she is my wife and I am proud of it!" That is what you or I would have answered. But the gauzy curtain that was covered over this foul tableau, has been lifted up, and you see it in all it hideous deformity. As I have before stated, you have seen, gentlemen, the flimsy evidence upon which is attempted to predicate a conviction for grand larceny. I am confident that in spite of all the attempts that have been made by a shameless wanton and her pretended husband, to crush this man, despite the meretricious trickery and villainous conspiracy which instigated, concocted and carried out this *persecution,* relying as I do, on your sense of justice, your strict integrity, and the independence of an American jury, that you will not permit our temples erected to justice, to be prostituted to the accomplishment of the designs of the polluted and the

114

infamous and that innocence will triumph, and your verdict be "Not guilty."

At the conclusion of Mr. Howe's address, Mr. Hutchings summed up for the people. Judge Russel proceeded to charge the jury. After recapitulating very carefully the whole of the testimony, told them that if they were satisfied that the prisoner Hemmings had taken these ear-rings from Mrs. Bethune, and had pledged them without her consent, then they should convict; but if they had any well-founded doubt arising from the testimony itself, and not engendered by the eloquent speech of the prisoner's counsel, then they should give the prisoner the benefit of the doubt and acquit him.

The jury then retired, and after a quarter of an hour's absence returned into court and rendered a verdict of NOT GUILTY.

Hemmings was accordingly discharged, and he quitted the court amidst the congratulations of his friends.

Mrs. Bethune also brought a charge of theft against Kate Fisher, which was heard at Essex Market Police Court. The New York *Herald* reported the proceedings next day as follows:

Essex Market court-room was this afternoon densely crowded with theatrical personages of all grades, apparently deeply interested in the progress of the case which concerns the position and honor of an actress so well known as Kate Fisher. The seats of the court would not contain more than half the number of the persons present, the remainder being compelled to stand around against the walls and in the nooks of the doors, etc. Among those present were W. B. Freligh, manager of the Bowery Theatre; John Jones, the treasurer; Clark, the stage manager; Deane, leader of the orchestra, and others. The court-room was at last found to be too small, and the whole party adjourned to examine the room on the second floor of the building, which was also found to be rather small, but yet more convenient for the purposes of an examination.

Justice Shandley then took his seat on the bench, and the parties concerned appeared in court. Mrs. Bethune was rather flashily dressed, and evidently intended to make a show. Kate Fisher was quietly dressed in black, and was very modest in her demeanor; attracting no attention, except from those who were acquainted with her. Mr. Bethune accompanied the complainant, and Messrs. Howe and Hummel, appeared for Miss Kate Fisher.

Having taken their respective seats, the case of Eliza Bethune, of Centreville, Long Island, against Kate Fisher, for the larceny of a gold watch and chain, valued at $200, was then called on.

Mrs. Bethune, the first witness, was then examined by her counsel. She stated that her name was Eliza Bethune, and that she resided at Centreville, L. I. She knew Kate Fisher, and knew her on the 16th of last November. She was then living in East Fourth street. On that day she missed her watch, and her daughter told her that Miss Fisher had taken it. Acting on this information, she sent for Kate Fisher on the afternoon of that day. Mrs. Bethune then asked her where her watch was. Kate Fisher was very much intoxicated at the time, but understood all that was said to her. She answered that she had taken it, and had given it to Hemmings. The watch and chain was worth $200. Mrs. Bethune subsequently learned that the watch had been pledged. Some time after, she, Mrs. Bethune, caused the arrest of Kate Fisher at Pittsburgh, but the case was dismissed for want of jurisdiction.

Mr. Howe then asked if the counsel had closed his case, but received an answer in the negative, as there were more witnesses to be examined. Mr. Howe stated that he was sorry that the case was not closed, as before he desired to commence a cross-examination he would take all the evidence to be exhausted. His case was a revival of one which had already been settled at the General Sessions, and bore on its very face the evidence of a malicious prosecution to injure the character and spotless reputation of a lady whose profession brought her constantly before the public, and whose good name became thereby part of her business capital. He regretted it, therefore, that the counsel for the complainant would not exhaust his case, as it made it necessary to adopt a course of procedure in his cross-examination that he should have preferred not to have done.

The counsel for Mrs. Bethune persisting that the cross-examination of each witness should go on in regular order as each witness appeared on the stand, Mr. Howe then proceeded by asking the witness her name.

My name is Eliza Bethune.

Are you married?

I am.

To whom?

Mr. Bethune.

What is his first name?

That is not your business.

Counsel appealed to the court, when the magistrate said the question was a proper one, and she answered:

My husband's name is Bethune. His first name I do not choose to give.

After further questioning, she at last replied:

My first husband's name was John Bethune.

What is the name of your present husband?

That is not your business.

Is he here in court.

He is. He represents me here.

What is his first name?

After a great deal of cross-firing the answer was elicited that it was George Bethune.

Were you ever married to George Bethune, the one who is now in court?

Objected to by counsel.

Justice Shandley: That is a proper question, and must be answered.

That is my business. He has been my husband for over ten years.

Were you ever married to him?

Objected to. Objection overruled.

I have answered already. I have answered all I am going to do.

Justice Shandley insisted that she must answer the questions, but when she still refused, almost in a defiant manner, he rose from the bench, and declared the case dismissed. His action was received with rounds of applause from the persons assembled.

CHAPTER X

A MARINER'S WOOING

Aforetime, when the mariner was entirely dependent on the winds and the tides to make his voyage, he was, as everybody knows, a peculiarly impulsive, generous, faithful and credulous mortal in his love affairs. Once ashore, he spliced the main-brace, sneered oathfully at land-lubbers, hitched up his trousers and ran alongside the first trim-looking craft who angled for his attentions—and his money. These fine salt-water impulses, begotten of a twelve or fifteen-months' voyage, have mostly vanished. Steam has greatly revolutionized Jack's sweet-hearting. He comes to port every fortnight, or so; he wears dry goods and jewelry of the latest mode; and he marries a wife, or divorces a wife, with the same conventional *sangfroid* of any mercantile "drummer" who travels by railroad. The conjugal history of that distinguished son of Neptune, Captain Oliver Perry Hazard, now to be related, haply has a delectable smack of mercantile jack's old-time methods, mingled with the shrewder utilitarianism of the steamship Jack of to-day.

Up in the estuary called the Y, and at the mouth of the river Amstel, lay, some years ago, the good American ship which had safely borne young Hazard across the Atlantic. He was a handsome, a tall, and a lively young man of five and twenty; and, with a vivacious young mariner's curiosity, he went ashore to sample the "Holland," for which the Dutch are so famous, to stroll across the two hundred and ninety-odd bridges, and to take an observation of the pretty girls that loomed up in sedate but ample old Amsterdam. There, in a saloon where the gin was a most divine Hippocrene, and the cigars fragrant, Oliver beheld a tight little craft, and straightway ran up his flag as a salute. She was a brunette, with as pretty a form as the sun had ever kissed. Her dark, dark eyes were large, lustrous and superb. Oliver shares Lord Byron's weakness for handsome eyes. He's very fond of them. The name of the Amsterdam divinity was Marie. He resembled the same illustrious poet in his predilection for the name of Mary or Marie. He thought there was a sweetness in it. And so he sank into the quicksands of Eros, right over his tarry toplights, and, nothing loth, Marie accompanied him in the Avernian descent. Every morning that he lay in the Dutch port our mariner squared his yard-arms and trimmed himself for bringing-to alongside Marie. Every night the tics were getting tauter, and when he proposed that she should cross with him to England there was no pitching on her part worth speaking of. And so they voyaged to Albion and to several ports in Gaul; and there was no lee-way in their love, but still the tics were getting tauter, evidencing strong probabilities of a life cruise together.

A year or two after, both Oliver and Marie were in New York, and, according to the affidavit of Captain Hazard's mother, Marie called upon the matron and told her "that she had been living with her son Oliver; that she had first met him in Amsterdam, and had traveled with him as his wife in England and in France, and that he had brought her to America." Marie assured the old lady that she loved him dearly, that she had been faithful and true to him ever since their intimacy, and hence she was anxious that Oliver should marry her and make her an honest woman in the eyes of the law and of the world. Whereupon, the mother persuaded the son to marry the pretty, young, gazelle-eyed girl, who could speak American and write like a born citizen.

Oliver's own account of this momentous event, as chronicled in his affidavit, is not materially different. He affirms that he first met Marie in a liquor store in Amsterdam, "which she was in the habit of frequenting. At this time she was of loose character;" she "lived with him and traveled to England and France, and he was going to send her back to Holland, when his mother urged him to marry her, which he did reluctantly."

In what way or to what extent, if any, the relations between the young mariner and his wife were affected after Hymen had stepped in and chained them together, there are data for determining. If we are to unqualifiedly accept the averments of the captain's affidavit we should come to the conclusion that Marie's nature and disposition were woefully transformed when she could legally designate herself, "Mrs. Captain Oliver P. Hazard." She then discovered "a jealous disposition" and "an ungovernable temper." When he returned from his various voyages she "did not receive him kindly;" but, contrariwise, sometimes received him on the side of "a poker," on the end of "a dirk" or at the muzzle of "pistol." Moreover—and this is dolefully comic—"she repeatedly left this deponent imprisoned in the house for hours under lock and key!" What a situation for a foaming mariner, accustomed to roam the vastness of the majestic, the free, the uncontrollable deep! Probably the next arraignment is still more exasperating. "She kept a servant to act as a spy and treat this deponent with disrespect." With the lapse of years, and with the peculiar hue which strife assumes in its backward prospective, his once happy-home and connubial comforts wore a jaundiced and sickly aspect. He ceased to recall the days when his heart was linked unto Marie's as a rosebud is linked to its stem.

Mrs. Hazard possessed some letters, written to her by her whilom amorous husband, which will enable the reader to form a pretty correct idea of the estimation in which, until quite recently, the captain held his pretty wife. For example, one Fourth of July, he writes from "On board the U. S. Steamer John Rice," from Fortress Monroe to "My own dear and precious wife," informing her that the ship has been landing troops, that he feels rather seedy and low-spirited, and wishes he was at home to spend "the glorious Fourth" in her company. In a postscript he blazes into amorous enthusiasm and exclaims, "Write your dear Olly!" and in the bottom left-hand corner, within a sort of fairy circle, about the size of the orifice of a quart-bottle neck, appeared the gushing invitation, ("Kiss me.")

Nearly a year afterward he writes from Havana, "On board the steamer Liberty, May 6, 1865," to "My own dear precious wife," informing her that he is safe from New Orleans, with other personal matters not necessary to rehearse. He subscribes himself, "Your affectionate and loving Olly." Over ten years afterward we find the captain writing another letter from on board the same steamer, October 13, 1875, lying in Savannah, to "My darling beloved wife," in which he graphically tells her the sort of dog Jocko is. "Jocko came on board all serene," writes the captain, "He is asleep under my sofa all the time when he is not hunting beef, and I keep my room very warm. So that is the kind of dog Jocko is. If he was a half decent dog I would keep him on board, but he is asleep all the day under my sofa, and hates to be on deck. So he is good for nix, the worse cur I ever saw. I will leave him with a good keeper, and glad to lose sight of him."

At this period Mrs. Captain Hazard was in the habit of sub-letting a portion of her house; and in the tail-end of the letter from which we have just quoted reference is made thereto. "Have you advertised in the *Tribute* yet? Try fifty cents' worth for two days, you may catch a sucker. May God, in his infinite mercy, ever bless, protect and make you well and successful, my darling wife, is the prayer of your ever-loving and affectionate husband, Oliver P. Hazard." In the usual corner appears the magic circle, with the imperative ("Kiss me.")

In the early portion of the year 1876, he had so persistently coaled up the fires of his love boilers that he couldn't wait until the steamer sailed, but plunges into glowing correspondence as soon as he reaches "Pier 2." He is now the captain of the Ocean Steam Navigation Company's vessel, San Jacinto, and on April 22 he writes, "My own darling good wife," before sailing, advising her to take good care of herself. The usual circular, hieroglyphic and osculatory invitation appears at the lower left-hand corner.

Four brief days afterwards our Strephon has reached Savannah. Again he writes, April 26, 1876, "On board the steamship San Jacinto." To "My blessed good darling wife," informing her that he has "no aches, no pains," and assures her that he is "growing stronger." Then he rushes into particulars in the following unique manner: "I still keep my oatmeal diet and Pepson. God's blessing and infinite mercies on you, my darling. . . . I have had all kinds of horable imaginations about you. . . . I hope Mr. C. K. Garrison will permit you to make next trip with me. Eat no salt smoked meats or fish, or drink no strong tea, but cat oatmeal and what will easily digest, to keep your bowels open. . . . I will, with God's help, be with my dear Marie on Tuesday. I have the Harriet Beecher Stowe and Crane family to bring North this trip, about the last of the crowd. I wish they were landed in New York, as I don't like any of them, but will fight through in a quiet way." This epistle occupies six closely-written and carefully-numbered pages of note-paper, and the lip sign-manual is emblazoned in the usual corner. It ought to be remarked that the captain is an admirable penman, moderately seaworthy as to syntax, but in need of overhauling in an orthographical aspect.

While we are busy with the correspondence, it may be *apropos* to quote the last amorous letter he penned to his Marie before a cyclonic storm from the nor'east struck the Hymeneal ship, and carried away her masts and rigging, leaving a pair of plunging, leaky bulk-heads on the weary waste of the censorious world's waters. The envelope of this letter is indorsed in a female hand—evidently the forlorn hand of Marie: "Last letter received from my husband." It purports to have been written "On board the steamship Herman Livingston, Savannah, Jan. 5, 1878." It begins, in a modified form, thus: "My darling wife," and takes a flatulent turn almost immediately, "we had a fair wind all the way; a few passengers, and only one lady, which was Lydia. She was very pleasant and no trouble, as she was not sea-sick, and sat in the pilot-house most of the time. I am feeling very well now. . . . It is not necessary to say that I have not drank any strong drinks; that, of course, is finished. I am all right now, you know. . . . I hope, my darling good wife, that you are feeling much better than when I left you, and that your sore throat is quite well by this time. . . . I hope you will take good care of yourself and not get cold. I shall take good care of myself. Little Maria sent me a pretty mug for my New Year's. I will not use my new napkin ring, as it is too nice to be lost or broken here. May God ever bless and protect you, and ever make you well and happy, is my ever prayer of your loving husband, OLLY."

Let not the reader imagine that Olly's love was all of the lip-and-epistolary cheap style. Even as faith without works is dead, being alone, so professions of affection without exemplification would be simply worth "Jocko," and that worthless creature, according to the mariner, was good for "nix." No; the captain had presented his darling with diamonds—a cross, for example, which cost $1,000, and a watch and chain and other jewelry, amounting in the whole to $2,800.

The impartial reader, therefore, from the excerpts of his correspondence and the summary of the jewelry, will be enabled to form a pretty fair idea of the esteem in which the captain formerly held his wife. Ah! but then the reader is not aware that Olly is very handsome, and so very, very gay! Olly's immaculate shirt-bosom was in the habit of bristling with diamonds, in the midst of which, like a headlight at the mizzen-top, coruscated a diamond cluster pin.

Marie was not jealous without a cause. Of this, every lady who has read thus far is morally convinced. Marie and her "spy" had discovered the cause, just sixteen brief days after Olly had penned that remarkable letter, with a benediction and a "kiss-me" lozenge at the end, Mrs. Hazard and her maid, Esther Doerner, hied them down and across town until they reached a boarding-house on West Ninth street. What happened in this high-toned hash dispensary let Miss Margaret Gilman, an eye-witness, proclaim by her affidavit:

"At half-past eight in the evening, Mrs. Hazard came in and went to a hall bed-room in the front, and knocked at the door of said room. She was accompanied by her maid, Esther Doerner. After she knocked, the door was opened from within by Lena Kimball. Lena attempted to close the door, but Mrs. Hazard's superior strength forced an opening, and she and her maid entered." Now let lynx-eyed Esther take up the narrative for a brief space: "Lena was but slightly clothed, having only a skirt and a sacque on. Lena asked: 'Who is this woman?' Mrs. Hazard replied, 'I am his lawful wife—you are his mistress!'" Then ensued a scene which Margaret and Esther are in accord in describing: "Lena attacked Mrs. Hazard, slapped her in the face and pulled her hair, said captain, meantime, holding his wife's hands and thus preventing her defending herself!"

Let us hear Miss Margaret C. Gilman, who is a dressmaker, a little further: "About the following Thursday I visited No. 106 West Sixteenth street, at request of said Lena Kimball, to arrange about a dress for her, when I saw said Captain Hazard enter the room of Lena. I left them together, alone. Lena told me that the captain would commence proceedings for a divorce from his wife."

Progressing chronologically onwards, we come to another day when Olly and his wife were quarreling at a great rate in their home up-town. It appeared that the captain had between $4,000 and $5,000 deposited in the Seamen's Savings Bank, and his wife was anxious that the money should be drawn and be equally divided between them. To this Olly demurred, whereupon the irate wife locked her faithless lord in the house, and kept him a close prisoner till he threw up the sponge and promised to accede to her demands. He obtained his liberty, and ostensibly left the house for the purpose of drawing the money and transferring $2,000 of it to his wife's account. What he did do was to draw the cash, go to his brother-in-law's, pay some debts, and then hand $3,000 to Lawrence Phillips, an insurance broker, at 85 Beaver street.

Of course, Olly did not return to his "blessed and darling wife" that night, nor the next, nor ever again. He had, no doubt, an attack of the old "horable imaginations," and deemed it advisable to put himself on an oatmeal diet somewhere in New Jersey. What he did do, as Marie's detective discovered, was to proceed with Lena to Taylor's Hotel, Jersey City, where they registered as Mr. and Mrs. James Peake, of Philadelphia. While enjoying this voluptuous seclusion with the fascinating young blonde, Olly was plotting mischief and otherwise conspiring against the forlorn Marie's peace and happiness. The following documents disclose the form their unchaste deliberations assumed. On the eleventh of February, the ill-used Olly sent a freezing letter to his wife, from which we quote:

"In view of the unhappy relations which exist and have for many years existed between us, I have reached the conclusion that it is impossible for us longer to live together as man and wife. Your manner of treating me has been so outrageous that it is necessary, in order to live with you that I should sacrifice my manhood, my independence and my self-respect, as well as the respect of all the members of my family and of my friends. While I believe your conduct would, in the eyes of the law and society, warrant me in refusing you all support, still I am inclined to deal liberally with you, and I have clothed Mr. Stanton, my counsel, with power to arrange the details of a separation." He then goes on to state that, in such an arrangement, certain considerations should have full weight, to wit: "That I am at present suspended from my situation, and that you assert you brought about my suspension; that you have a very comfortable home, for which I pay the rent, with about $5000 worth of furniture, which I would be willing to turn over to you; that you have valuable diamonds, and that I have given you a great deal of money of late."

Marie was, no doubt, pondering over her frigid Olly's proposal, and making up her mind how to proceed, when another letter reached her. It was written in a bold, clear, round hand. It bore no date or superscription, but the envelope is stamped: "New York, Feb. 12, 12 o'c." The letter might have been written by a love-crazed Cassandra. It was as follows:

> "You imagine me in Philadelphia. Not so. I am in the city, and will remain here until I accomplish the ruin and destruction of the old fool, your husband, and yourself. I have sworn revenge on you and I shall keep my oath. I do not care a damn for the old man. You expect him home to-night, but you will be disappointed. The old fool is trying to get a divorce from you now. My vengeance being accomplished I will leave the city, and not until then.

> "With hatred and revenge, I am your enemy until death, LINA KIMBALL."

Mrs. Hazard had been acting under legal advice, so far as the discovery and proof of her husband's unfaithfulness were concerned. But determining upon a more active and aggressive warfare, she was prudently advised to intrust her interests to Messrs. Howe & Hummel. The conflict was speedily begun. On February 16th the first papers in the case were served upon Captain Hazard at his lawyer's office, 198 Broadway. On the same day Mr. Henry Stanton promptly gave notice of his appearance in Olly's behalf. On the twentieth of February, on the application of Howe & Hummel, an order of arrest was granted by Judge Donohue, on the ground that the defendant intended to leave the city, and that any order for alimony would thereby be ineffectual. On the following day the captain did leave the city for Boston, and registered at the Parker House. It is alleged that he was seen with Lena Kimball in the Hub; but the captain explained afterwards that he had not vamoosed on purpose—he had gone to inspect a ship, with the possible intention of buying a captain's share.

On February 28th, Mr. Stanton served upon Messrs. Howe &

Hummel a copy of a petition and notice of motion returnable the third Monday in March. On the same day the complaint was served upon defendant's lawyer. Meantime, detectives were on the *qui vive* for Olly. They had his portrait on tin imperial size, and they had a lock of his hair in an envelope. There were certain lager-beer saloons in the vicinage of Sixth avenue and Sixteenth street he was said to frequent. A sharp lookout was kept on his brother-in-law, Bradbury, as well. On March 19th the sheriff tapped the distinguished son of Neptune on the shoulder and exhibited a momentous piece of paper. The captain took an observation and hauled down his colors as a free man. He was a prisoner and put himself promptly in tow. After a short run and a few tackings they ran into Ludlow Harbor, and all was made taut for the captain.

Next day the petition and motion was argued for the prisoner, by Mr. Stanton, before Judge Lawrence. Mr. Hummel opposed on behalf of Mrs. Hazard. It was argued that the alleged acts of adultery had been condoned; that the defendant had no intention of leaving the state; that when he separated from the plaintiff he went to live with his brother-in-law and mother; and that he went to Boston for the purpose already stated. The alleged pokerings and dirkings and pistolings were dilated upon. Esther, the spy, was denounced. It was affirmed that "on one occasion, when he returned," with the odor of the sea fresh upon him, "plaintiff had a baby." It has never been claimed that he was the father of it. Nor does he know who is the father. He has never been able to find out the paternity of that babe, "nor does he know who the mother is." Notwithstanding that he has been suffered to swell almost to bursting with ignorance of these bottom facts, he "has been forced to support it." He showed that Mrs. Hazard possessed diamonds and furniture and twenty-one building lots on Long Island; that she had been extravagant as to crayon portraits and carriage hire; that for the last-mentioned item alone her expenses for February had been about eighty-seven dollars. Wherefore, counsel argued, the court ought either

128

to dismiss the arrest or reduce the bail from $6,000, at which it had been fixed. Mr. Howe had an equally affecting story to rehearse. He showed that Mrs. Hazard had been compelled, through her husband's neglect to provide her with money, to pay several visits to a relative of hers, to whom the adage "Blood is thicker than water" does not apply. With this personage she had left, for pecuniary considerations received, her diamond cross and other valuables.

The judge took the papers and, a few days afterward, ordered the parties to the suit to appear before a referee, who was instructed to take proof as to the defendant's ability to pay alimony, and to determine what amount should be paid. On the evidence taken before the referee, Lamberson, who died before the testimony was all in, both sides agreed on the question of alimony.

Thus far Mrs. Hazard's lawyers had carried all before them like an irresistible flood. They now turned their attention to Lena Kimball. Mrs. Hazard had not forgotten nor forgiven that face-slapping and hair-pulling in Ninth street. Lena's maledictory epistle had added brimstone to the fire. And so it came to pass that Messrs. Howe & Hummel brought an action in the Supreme Court against Lena for the assault and battery of their client. An order of arrest was promptly issued by the court, holding the ravishing young blonde in bail in the sum of one thousand dollars. After she had enjoyed the hospitalities of the warden for two days, the captain planked down a thousand dollars in the hands of the sheriff, and Lena was free.

Behold, now, how tribulation followed tribulation!

Two days after Lena had breathed the air of freedom, Mrs. Hazard and her lawyers went before a police magistrate, and had the fair creature arrested criminally for the same offense of assault and battery. Being produced, Mrs. Kimball gave the required bail to answer at Special Sessions. A fortnight afterwards the case came up. Lena pleaded guilty, and was fined.

After a good deal more litigation, an order was entered in the

Supreme Court referring the many issues of the case to James P. Ledwith, Esq., to take testimony and report thereon to the court. Many hearings were had before the referee, and finally his report was in favor of the plaintiff, Mrs. Hazard, who was awarded an absolute divorce, with a liberal allowance of alimony and costs.

CHAPTER XI

THE BARON AND "BARONESS"

During one October, our offices were visited by a lady who had achieved considerable distinction, as well as notoriety, in Parisian society. This was Mrs. Helene Cecille Stille, otherwise the "Baroness de Reviere," and sometimes designated "The Buckeye Baroness," She came for the purpose of prosecuting a charge against the Baron de Reviere of "wrongful conversion and unlawful detention of personal property," arising from circumstances which will appear further on.

The "Baroness" was then, as she still is, a handsome woman. She was then somewhat on the youthful side of thirty. Highly attractive and fascinating, her every movement and gesture bespoke a vigorous physical organization and perfect health. While the curves of her fine form partook more of Juno's majestic frame than Hebe's pliant youth—while the full sweep and outline of her figure denoted maturity and completeness in every part, the charming face, the large, gazelle eyes, the voluptuous ease of her attitude, the gentle languor of her whole bearing, constituted a woman which few susceptible young or even mature men could have looked on without misgivings that they might but too soon learn to long for the glances, the smiles, the witcheries which had made Helene Cecille Stille, in many respects, a counterpart of Helen of Troy.

We were not acquainted with the lady's antecedents nor with her remarkable history; but she told a plausible story, and was very fluent and indignant, as may be gathered from the following extract from the affidavit which was drawn under her instructions at the time:

Superior Court of the City of New York: Helene Stille, plaintiff, against the Baron Henri de Reviere, defendant. City and County of New York, ss.—Helene Stille, of said city being duly sworn, says that she is the above-named plaintiff, and that she has a good cause of action against said defendant for wrongful conversion and unlawful detention of personal property, arising on the following facts, namely:

In the summer of 1865, in the French empire, the above-named defendant, giving himself out to be a French nobleman of princely fortune, and then representing himself to deponent as an unmarried man, but being in truth, as deponent has since discovered, then a married man and a common plebeian, swindler and common *chevalier d' industrie;* by divers arts, devices, false pretenses and allurements, gained this plaintiff's affections and confidence, and did, by false, wicked and fraudulent devices, debauch this plaintiff and induce her to live with him as his wife; and having thus basely obtained ascendancy over her and won her confidence, did, by trick and device, induce this plaintiff to deposit with him for safe keeping on the tenth day of September, at the city of Paris, in France, the sum of twenty-seven thousand five hundred francs in gold coin, and of the value of seven thousand five hundred dollars of American money, belonging to this deponent; and said defendant then and there promised and agreed to return the same property to this deponent on request.

And this deponent says, that having ascertained the defendant's real character, she demanded the restoration to her of said money by said defendant, when said defendant absconded from France and is now in this City and wholly refuses to return said amount of seven thousand five hundred dollars to deponent, or any part thereof; but said defendant has wrongfully converted said property to his own use, and now unlawfully detains the same from this deponent, at said city of New York, and is now, as deponent is informed and verily believes, about to quit this city, said defendant being only a transient boarder at the New York Hotel in this city.

Judge Freedman granted the application for an order of arrest; the warrant was placed in the hands of Sheriff O'Brien; and Deputy Sheriffs Laurence, Delmore and the present elegant police court clerk, John McGowan, proceeded to the New York Hotel, and just as the guests were assembling for dinner, the haughty aristocrat was made a prisoner, despite his indignant protests.

In the newspapers of the day Mrs. Stille was described as "a beautiful woman, twenty-eight years old, who has seen more life all over the globe than any woman of her age now living." She was born in Cincinnati, Ohio, the daughter of respectable and well-to-do parents. Superbly developed and precocious, at a very early age Helene began to sound the chords of feeling and to taste the Circean cup that promises gratification and excitement, mingled with so much after-bitterness. When she was yet seventeen, she was married to George Stille at Philadelphia, after the briefest kind of an acquaintance. With him she came to New York, living in a style of careless gayety. Early in 1867, she gave birth to a child, named George after his father, and in June of that year Mrs. Stille, and Georgie, and his nurse, Mrs. Demard, were living in Saratoga. The dashing young wife's flirtative proclivities led to a quarrel with her husband, and he left her in a huff. His desertion did not perceptibly disturb the serene elasticity of her mind. She possessed expansive tastes and a capacious heart, and she was speedily consoling herself by the attentions of George W. Beers in the gay watering-place. When Helene, Mr. Beers, the baby and the nurse returned to New York in September, they occupied a suite of rooms at the Prescott House. Not unnaturally, the presence of the dashing woman in the hotel created a sensation, as such a presence always will, as long as men continue to be the weak, erring, susceptible creatures they are. So Helene was flattered, and courted, and admired; and as usual, some she fancied, some she liked, some she laughed at, and some she reserved for her more precious favors. Then, of course, Beers mounted up on his ear, and there was a quarrel, which resulted in the party leaving the Prescott House for quarters over the club house at the corner of Prince and Mercer streets. More quarrels for the same cause eventuated here, and then Beers left her for a while. Not at all disconcerted, she took the child and his nurse to the St. Denis Hotel, where Beers again returned, magnanimous and forgiving. But alas, it was no use. Helene's craving for admiration, masculine attention and money were insatiable. So Beers became wildly jealous and indignant, and left her for good. When next heard of, she was in Paris, where she had succeeded in making the acquaintance of the Due de Morny, and sometimes figured as *la Duchesse*.

Baron Henri Arnous de Reviere was the eldest son of Baron William Arnous de Reviere, Counsellor-general of the Department of the Loire Inferior. The title is hereditary; the family estate is situated at Varades; and the ancestral records are kept in the archives of the ancient city of Rennes in Brittany. The Baron first cropped up in this country about the outbreak of the rebellion, when people here and in England were in great excitement over the steps taken by the general government in securing the arrest of Messrs. Mason and Slidell. He had apparently made one of the elder Dumas' heroes his exalted ideal, for at the period we speak of he had set the fashionable world of Gotham agog by making a romantic conquest of a Mobile belle, who, after becoming thoroughly infatuated with him, eloped to a prominent watering-place. The interference of her friends prevented the consummation of a wedding; but his escapade formed the subject of a book, afterwards dramatized, and acted at Wallack's Theatre. Subsequently the Baron married Miss Blount, the daughter of a rich Southern lawyer.

When he returned to Paris, his fame had preceded him. Society in the gay capital under the empire was of the kind to appreciate his exploits and to exalt him into a sort of rivalship of Monte Cristo. He assiduously attended the theaters and salons, receiving homage everywhere-even from the emperor himself. Finally he mounted the rostrum, and his lectures on *L'Amour* were the talk of the gay city.

Among those who had rushed to listen to the Baron's impassioned eloquence was Helene Cecille Stille, now the proprietress of the handsomest hotel on the Rue Mont-martre. It need scarcely be premised that the wandering and appreciative eyes of the lecturer had rested on the beautiful American, as she sat before him in an attitude expressive of dormant passion, tinged with an imperious coquetry which was one of the most alluring of her charms. The Hotel Montmartre was then the fashionable resort of Louis Napoleon's dissolute nobility, and the Baron de Reviere soon found himself a worshiper in the luxurious retreat. He was not a man who courted by halves. He fell madly in love with the voluptuous Helene, and yielding to an irresistible penchant, the soiled beauty threw herself and her accumulated francs into his arms.

The Baron was one of those few men whose manners were perfect and whose dress never strikes the eye, but which seems to have developed on them as the natural foliage of their persons. He had a high appreciation of the enjoyments of life—vanity, ostentation, good eating, and even the austere joys of the family. At home with his wife he illustrated the tender assiduity of the young husband; abroad he was the personification of a youth just freed from parental discipline. While his wife was the happiest woman in Paris, he was rendering Miss Stille equally felicitous. The dinners he gave at home were unexcelled except by those banquets which he gave at the hotel in the Rue Montmartre.

So complete had become the Baron's infatuation with the fair Helene in September, that he took her to Biarritz, and, according to her own story, introduced her to the Emperor Napoleon. "Then," to use her own language when examined under oath, "I came back to Paris; stayed there about a week, and then went to London with de Reviere. After spending ten days in London, we went back to Paris and stopped at the Hotel de Louvre. We then went to Bordeaux, where I remained a few days, and whence I went to Lisbon, Portugal, staying six weeks, and went back to Paris by way of Marseilles, traveling part of the distance in the yacht of the Bey of Tunis. From Paris, I went with de Reviere to Nantes, thence to Nazarre, where I stayed two days with de Review's sister."

At this time the lady described her possessions as follows: "I had two hundred thousand francs worth of furniture, fifty thousand francs of *objects de vertu,* nine horses, five carriages, a hundred thousand francs worth of jewelry, many India shawls, twenty thousand francs worth of furs of every kind and description known in the world, any quantity of laces, twelve velvet dresses of different shades, and a toilet-set worth eighty-thousand francs, besides an income derived from my family in America of sixty thousand dollars," received regularly through the hands of her banker Mr. John Monroe of 5 Rue de la Paix.

Helene Stille then disposed of her *maison* and started with the Baron de Reviere on a trip to South America. A full account of that trip would read like a supplement to the Arabian Nights. For the purposes of this tour the lady became the Baroness de Reviere, and the pair traveled through the land of Cortez and Pizarro like some fabled Eastern conquerors. A courier rode ahead, and engaged nearly the entire apartments of every hotel at which they condescended to stop. Postilions and outriders accompanied their entrance. In the hotels the Baron and "Baroness" had their magnificent court dresses unpacked to impress and bewilder and confound the guests, while the gaping domestics would spread the news abroad until the entire population of the town would be assembled open-mouthed in front of the Baron's hotel, watching his movements and admiring in no stinted terms the statuesque beauty of the "Baroness."

This extensive triumphal procession cost a lot of money, every cent of which is said to have been paid by the infatuated woman.

It was during their progress through Peru that she seems to have first made the discovery that the Baron already possessed one legal wife. From that hour, it is related to her credit, she stopped all marital relations. She parted from her companion then and there, and returned to Paris. She had two children by the Baron, as she testified in the legal proceedings brought by her. The eldest, a boy, was named "Monsieur le Comte Edmond Viel d'Espenilles; the girl, Santa Maria Rosa de Lenia—names given them by the Baron; for," added the lady, "he is fond of long and sonorous names."

After the separation the Baron and Helene Stille were at daggers drawn. They had some virulent litigation in Paris, and when the Baron came to New York with his family, consisting of his wife, two children, two men servants and three maid servants, she quickly followed. The Baron and his establishment were sojourning at the Clarendon Hotel, when he received the following letter:

"Monsieur Henri de Reviere:

I wish to know whether you intend doing anything toward the support of your child? She is a poor, delicate little thing, being afflicted with curvature of the spine. I have had her under treatment of Dr. Taylor for the last three months and his charges are five hundred dollars, which for me, with my other expenses, is a great deal. I hope you will consider my claim a just one and act accordingly. Rosa de Lenia is one of the most beautiful children in the world, and I love her with such a love as you could never dream of. Reply by bearer, or send reply later in the day, just as you feel disposed; but a reply I must have. I should think your *amour proper* would not allow you to abandon your child, as you have done for nearly three years.

Hoffman House, Sept. 26
Helene De Stille"

137

The rejoinder was insulting, and so she had him arrested in order that "he might disclose those dreadful things he pretended to know about me."

There was a hearing of the lady's case before Judge Jones of the Superior Court, when most of the foregoing particulars of Miss Stille's history was drawn from her in cross-examination by the defendant's counsel. At a subsequent hearing the Baron contributed an affidavit containing many startling assertions accompanied by big figures.

"I left Paris in April for Madrid," he began, giving exactly the same route already described by Miss Stille. Continuing, he said, "Further, I have had an office as government contractor for artillery and ships of war. I also contracted with a Liverpool ship-builder (Laird) for two iron-clads and four steam corvettes for twelve million francs. I acted as agent and partner of L. Arman of Bordeaux and Vous of Nantes, and received in one year for my share eleven hundred thousand francs profit. I sold forty guns to the Danish government, receiving as my commission forty-five thousand francs. I sold in 1884, to the Prussian government, an iron-clad and two steam corvettes for seven million five hundred thousand francs, and received five per cent, commission." Then he professed to have had gigantic contracts in Chili, Peru and other parts of South America for artillery and guano. Altogether his story was of the Brobdingnagian type.

The case, however, never came to trial, the friends of both parties to the action suggesting an amicable settlement of their differences, which being adjusted to everyone's satisfaction, the Baron went his way, lecturing on "Love," a theme on which he was most conversant, and the fair Helene spent her time flitting between this city and gay Paris, in both of which cities she is thoroughly at home. And so the somewhat famous episode ended, so far as the office of Howe and Hummel was concerned.

CHAPTER XII

THE DEMI-MONDE

Reader, did you ever try to estimate the malign influence upon society of one single fallen woman? Did you ever endeavor to calculate the evils of such a leaven stealthily disseminating its influence in a community? Woman, courted, flattered, fondled, tempted and deceived, becomes in turn the terrible Nemesis— the insatiate Avenger of her sex! Armed with a power which is all but irresistible, and stripped of that which alone can retain and purify her influence, she steps upon the arena of life ready to act her part in the demoralization of society. As some one has remarked, "the *lex talionis*—the law of retaliation—is hers. Society has made her what she is, and must now be governed by her potent influence." Surely the weight of this influence baffles computation! View it in shattered domestic ties, in the sacrifice of family peace, in the cold desolation of once happy homes! See the eldest son and hope of a proud family, educated in an atmosphere of virtue and principle, who has given promise of high and noble qualities. He falls a victim to the fashionable vice, and carries back to his hitherto untainted home the lethal influence he has imbibed. Another and another, within the range of that influence, suffers for his lapse from moral rectitude, and they in turn become the agents and disseminators of fresh evils.

This promiscuous association is tacitly regarded as a necessary evil, the suppression of which would produce alarming and disastrous effects upon the community at large. The passions, indolence, and the love of dress and display are the main agents in producing the class of women we have under consideration. It is a vulgar error and a popular delusion, that the life of a fallen woman is as revolting to herself as it appears to the moralist and philanthropist. Authors of vivid imagination love to portray the misery that is brought on an innocent and confiding girl by the perfidy and desertion of her seducer. The stage presents the picture with all its accessories of light, color and morbid emotion. The pulpit takes up the theme and howls its evangelical horrors, picturing those women as being a continuous prey to "the long-beaked, filthy vulture of unending despair." Women who in youth have lost their virtue, often contrive to retain their reputation, and even when this is not the case, frequently amalgamate with the purer portion of the population, and become, to all outward appearance, good members of society.

The love of woman is usually pure and elevated. But when she devotes her affections to a man who realizes her ideal, she does not hesitate to sacrifice all she holds dear for his gratification. Actuated by a noble self-abnegation, she derives a melancholy pleasure from the knowledge that she has utterly given up all she had formerly so zealously guarded, and she feels that her love has reached its grand climacteric when she abandons herself, without redemption, to the idol she has set up in the highest place in her soul. This heroic martyrdom is one of the recognizable causes of the immorality that insidiously permeates our social system.

The crime of prostitution can be witnessed in New York in every phase in which it invites or repels the passions of men. There are the splendid parlor houses distributed in the most fashionable parts of the city; there are the bar houses; there are the dance houses; and there are the miserable basements where this traffic is seen in its hideous deformity, divested of the gaslight glare and tinsel of the high-toned seraglios. The internal arrangements of the palatial bagnios are in many instances sumptuous, magnificent and suggestive. The walls of these seductive arsenals, too, are frequently of a color calculated to throw the most becoming shade over the inmates, while the pictures on the walls usually suggest resplendent sensuality. Many of these gilded palaces are patronized by prominent citizens, officials in the government, state and civic employ. Many of them, already married, keep mistresses in these establishments, while others are content to be recognized as "lovers" of the inmates. Many of the country merchants who periodically visit New York insist on being taken the "grand rounds," as it is termed, before they will order goods or attend to business at all. The salesmen in our leading houses are expect to be posted, and to act as escorts sad chaperones in this wine-guzzling tour. Indeed, so much is this disgraceful feature recognized in some large business houses, that the proprietors make an allowance to their salesmen for this purpose.

The proprietresses of these houses are all impervious to shame, and carry on their trade with the sole ambition of realizing money. Many of them have summer establishments and suburban villas at the watering-places, and carry on their nefarious business at Saratoga, Long Branch, Coney Island, Newport and Cape May during the summer mouths. Many of them own handsome equipages, in which, gorgeously attired, with liveried menials, they show themselves in Central Park to the envy of the virtuous and honest of womankind. It is in the places kept by these women, where the inmates are usually handsome young girls between the ages of fifteen and thirty, that the precocious and well-to-do young men of this city fall an easy prey to vice, and become in time the haggard and dissolute man of the town, or degenerate into the forger, the bank defaulter or the swindler.

The bar and basement brothels, profusely scattered over the lower portions of the city, present the most miserable phase of this disgusting evil. Nearly all these places are kept by men, though nominally under control of their mistresses and wives, who are generally hideous specimens of womanhood, and whose features present the traits of sensuality, cruelty and avarice as clearly expressed as if traced there by Belial himself.

The men, flashily dressed and bejeweled, their flabby features decorated by a huge dyed mustache, frequent race courses and other places of public resort, and loud in appearance as they are obscene in talk, are, in the estimation of every self-respecting man, eminently fitted by Lucifer for laboring in the State-prison quarries for the term of their natural lives.

The inmates of these basement brothels invite the pencil of a Hogarth. Their bloated forms, pimpled features and bloodshot eyes are suggestive of an Inferno, while their tawdry dresses, brazen leer, and disgusting assumption of an air of gay abandon, emphasizes their hideousness and renders it more repulsive. Most of them have passed through the successive grades of immorality. Some of them have been the queenly mistress of the spendthrift, and have descended, step by step, to the foul, degraded beings of those human charnel-houses. In some instances fresh-looking girls will be seen, and careful inquiry will discover the fact that they were either emigrant or innocent country girls, who have been inveigled into these dens by the arts of procuresses or brought there by their seducers. Unsophisticated and unacquainted with life in a great city, without money or friends, they have been entrapped and compelled to submit to a life of shame by the coarse words and frequently the brutal violence of their captors.

Between the two extremes of unfortunates already described, there is another class nomadic in their habits. Some of these are street-walkers, some frequent dance houses like The Allen's, Billy McGlory's, Owney Geoghegan's and Harry Hill's, while others circulate around such up-town, west-side houses as the French Madame's, the Haymarket and Tom Gould's. They usually live in furnished rooms, in houses owned by wealthy and respectable citizens, let to them by agents who lease them at exorbitant rents, paid in advance. In both the eastern, western and central portions of the city they may be found occupying rooms on the same floors with respectable families. These women seldom conduct the prey that they have allured to their home, but to some assignation house or fourth-rate hotel, of which there are a large number scattered over the city.

Most of this class of unfortunates have a "lover"—a gambler or pimp, who occupies their room and assumes the role of husband and protector for the nonce, with the privilege of spending the girl's blood money in drink or dissipation, and unmercifully beating her when he feels inclined that way. The pair call this place their home, and as they are shiftless in their habits, and careless of sickness, they are frequently in a condition of chronic impecuniosity and are thus liable to be "fired out" by the heartless agent. Many of these girls, from their association with vicious society, become thieves, and ply their light-fingered privateering while caressing their victim. It is a favorite dodge of some of the more comely and shapely of this class, especially the frequenters of such places as Gould's, the Haymarket, the French Ma-dames, the Star and Garter, and the Empire, to ask gentlemen on whom they have been unavailingly airing their becks and nods and other fascinations to put a quarter into the top of their hosiery "for luck." They usually get the quarter, and sometimes the man as well.

The assignation houses are usually located convenient to the great arteries of travel, and, as we have already hinted, they are largely patronized; while the number of "flash hotels" which are frequented by the "soiled doves" and their mates, is also numerous and scarcely less notorious than the assignation houses. The proprietors of these "convenient" hotels invariably keep the hotel register required by law, but agreeably fail to ask their lodgers for the time being to chronicle either their own or even a fictitious name, thus, day after day, violating a specific statute.

Besides these, there are assignation houses of a far different character. By these we mean the introducing houses, such as ostensible millinery establishments and the like in fashionable but retired streets, where ladies meet their lovers. Married women of the *haut ton,* with wealthy, hard-working husbands courting Mammon downtown, imitating the custom of Messalina, not uncommonly make use of these places. Sometimes the lady will even take along her young child as a "blind," and the little innocent will be regaled with sweetmeats in the parlor while the mother keeps her appointment up-stairs.

Liberally, every woman who yields to her passions and loses her virtue is what Tom Hood would have called "one more unfortunate," but many draw a distinction between those who live by promiscuous intercourse, and those who merely manifest, like the ladies referred to above, a *penchant* for one man. There is still another denomination of this latter kind, whom all the world has heard of as kept mistresses. These women exercise a potent influence upon society and contribute largely to swell the numbers of well-to-do young men who manifest an invincible distaste to marriage. Laïs, when under the protection of a prince of the blood; Aspasia, whose friend is one of the most influential noblemen in the kingdom; Phryne, the *chere ami* of a well-known officer, or a man of wealth known on the stock exchange and in the city—have all great influence upon the tone of morality, while the glare of their dazzling profligacy falls upon and bewilders those who are in a lower condition of life, and acts as an incentive to similar deeds of licentiousness, though necessarily on a more limited scale.

The prevalence of the kept mistress surpasses the wildest imagining in this city, although in many a home her dire influence has extinguished the Hymeneal torch, and left nothing but ashes and desolation. It is a great mistake to imagine that these kept women are without friends and debarred from society. On the contrary, their acquaintance, if not select, is numerous. They are useful, good-looking, piquant, tasteful and vivacious. Many of them have more than one lover, and conduct their amours with singular *finesse,* generally escaping detection. They are rarely possessed of more than a smattering of education, because their ranks are recruited from a class where education is not in vogue. They are not, as a rule, disgusted with their mode of living—most of them consider it as a means to an end, and in no measure degrading or polluting. Most of them look forward to marriage and a certain state in society as their ultimate lot. Many of these women reside in the most fashionable apartment houses up-town, and successfully conceal their shame from the inquisitive eye of the respectable matron. They may also be seen in the most fashionable hotels and boarding houses, while they have even crept in as members of institutions and organizations which were incepted solely for the benefit of high-toned and virtuous women. Moreover, they are to be seen in boxes at the theatre and the opera, and in almost every accessible place where wealthy and fashionable people congregate. In point of fact, through the potent influence of their more or less wealthy protector, they possess the open sesame to all places where admittance is not secured by vouchers, and in many instances those apparently insuperable barriers fall before their indorser's tact and address.

CHAPTER XIII

PASSION'S SLAVES AND VICTIMS

Our practice has furnished many illustrations of Thackeray's shrewd remark, that "Most men have sailed near the dangerous isles of the Sirens at some time of their lives, and some have come away thence wanting a strait-waistcoat." The following is a case in point, which occurred in the time of the Tweed *régime*. The position, wealth and influence of the somewhat mature Lothario, backed by the more or less corrupt judiciary of those days, prevented the ventilation of this most remarkable and sensational scandal of our times in the newspapers. Begun as a piquant flirtation, the intimacy, so far as the principal actor was concerned, traversed all the stages between bliss and rapture on the one side, and fear and remorse on the other—between garlands of roses and the iron link, forging a clanking manacle of the past. A man of singularly graceful presence and attractive mien; a leading member of the bar, whose Corinthian taste and princely hospitality nominated him as a fitting host of the Queen of England's eldest son, when he visited this city; a prominent figure in the returning board that conferred the Presidency on Hayes; and finally his country's representative at a leading European court; he now sleeps the sleep which sooner or later comes to all—to victim as well as to victimizer.

It was about sundown of a beautiful evening in the early autumn of 1865, that the aristocratic lawyer first beheld the lady with whom he was to become so insanely infatuated. But slightly advanced in the thirties, the widow of a leading officer of the Confederate Army Medical Staff, and formerly a leading

Baltimore belle, she was a fascinating and beautiful woman, when meeting the lawyer that evening on Fifth avenue, near Delmonico's old place, she met Fate. It seems to have been a mutual infatuation—a case of love at first sight, and in a moment of delirium, under an impulse which was perhaps uncontrollable, she sacrificed her virtue and her self-respect.

The story of her infatuation reads like the distempered dream of an opium-eater. It was a case of fervent love on both sides. They met on the avenue, looked, spoke and, without more ado, proceeded to Delmonico's to sup. The amour thus begun soon assumed a romantic intensity. When she left the city, he dispatched ridiculously "spoony" telegrams to her in Baltimore, and in his daily letters indulged in a maudlin sentimentality that might have inspired the envy of a sighing Strephon in his teens.

During the summer of 1866, while his wife was in the country, he brought his Baltimore inamoretta to New York, and established her in his splendid mansion on the Avenue. With an impudence and infatuation perfectly astounding in so shrewd a man, he took no pains to conceal his conquest. Jauntily would he pace down Broadway with her on his arm in the morning, and in the evening she would be in waiting to accompany him home.

Tidings of this open *liaison* reached the lawyer's wife in her retreat among the Vermont hills, and she promptly came to New York and dislodged the mistress *pro tem*. Relatives of the infatuated widow also appeared at this juncture and strongly urged her to conquer her mad infatuation, while a like appeal was made to the lawyer. But he was deaf to reason. He refused to give up his idol, and the widow declared her intention, to use her own language, "of sticking to him as long as he had a button on his coat."

Time sped on. The lawyer's passion began to be exhausted, and the unending insistence of her's began to excite his repugnance. As Ouida happily remarked, "A woman who is ice to his fire, is less pain to a man than the woman who is fire to his ice." There is hope for him in the one, but only a dreary despair in the other. In the latter part of 1867, the lawyer began to realize the force of this philosophy. The amorous widow was then boarding at the Metropolitan Hotel, and he began to take the initiatory steps to be rid of her. After two years of madness, during which she had sacrificed the respect of every relative she had, including her own daughter, a pretty girl in her teens, it was hardly likely that he would evince the moral courage to declare openly and straightforward to her that their relations must end. On the contrary, he invoked the aid of three lawyers—two of them her own cousins, the other bearing an historic name—to kidnap and spirit her out of the city. First they forcibly conveyed her to police headquarters. Then, in spite of tears and protestations, she was kept all night in a dark room. Her screams and entreaties might have moved a heart of stone, but they were unavailing. In the morning she saw Superintendent Kennedy, and demanded the cause of the outrage. He informed her that she had been brought there on a charge of being insane about the lawyer. A physician was summoned, and by his direction, after he had submitted her to an examination, she was sent back to her hotel. During the same afternoon, the lawyer called and emphatically denied having had any hand in her contemplated imprisonment, and secured her release, conveniently imputing the conspiracy to the jealousy of his wife.

Meantime, however, the lawyer and his fellow-accomplices of the law were plotting to get the wretched woman placed in some private asylum. Bloomingdale and Flushing asylums were full, and as she continued to follow her whilom lover and importune him to visit her, he found it politic and convenient to renew his attentions and to feign a revival of his passion. In a certain sense, he was to be pitied. Love of this kind begins as a gift; but a woman of this temperament does not leave it so. She promptly turned it into a debt, and the more she loved the debtor, the more oppressively and inexorably did she extort the uttermost penny from him. About this time she was introduced to an eminent medical specialist in mental diseases, who, by some inexplicable means, was induced to give a certificate of her insanity. Then her cousins took her before a justice, and swore that she was an indigent lunatic, upon which showing the court issued an order of committal to an asylum. A few days before her contemplated abduction, the lawyer induced her to board at the Astor House, and on the morning of February 26, 1868, he being engaged in the Federal court, while she was leisurely sauntering along Broadway looking for him, as was her wont, she was suddenly seized by three hired ruffians, hustled into a carriage, gagged and driven rapidly up-town to Central Park, when the bandage was removed from her mouth. For four mortal hours she was driven about the park in the company of her brutal captors, and afterward placed on board the afternoon train for Albany at the old Hudson River depot. "All along the road," as she subsequently told the writer, "I implored the conductor to furnish me with paper and pencil so that I might telegraph to New York, but it was only when we reached the end of the journey that he did so. I gave him money to pay for the dispatch, but he probably never sent it. When I reached Utica I was placed in a pretty bad ward, and when the physician, Dr. Kellogg, saw me he went and reported to Dr. Gray, the director of the place. When he came up he said I must not be treated so, and I was at once removed to the well ward; I remained there two weeks, when I was discharged." Yes, she was discharged, and was received with crocodile congratulations by the lawyer and one of her lawyer cousins, and triumphantly, as it were, transported back to New York.

She was now placed in elegant apartments in the Hoffman House, and her lawyer lover resumed his visits as formerly. During the summer she went to the country at his expense, and when, in September, 1868, she returned to the city, he finally ceased to visit her. She was frantic with disappointment, and her insane infatuation led her into all manner of indelicate demonstrations. She dogged him in the streets; she followed him into court and interrupted him in his pleadings. Sometimes she sat on the stoop of his elegant mansion all night. Once she dressed herself as a soldier, and tried to gain access to him. Frequently she waylaid him, and sunk upon the pavement in real or assumed paroxysmal fits when he approached. There were other demonstrations that no decent pen could describe, except in a medical book for purposes of science. Naturally the unfortunate lawyer was driven to the brink of desperation, and at this time he never went out of doors without being accompanied by two detectives to protect him from her indelicate approaches.

On November 16, 1868, he caused her to be arrested for disorderly conduct and thrown into the Tombs. The lawyer with the historic name appeared against her, and, to use her own language, "without any examination, I was committed by Judge Dowling." Her gentle bearing and lady-like address again stood her good stead, however, and in a few days she was released.

She now consulted the late James T. Brady, the greatest lawyer who ever practiced at the American bar, and after listening carefully to her statement, he promised to see her "righted." Pending legal action that eminent advocate died, and in the beginning of February, 1869, she took the opinion of Edwin James, the English barrister, and a suit was immediately instituted against her whilom lawyer lover in the Court of Common Pleas, damages being laid at $100,000. When the defendant received notice of the suit he hastened to see Mr. James, and during several conversations offered any reasonable compromise to procure a stay of proceedings. The lady's version of the suit and the subsequent negotiations is as follows: "The suit was never placed on the calendar. It was arranged with Mr. James to allow the case to proceed a certain length and then obtain a release. Mr. James got no retainer, but took my case on speculation, with the understanding that he was to have one thousand dollars at the end of the suit, if there were any proceeds from the same. He continuously urged me to go to Europe with my daughter for two years, and they would advance the money; but I declined. An order was obtained by the defendant's lawyer to examine me; whereupon Mr. James advised me to leave the city in order to avoid the examination. On my return Mr. James advised me to release the suit on the payment of a certain sum by the defendant, he, the defendant, at the same time to make an apology for what he had done and to express regret for my sufferings."

Accordingly, on May 27, 1868, she wrote a letter by advice of her counsel, authorizing him to withdraw the suit on these conditions, and early in June she signed a "general release," professing afterwards to be entirely ignorant of the nature of the instrument. Indeed the unhappy woman cared more for an expression of regret from her enslaver than for any pecuniary solace, and she received no money, although her lawyer did, when the general release was signed. When she discovered the nature of the instrument she was extremely indignant and demanded from Mr. James the telegrams and letters in his possession which had been sent to her by her worshiper in the heyday of their passion. The lawyer hesitated and delayed, and finally, being pressed by a friend and kinsman of the unhappy lady, said, "I won't give them up unless I have an order from the court." Subsequently he claimed that he had destroyed these tell-tale documents, and that the "general release" authorized the proceedings.

She now consulted another law firm, but her case came to nothing, and meantime her former adorer, now grown fiercely hostile, instituted proceedings in the Supreme Court, for the purpose of procuring a perpetual injunction to forever restrain her from harassing him with such suits. This was in 1870, in the early days of March, when the writer saw her last, and conversed with her on her wrongs. Her picture lives in his recollection yet: The soft, large brown eyes, half sad and half voluptuous in their tenderness; the soft, pleading face, with a refinement—even a sort of nobleness—that had outlived the sacrifice of her virtue and reputation. To the last she was a lady of extreme sweetness of manner, and a fascinating and interesting conversationalist.

Another notable man, now also a member of the "great majority"—a renowned Shakespearean critic, author and censor in the domain of *belles-lettres*—brought great trouble and humiliation upon himself by an amour with a ridiculously plain-looking and by no means young woman. He had naturally, perhaps, a *penchant* in that direction, for on the appearance of the Lydia Thompson troupe of original British blondes in this city, he wrought himself into a fervor of passionate folly over the statuesque Markham, and designated her in his Erosian outpourings as "she of the vocal velvet voice." There may have been some excuse for this passing delirium, and many others were touched by it, Pauline Markham was a singularly beautiful girl, and she never looked so well as when she sang; it sent warmth into her lips and took the hardness from her face. But the lady with whom he became involved in a scrape, with the attendant litigation, payment of damages, danger of publicity and total ruin of reputation in the exclusive places where his character was respected and his judgment esteemed, was in every respect different from the lady of burlesque opera. Bitterly did he regret his follies, for the facts were given to a newspaper famous for its sensations, and the great *littérateur* was compelled literally to go down on his marrow bones to induce the editor to withhold the particulars of his seduction of the lady from publication. The sword of Damocles was suspended for weeks, during which the high-toned censor's condition was sometimes pitiable to see. His entreaties finally carried the point, and the case became one of those scandals of the existence of which the public never dreams.

CHAPTER XIV

PROCURESSES AND THEIR VICTIMS

The revelations not long since published in the London *Pall Mall Gazette* revealed fashionable aristocratic depravity in the British metropolis in a shamefully disreputable light, and disclosed the services of the professional procuress in all their repulsive loathsomeness. Although we do not possess titled libertines at elegant leisure here, there can be no manner of doubt that the procuress plies her vocation among us, and thrives on a liberally perennial patronage. Whatever may be her characteristics in other respects, she is invariably an elegantly-dressed woman, with persuasive address, suave speech and attractive mien. In most cases procuresses possess houses of their own, where they procure desirable ladies for their patrons. Sometimes these establishments are termed "Introducing houses," and, as may be imagined, are exceedingly lucrative to their proprietors. Sometimes ladies are boarded and lodged in the house; but they are usually "independent," or, in other words, living under the protection of some patron of the establishment. Some of these procuresses possess a list of ladies whom they can send a messenger for on demand. Take the case of a well-known establishment in one of the most fashionable quarters up-town, for example:

A wealthy broker, speculator, or attache of Uncle Sam, calls upon the lady of the house at a fashionable afternoon hour, orders wine, and enters into conversation about indifferent matters, until he is able delicately to broach the subject he has in view. He explains that he wishes to meet with a quiet lady, whose secrecy he can rely upon, and whom he can trust in every possible way. He intimates his preference for an elegantly-formed, young and fairly good-looking acquaintance, and would like her, in addition, to be vivacious, witty and a little gay. The lady of the house listens complacently, and replies that she is acquainted with a lady who will suit him to a nicety, and offers to send a message for her at once, if he wishes; but he must take his chance of her being at home. Should she be out, she intimates an appointment will be made for next day. In the meantime, a messenger is dispatched to the lady in question, and more wine is ordered and drank. When the lady arrives, the introduction takes place, and the business is transacted, as far as the procuress is concerned. Sometimes the gentleman pays the professional fee, and sometimes the lady gives half the money she receives from the patron to the madame of the house.

Not infrequently these procuresses will write to men of means of their acquaintance, informing them in some cipher or slang phrase that they have a new importation in their house awaiting eligible disposition. Large sums are often paid under such circumstances, and the fresh importation is usually sold in this way five or six times. In other words, she is represented as a maid and imposed upon men as a virgin; which fabrication, as it is difficult to disprove, is believed, more especially if the girl herself be well instructed.

To the house up-town, to which reference has been made above, both married and unmarried ladies repair, in order to meet with and be introduced to gentlemen. This sort of clandestine meeting is greatly on the increase in New York, as it is also in Paris and in London. Some curious facts have come to us in a professional way, to which we can only refer in a general manner here. The following is a case in point:

A brilliant and handsome lady, belonging to the best society in Gotham, married to a man of wealth, found herself unhappy in his society, and after some time unwillingly came to the conclusion that she had formed an alliance that was destined

154

to make her miserable. Her passions were naturally strong and her education had -not been of the kind calculated to enable her to control them. She had been, pampered and petted, and had been accustomed to have every desire gratified. One day the name of the "Introduction-house" madame came up in conversation at a lady friend's house, and the naughtiness of the topic was discussed with the freedom characteristic of progressive society ladies, safe from intrusive masculine ears. A few days after, she ordered a cab and drove to the house in question. She was received with *empressement,* and informed that it was not necessary to explain the nature of her business. That, she was assured, was understood. She was shown into a handsome drawing-room, elegantly furnished and upholstered, and requested to wait a few minutes.

After waiting, in uneasy suspense, a little time, the door opened and a gentleman entered. The heavy curtains of the windows and the thick blinds caused only a "dim, religious light" to pervade the apartment, preventing the lady from seeing distinctly the features of her visitor. He approached her with well-bred politeness, and, in a low tone of voice, began a conversation with her about the beautiful weather New York was then enjoying. She listened for a brief moment, and then, with a cry of astonishment, recognized her husband's voice. He, equally confused, discovered that he had accidentally met in a house of ill-fame the wife whom he had sworn to love and honor, but whom he had condemned to languish at home while he enjoyed himself abroad. This remarkable rencontre had a happy termination, for, after a little legal sparring, it ended in the reconciliation of husband and wife, who mutually admitted that they were both to blame.

CHAPTER XV

QUACKS AND QUACKERY

The vile practices, the monstrous impudence, the cruel rapacity and enormous gains of the obscene tribe of quacks, together with the mischief they do, and the ruin they work, would require much more space to adequately ventilate than we can devote to it here. The healing art is a noble one, and duly qualified men, interested in their profession, are public benefactors; but the despicable race of charlatans not only rob their victims, but frequently ruin their health, and drive them to the verge of insanity. There is probably hardly a reader of this page who has not met, within the circle of his or her acquaintance, some unfortunate individual whose hopes in life have been wholly or partially blighted by the adroitly-worded insinuations of those advertising quacks. We all know that "fools are the game that knaves pursue," and no well-informed member of the community needs to be informed that the victims captured by quack advertisements are not among the wiser portion of the community. Many of them, however, lie open to be allured into the quack's net, not by mere congenital and absolute folly, but because of the inexperience of youth or lack of knowledge of the world, or perhaps in some cases from a natural deficiency in the faculty of deciphering characteristic expression. There are some who fail to recognize a quack advertisement when it meets their eye, from a defect in perception similar to that which incapacitates certain persons from distinguishing a pocket-book dropper, or a bunco steerer, or a billiard sharp, or a sporting "gent."

Of course, there are degrees and varieties of quacks, as well as in the character of their announcements. The street-vender of a "magic pain-reliever," who, by dint of talk and manipulation, convinces some credulous sufferer that his rheumatism is banished, is a quack. So are those who advertise such preparations as sarsaparilla, blood-mixtures, and a variety of pills, potions and lozenges too numerous to mention. So also are those marvelous discoverers of "hair restorers," "removers of freckles," and so on. Most of these do little harm beyond lightening the purses of the purchasers, and in some cases the administration of an inert substance, by exciting the victim's imagination, produces a cure. But the great injury, so far as these innoxious preparations are concerned, lies in the fact that they prevent the sufferer from seeking proper professional treatment. Still this class of quacks is rather to be reckoned among swindlers who obtain money under false pretences, than among the *bona fide* medical quacks that we have in view. The great aim of this pernicious class is to get people in fair, ordinary health to consult them by means of newspaper advertisements, almanacs, pamphlets and circulars filled with details of the character and symptoms of various diseases, scattered broadcast through the land. We will not contaminate our pages in giving samples *in extenso* of this prurient and abominable literature, but a few of the typical advertisements to be met in even respectable newspapers, can hardly be omitted if the exposure is to be thorough:

MEN ONLY.
A quick, Permanent Cure for Lost Manhood, Disability, Nervousness and Weakness. No Quackery.

To Weak Men,
Suffering from nervous debility, weakness of body and mind, loss of memory, mental and physical exhaustion. On receipt of stamp we will send you a valuable treatise upon the above diseases, also directions for home-cure.

Any Part of the Body when deprived of growth, weak and undeveloped, lacking in proper size, form and vigor, may be enlarged, developed and strengthened by simple scientific self-treatment. We will prove this free to any honest person. Write for sealed circulars, description, references.

Nervous Debilitated Men
You are allowed a free trial of thirty days of the use of ———'s Celebrated Voltaic Belt with Electric Suspensory Appliances, for the speedy relief and permanent cure of nervous debility, loss of vitality and manhood, and all kindred troubles. Also for many other diseases. Complete restoration to health, vigor and manhood guaranteed. No risk is incurred. Illustrated pamphlet in sealed envelope mailed free by addressing Voltaic Belt Co.

Nervous Debility, weakness of body and mind, loss of memory, nervous and physical exhaustion permanently and quickly cured. I will send you a valuable treatise upon the above diseases, also directions for home-cure, free of charge.

Weak Men
Can be promptly and lastingly cured, secretly and without nauseous drugging, by the French Hospital Treatment Board of six regular physicians. Consultation free. Full restoration to vigor and strength, however lost.

The list of lewd and brazen manifestoes might be indefinitely extended, but as they all bear the same disgusting ear-marks, the foregoing must suffice. As for the pamphlets sent through the mails in "sealed envelopes" by these harpies, the following titles will sufficiently indicate their character: "The Friend in Need;" "A Medical Work on Marriage;" "The Tonic Elixir;" "The Silent Friend;" "Manhood;" "A Cure for All;" "The Self Cure of Nervous Debility;" "The Self-adjusting Curative;" "New Medical Guide;" "Debility, its Cause and Cure;" "A Warning Voice;" "Second Life," and scores of others of a similar stamp. This disgusting literature corrupts and pollutes the mind and morals of a large class of people who have not the courage to disbelieve its monstrous exaggerations, or the good sense to despise its revolting indecencies. Nor is this strange, when we reflect that the reading of even a standard medical work has a tendency to excite belief in the reader that he is afflicted with the malady whose grim description he is perusing. His apprehension being alarmed and his imagination excited, he has no difficulty in detecting all or a great many of the symptoms in himself, although at the same time none of them may exist. The quack, in his advertisements and publications, frequently warns the reader against quacks and quackery, as, for instance, take the following cheeky extract:

"The object in writing these pages is to teach the public at large to discriminate between the legitimate, duly-qualified practitioner and the legion of charlatans who infest every important city and town of the United States, and particularly New York. That this is a subject of the gravest importance cannot for a moment be doubted when it is considered that, dating from our entrance into the world, 'from the cradle to the grave,' we too often require the valuable services of the accoucheur, doctor, surgeon, or physician, in consequence of departing from Nature's laws, increased state of civilization, and overtaxed condition of the mental and bodily systems, necessitating from time to time the knowledge and attendance of the medical man. Under these circumstances it behooves

159

each individual to be placed on his guard, so as to be made cognizant of the means to detect the nefarious, unqualified, and dishonest charlatans, in order to save the one in search of health from falling in their meshes, and thus jeopardize the welfare of his nearest and dearest objects. The laws of the country, public opinion, and private information, have and are doing much to save the reputations of those who have made choice of the medical profession, thereby exposing themselves to be placed on a level with some with whose names we will not soil our pages, *nor indirectly offer the advantages of publicity,* for it has well been remarked that to be mentioned with disparagement is to these preferable to not being mentioned at all, and thus it very often happens that the veil to hide a motive is so flimsy that even the uninitiated are unable to catch a glimpse at the mystery within."

Here are the strains of another disinterested Mentor in the same field, who once had an office on West Twenty-second street in New York City:

"Country patients are informed that they can have the necessary remedies sent to any address, or directed to be left at an Express Office *till called for,* in a portable compass. The medicines are carefully packed, *and free from observation;* and may be taken without confinement or any restraint. Patients should be as *minute* as possible in the details of their symptoms, age, general habits of living and occupation in life. *The Communication must be accompanied by the usual* CONSULTATION FEE OF FIVE DOLLARS, which may be sent in bank note, or by Post-office order, without which no notice can be taken of the application. In all cases *secrecy is to be considered as inviolable,* all letters being, if requested, either returned to the writers, or destroyed.

"Dr.—— begs to impress upon patients the importance of ONE personal interview, even when resident at a distance.

160

The advantages are manifold, when compared with mere correspondence. A single visit will, in most cases, enable Dr.—— to form an instantaneous and accurate judgment, *and thus expedite the patient's recovery.* In the first place, many important questions affecting the patient are likely to be suggested by a personal interview, which might be lost sight of in correspondence. Secondly, more correct diagnosis of the disorder and a better appreciation of the patient's constitution can be arrived at, *whilst a microscopic examination of the urine, where necessary, will render any mistake impossible,* especially in cases of Spermatorrhœa. And thirdly, where the patient is laboring under urethral discharges, which may or may not be produced by impure connection, one personal visit with a view to a urinary examination is eminently advantageous. In a word, the correspondent will be more than repaid for the trouble and expense of his journey by the increased rapidity of the cure. * * * * *

"Such patients, although they may be reaping the rewards of their own folly, are, nevertheless, the very ones who have special need of correct counsel, and are, for the most part, in just the frame of mind to appreciate advice fitly rendered by a judicious medical man. In my experience, it has always appeared strange to me why the treatment of this affection should remain abandoned by respectable members of the profession to the benefit of quacks and those vile harpies who play on this class of victims.

"Medical men are too apt treat the complaints of such patients lightly, making no effort to allay their anxiety—a course which often leads them to apply for aid in illegitimate quarters, and to become the victims of unprincipled men."

161

In some instances it is a clergyman who is the reputed advertiser, who, as in the following unabridged "Ad," widely circulated in the country papers, wishes to communicate to suffering humanity "the recipe that will cure you free of charge":

A CARD

To all who an suffering from the errors and indiscretions of youth, nervous weakness, early decay, loss of manhood, etc., I will lend a recipe that will cure you, FREE OF CHARGE. This great remedy was discovered by a missionary in South America. Send a self-addressed envelope to the Rev. * * * * Station D, New York City.

Then there are the "Retired Philanthropic Physicians," and the "Patients Who have been Cured," *et hoc genus omne,* who, with such rare disinterestedness, incur large weekly expenses in advertising their willingness to forward to sufferers the means of self-cure "on receipt of two postage stamps." In a word, one and all of these pirates have only one common aim and aspiration— to fleece the fools who are credulous enough to seek their aid.

The main point to attain in this business is to decoy the victim to the advertiser's den or office. Once there, he is impressed with the multifarious engagements of the human decoy-spider who is probably appraising his prey through a peep-hole. By and by, the patient's anxiety is dissipated by the appearance of the pretended Medicus, and he proceeds to give all the painful details of his case, while the listener, by looks and words, does everything to increase his alarm. The history finished, questions will be asked him as to his avocations, position and income, all apparently with the view of elucidating the points of his case, but in fact for the purpose of estimating the "size of his pile," with the object of ascertaining to what extent he can be "bled." This essential information obtained, the quack at once sets his moral rack to work. Everything will be said not only to confirm the patient's fears, but to increase them. A pretended examination of urine will be made, and he will be gravely told that the quack's worst fears are confirmed, ocular demonstration being offered the dupe. The effect of this ordeal may be imagined. The unfortunate victim believes that he has received "confirmation, strong as proof of holy writ," of his dangerous condition. Glibly the quack discourses on the consequences of neglecting the terrible symptoms, and the great difficulty of combating them. He is told that he will be liable to spinal disease, softening of the brain, or insanity. Sometimes a collection of plates, containing hideous representations of dreadful eruption, and sores covering all parts of the body, are submitted to the patient's horrified inspection. Frightened by the hideous pictures before him, and at the same time soothed and charmed by the high-flown encomiums which the quack pronounces on his particular "non-mercurial mode of treatment," the patient becomes anxious to submit himself to the process. The quack is equally ready to take the case in hand, and the only stumbling-block likely to be in the way, may be the patients' inability to pay the large fee demanded. When the victim, however, is manifestly pecunious, the remedy employed in the treatment is correspondingly expensive. In some cases "a preparation of gold" has been used, and the patient has been instructed that it would be absolutely necessary for him to remain in bed for the six weeks during which he would have to take the remedies, and that he must have a nurse to sit up with him at night, in order to wake him and give him the medicines regularly!

We presume no intelligent person need be told that the pretensions as to the "golden" and other "secret and valuable medicines" which these quacks boast themselves to possess, are absolutely without foundation. They no more possess such remedies than they possess any legitimate right to the names and medical titles which they too frequently assume.

In cases of indiscretion, the quack treatment is always with mercury—notwithstanding denials. Sometimes serious mercurial poisoning results, and not unfrequently, through the charlatan's ignorance of proper treatment in complicated diseases, irreparable injury ensues.

The quack advertisements and pamphlets are the source of incalculable evils to youths between the ages of seventeen and thirty. They are impelled by fear to visit the quack's den, where they are "played" as long as practicable. Sometimes exciting drugs, like cantharides, are given in the medicine, and thus intensify the evil. The quack, of course, ascribes the result to the patient's alarming condition, who is growing worse, in spite of his medicines, and who can only be cured by more powerful and costly drugs. Sometimes a seemingly candid but equally misleading offer of "no cure no pay" is offered. In this case the patient is usually required to sign a statement of his condition, in which his symptoms and his previous bad habits are fully set forth. It is stipulated that the "doctor" is to be paid a certain round sum when a cure is effected, and while the case is under treatment the patient pays for the medicines. If no pay is asked for the "stuff," the quack is seldom or ever a loser. Such a document few persons, with characters to lose, would care to run the risk of publishing, and hence they generally acknowledge themselves cured, or pay the doctor handsomely to redeem the document.

While wading through this dark morass of deception and fraud, the "anatomical museums" must not be overlooked. These Priapean establishments, in which is an exhibition of wax models of different organs and parts of the human body, are too vile for description. "Lectures" are delivered with the design of furnishing patients to the quack practitioners in whose interest the place is run. Thousands—we might have said millions—of copies of disgusting little books on "Marriage," or the "Philosophy of Marriage," or some cognate obscenity are distributed gratis, and it is no unusual sight to see a score of nervous, hollow-eyed patients waiting for treatment.

We have endeavored to speak plainly and to the point in

dealing with quacks and quackery, because it is a topic of sovereign importance and urgency. Hundreds upon hundreds of our population are plundered and poisoned by these medical pests of society, and if we have not made it plain that it is dangerous to have anything to do with the advertising doctors of New York or any other place, we have failed in our purpose. Their advertisements, their pamphlets, and their rascally little books, penetrate the remotest corners of the land. Curiosity leads the farmer's son or the apprentice to send for some advertised book to satisfy a craving for information, or to pander to an already diseased imagination, and the bad seed is sown. He is surprised, startled, and finally alarmed; and he writes. He is told in the reply that "I seek my remedies in far-off climes; some in the distant prairie, some in the ever-blooming balsam; in the southern climes, where eternal summer reigns, and on the top of the snow-clad Himalayas." Accompanying the reply is a recipe calling for articles having no existence, or for decoctions from plants unknown to botanists. But in whatever form the response comes, the result is uniform. Plunder, always plunder, in the first place; sometimes this is supplemented by murder; whole families are destroyed, insanity is engendered, and the victims of these vile knaves are driven headlong to destruction and an early grave.

It has always been the dearest wish of a quack doctor to possess a diploma of some sort, no matter where or how dishonestly procured. Sometimes it was forged; sometimes second-hand; but however or wherever procured it was framed and conspicuously displayed in the "consulting" room. By the recent and entirely wholesome amendment of the law, however, those beguiling documents are no longer available. It is now imperative that the certificate of every physician must be filed with the County Clerk. Until this provision is observed, no doctor—no matter how eminent or well-qualified—can practice in New York. Many a quack, flourishing like a green bay-tree, was summarily brought to the "end of his tether," by this most wise legislative enactment.

We would be derelict to the duty we owe to the public did we not here, and in this connection, state our emphatic opinion that the editors and proprietors of newspapers, as a rule, have hitherto looked too leniently on this subject of quackery and its baleful announcements. Happily some of our journals will not publish such advertisements, and no editor can excuse himself by saying that he is ignorant of the character of such announcements. It must be known to every man of experience that such advertisements are unfit for the perusal of young men or women, and it is surprising that the heads of families should permit newspapers containing those advertisements to enter their houses. As a well-known English author some-time since wrote:

"It is pregnant with matter for grave reflection, and this not only in reference to patients themselves, but also in regard to the reprehensible conduct of parents who so recklessly admit into their family circle newspapers which insert the obscene advertisements of the quacks. As I have said before, these advertisements are traps for their sons and an offense to the modesty of their daughters. Well assured am I that many cases of unaccountable suicide in youths and young men, which cause so much surprise and misery in families, are due to these unfortunates having become the dupes of quacks."

This is a very terrible picture of the evil wrought through the abuse of the advertising columns of the press, but experience has shown us that it is not by any means overdrawn. The responsibility of the health and comfort—even of the lives—of many of the rising generation thus rests with the newspapers. How careful, then, ought publishers to be that the columns of their journals should in nowise assist in disseminating that which pollutes the minds of the young, renders them unfit to fulfill the duties of society, or to enjoy its pleasures, and, in short, makes their whole life a burden and a misery.

CHAPTER XVI

ABORTION AND THE ABORTIONISTS

"Such is the fate of artless maid.
Sweet flow'ret of the rural shade!
By love's simplicity betrayed,
    And guileless trust.
Till she, like thee, all soiled, is laid
    Low in the dust."

—BURNS,
To a Mountain Daisy

Love's young dream—the dream of the ages—has sometimes a fearful awakening. In her "guileless trust" and unsuspecting ignorance, a young woman weaves a light web of folly and vain hopes, which one day closes around her like a poisoned garment, instantly changing all her fluttering raptures into a wail of the deepest human anguish. All at once the whole force of her nature is concentrated in the effort of concealment, and she shrinks with irresistible dread from every course that would tend to unveil her miserable secret. Overshadowed by a misfortune that is worse than death, in her half-benumbed mental condition, she hears of the professional abortionist, and braces herself for one of those convulsive actions by which a betrayed woman will sometimes leap from a temporary sorrow into the arms of Death.

The dark crime of abortion abounds in New York, as it does in all great cities. Yet this crime is conducted with so much care that rarely a case comes to light. Even when one of these ghouls is arrested and put on trial it is but seldom that conviction follows, because it is an offense extremely difficult to bring home to the perpetrator. Many indictments, for inexplicable causes, from time to time have been pigeon-holed; but as the transaction is committed in private, the victim is the only witness, and she is naturally averse to exposure.

It is only when the remains of some beautiful victim are found packed in a box, or jammed into a barrel, that the imagination realizes the imminent peril dishonored women incur by trusting themselves to the mercy of those sordid butchers. The author of her wrong usually makes the arrangement, under cover. The wily practitioner talks blandly and soothingly. If the operation succeeds, all is well; if not, the poor victim's body is secretly disposed of. She is chronicled among the mysterious disappearances, because every precaution had been taken that her friends should know nothing whatever of her condition, or of her whereabouts.

Naturally, the practice of child-murder hardens the hearts and petrifies the feelings of those systematically engaged in it. The tortures inflicted on the patient are, no doubt, in many cases unavoidable if the end is to be achieved; but many of these operators are cruelly ignorant and unscrupulous, and barbarously brutal and reckless. The mind shrinks from contemplating the thrilling honors of some of the scenes enacted within those deadened walls. Despite the tears and protestations of the suffering woman, the operation will sometimes be repeated two or even three times. But helpless and unprotected as she is, she is compelled to submit, because she is terrorized by her inquisitor's threats to send her to some hospital at once, to expose her condition to the world and to die.

When death appears only too probable, the abortionist generally has the victim either sent to a hospital or to some regular physician's premises, and leaving her before her condition or their connection with the case has been discovered.

If the death occurs on their own premises, a certificate from some doctor called in at the fast moment, and deceived as to the cause of death, may enable a quiet little funeral to take place. And again, the fact cannot be denied that from time to time regular, diplomated physicians have been found who would not hesitate, for a consideration, to give "crooked" certificates. Should it be found impracticable to dispose of the body in such a convenient and regular way, in some cases it is shipped by rail to a distant and fictitious address, without any clue by which it can be traced back to the "shipper."

The pitiable case of Miss Alice Augusta Bowlsby will occur to many readers just here. The facts in her case were simply these: One Saturday night towards the end of August, 1871, a trunk containing the remains of a young and beautiful female was found at the depot of the Hudson River Railroad, checked for Chicago. The remains were subsequently recognized as those of Miss Bowlsby of Paterson, New Jersey, and the trunk was traced, by means of the truckman employed to carry it, back to the residence of Dr. Jacob Rosenzweig. It was soon discovered that the death of the unhappy girl was caused by an operation tending to produce abortion. Rosenzweig was a burly fellow, with a forbidding aspect, and a bold, confident look. His large, bullet eyes looked defiantly from behind the deep-intrenched line of wrinkles that care or conscience had gradually drawn around them. He had, in fact, a forbidding aspect, and when he was placed on trial before Recorder Hackett, according to a newspaper reporter present,

"one eye was devoted to watching the Grecian bend of his vulture-hooked nose, while the other was on duty over a precocious lock of his curling red hair, which clung to the verandah of his left ear like a Virginia creeper."

Rosenzweig was convicted of manslaughter while treating a woman for abortion, and was sentenced to state prison for seven years—a sentence so obviously out of proportion to the enormity of the crime that a howl of public indignation went up to the skies. However, Recorder Hackett had awarded the utmost penalty of the then existing law, and Rosenzweig was sent to Sing Sing. Soon after, a law was enacted by the state legislature, making the penalty of crimes like Rosenzweig's twenty years in the state prison, with hard labor. After this law was passed, and when the abortionist had served about a year of his sentence, another charge of abortion was found against him, and he was brought down the river, again put on trial and sentenced. Mr. Howe, for his defense, in appeal, raised the natural objection that it was unfair and improper to try Rosenzweig in two cases at once. Consequently, he got a new trial, in which he was acquitted, because the old law under which he had been previously convicted had been repealed. Here was a manifest miscarriage of justice effected by a wise change in the laws. This prisoner escaped, but such a result could hardly, within the range of possibility, occur under the same law again.

In the majority of cases, the victims of abortion are gotten rid of by the practitioner before they die. The operation once over, they are hurried from the premises with all possible dispatch, even though the fatigue and exposure may imperil their lives. Many die a few days after reaching home, in which case the name of the abortionist is never known, and many more linger for a few months or years, mere physical wrecks of their former selves, till merciful Death folds them in his leaden arms.

Before the recent laws were passed, making it a punishable offense to offer to produce abortions, either by medicine or instruments, there were many nostrums, in the form of pills and powders, covertly advertised for the alleged purpose of producing miscarriages. When a person called on one of those quacks and explained the purpose for which the medicine was needed, he was told that it was very dear—from five, ten, to fifteen dollars a box. At the same time he would be assured that his lady friend was merely suffering from "an obstruction arising from cold." If he insisted on explaining, the hard face of the quack would grow darker and harder, and a mysterious gleam of intelligence would shoot from the speculative eye as he was told:

"I will not sell medicine for anything else but a cold; nor will I treat any lady for anything else. Your young friend has only taken cold, and if she is not relieved by these pills she had better come and see me herself."

No doubt most of those medicines were deceptive, fraudulent and futile. But they had the intended effect of advertising the person who sold them, whose "professional" services were generally brought into request when the pills proved inoperative. This was the secret of Madame Restell's reputation and immense accumulated fortune. Her occupation was that of a midwife, and in that assumed capacity she advertised her "Female Pills." As all the world knows now, her real vocation was the ante-natal destruction of unwelcome babies. To her gorgeous palace at the corner of Fifth avenue and Fifty-second street went for years some of the most wealthy and fashionable women of this metropolis. It is a dreadful admission, and a sad commentary on our boasted civilization, but the truth must be told. Some of her patrons were married ladies who, finding themselves likely to become mothers, and being too heartless and frivolous to desire the pains and cares of maternity, sought this woman's aid and, in some instances, paid her fabulous sums to have their innocent offspring destroyed before they saw the light. Others who sought her services were unmarried girls, who, having sacrificed their honor were prepared to pay any price to conceal their shame, by the destruction of the little life which would blazon it to the world.

Madame Restell's clients were all, or nearly all women of the higher orders of society, and of liberal means. Of this disgraceful fact there can be no manner of doubt. Her scale of charges was so extravagant as to positively prohibit her employment by any one unable to pay a handsome fee for the gratification of their murderous project. Sometimes a poor girl, ruined by some wealthy libertine, would be supplied by him with funds to pay for the terrible operation which would conceal her folly; but in the great majority of cases they were ladies of wealth and social standing who went dressed in elegant apparel, loaded with jewelry, and double veiled, to her palatial mansion to obtain her aid.

Madame Restell, whose name was a scandal and her Fifth-avenue house an outrage upon New York for years, was a native of Painswick, Gloucestershire. She was the daughter of a humble laborer named Trow, and first saw the light in 1813. Her educational facilities—as indeed were all those similarly or even better circumstanced in England seventy years ago—were of the humblest kind. But she was made to work, taught to use her needle, and "sent out to service" in her early teens. And so it came to pass that, at the age of sixteeen, she was "maid of all work" for a butcher in her native town. She was quite good-looking, with piercing black eyes and thick, luxuriant black hair, and shapely form. She had many candidates for her young affections among the young weavers of the place, but a journeyman tailor named Henry Somers was the successful wooer. A year or two after the wedding, Mr. and Mrs. Somers emigrated and came to the city of New York, settling over on the east side, about Oliver street. Somers was lazy, improvident and a tippler, and after a short sojourn in America Mrs. Somers found herself a young and blooming widow, with one child, a girl, to provide for. She had all along industriously supplemented her husband's earnings by her needle. She was now wholly dependent upon it for the subsistence of herself and child.

It was while in these pinched circumstances that she made the acquaintance of Charles R. Lohman, a printer poor as herself, and became his wife. There was no immediate improvement in their condition. Both were impatient of the pinchings of poverty. Neither was constitutionally disposed to work hard and patiently for an honest competence. The celebrated "Female Pills" formed the philosopher's stone which released them from this condition of chafing discontent and brooding unrest. From what source a knowledge of the ingredients requisite for the composition of a pill for such a diabolical purpose was derived, or whether, indeed, the pill was effective or diabolical at all, remains a mystery, inasmuch as none of her medicine seems to have been subjected to chemical analysis. Suffice to say that the couple rented a small room, and the first advertisement of the female physician was printed in the old *Sun,* and paid for with borrowed money.

Under such auspices the abortion business dawned upon this city, and in more than one of the daily newspapers, between the years 1836 and 1840, appeared glowing puffs of "the beautiful young female physician," as she was termed, accompanied by elaborate advertisements setting forth her specialty. No wonder this Upas tree flourished by the river of crime on whose banks it was fed. No wonder that her brother Joseph, who had been imported from madame's native English town, was kept busy in putting up medicines and compounds for the ladies of New York. No wonder that the Lohmans, *alias* the Restells, waxed fat and insolent, or that, with only thirty years actual existence, madame informed the public that she had been for "thirty years physician in European hospitals"!

By and by her boldness attracted the attention of the Albany Solons, and in 1846 a law was enacted which was intended to prevent the dark crime which Madame Restell had helped to make so fashionable. In September, 1847, a minion of justice invaded her Gehenna, then at No. 146 Greenwich street, and, upon an affidavit, she was arrested and put in prison. On the tenth of that month she was arraigned and, pleading "Not guilty," was sent back to jail to await her trial. At this preliminary proceeding it appeared that Dr. Samuel C. Smith had been called upon to attend professionally a young woman of Orange County, by the name of Mary Bodine, and, upon discovering evidences of foul play, communicated with the Mayor of New York, and Madame Restell's arrest followed. Public excitement rose to an intense pitch. A spasm of morality shook the city to its foundations. Nothing was talked of but the hideous crimes of the woman abortionist. People lost sight of the war, then raging in Mexico, while listening to the stories of imaginative people about heaps of babies' skulls supposed to be mouldering beneath the floors of the Greenwich-street Golgotha. There were threats of mob violence, and of incendiary proceedings. It was necessary to guard the premises, and Lohman kept himself religiously secluded from public observation.

On the twentieth of October, 1847, the abortionist was placed in the dock of the Court of General Sessions, before Recorder Scott and two aldermen. For the prosecution there appeared Ogden Hoffman, John McKeon and Jonas B. Phillips; for the defense, James T. Brady and David Graham, Jr. The prisoner was charged in the indictment with manslaughter in the second degree. Considerable difficulty was experienced in obtaining a jury. Mary Bodine, herself, was the first witness. She described her engagement as a servant with a person of the name of Cook; her seduction three days after entering upon her duties, and the consequences that followed her visit to Madame Restell's establishment; the conversation that took place; her sojourn in an apartment of the dreadful den; her diet and treatment, and all the revolting details were given with a pre-Raphaelite sharpness of outline that carried the conviction of truth. It was a long trial, and not before November 12th did the Recorder sum up, when the jury, after a brief retirement, found the prisoner "Guilty."

She was sent to the penitentiary on Blackwell's Island, and popular excitement was allayed, while the spasm of public morality, with a soft sigh, fell asleep. When Madame Restell's term of imprisonment expired she came back to the city and, purchasing a new property on Chambers street, hung out her "Midwife" shingle, and carried on her business with nearly as much effrontery, and with quite as much success, as before her prosecution and sentence.

A craving for pomp and ostentation was one of the peculiar phases of Madame Restell's character. To gratify this kind of ambition, she purchased, through a real estate agent, ten lots on Fifth avenue, between Fifty-second and Fifty-third streets. They cost at that time $1,000 each—$10,000 for the ten. When it became known that this woman was the purchaser of the ten lots, a movement was at once made by reputable citizens interested in the respectability of New York's leading avenue to repurchase the property. Five thousand dollars were offered for her bargain without avail. When, many years later, the horrified residents of the fashionable thoroughfare beheld ground broken and the abortionist's mansion gradually raising its brazen front, their indignation knew no bounds. Large sums of money were offered the woman to forego her intention, but she haughtily answered that "there was not money enough in New York" to prevent her. No expense was spared, either in the construction or decoration of this palace of infamy. The frescoed ceilings were works of art. Two Italians worked at them for a twelve-month, at an expense of twenty thousand dollars. The carpets and upholstery, ordered through the house of A. T. Stewart & Co., were manufactured specially in Paris. The paintings were selected from the productions of the greatest artists of the period. Her stable was erected at a cost of twenty-eight thousand dollars. The Osborne House, another of her investments, erected on the ground adjoining her own residence, cost about two hundred thousand dollars.

In February, 1878, evil days again fell upon Madame Restell. On the eleventh of that month she was arrested by Anthony Comstock, of the Society for the Prevention of Crime, and taken to Jefferson Market Police Court, before Justice Kilbretli. She desired her release upon bail, pending examination. The bail was fixed at $10,000, and although she offered to deposit with the court that amount in government bonds, Judge Kilbreth refused. Satisfactory bail not being forthcoming, she was committed to the Tombs, and assigned to a cell on the second tier of the women's prison. By and by, she was released on bail and, pending her trial, some time early on the morning of April

1, 1878, she committed suicide, by cutting her throat from ear to ear, in her bath-tub. The scene was described in that morning's *Herald,* as follows:

"Mme. Restell's chambermaid, Maggie McGraw, went to her mistress' room at about eight o'clock this morning, but not finding her there she went to the bathroom, which is on the second floor. There, hanging on the door, she saw her mistress' clothes. Thinking that she was taking a bath the girl went downstairs, but soon returned and, seeing the clothes still there, she looked in. Not seeing the madame, she became alarmed. A peculiar smell then attracted her attention and, looking in, she saw that the bath-tub was filled with bloody water, and at the bottom of the tub lay the body of her mistress, with her throat cut from ear to ear. The instrument of death, a large carving-knife, was lying at her side. The bath-room is fitted up with Oriental splendor, being frescoed and decorated handsomely."

The suicide was buried next day, being conveyed from the Fifth-avenue mansion to the Grand Central Depot, and thence to Tarrytown, the place of interment. The funeral procession consisted merely of the hearse carrying the body and one carriage. It is a strange, revolting story, carrying its own warning and moral, besides furnishing an admirable instance of the unexpected forms in which the great Nemesis manifests herself.

CHAPTER XVII

DIVORCE

A large proportion of the marital infelicity now so alarmingly prevalent in this country is no doubt caused by the mal-administration of our divorce laws, and by the demoralizing discord between the legislative statutes of the various States on the subject of divorce. While in the middle and a portion of the Eastern and Southern States, the conditions legally imposed, before a dissolution of marriage can be judicially obtained, are wholesomely exacting and in accord with the strict Scriptural standard, in certain of the Eastern, Southern and Western States the most trifling alleged causes of disagreement or "incompatibility" are sufficient to secure the law's disseverance of the marriage tie. The divorce business of certain courts in Illinois, Iowa, Utah, and some of the territories, enjoy an infamous notoriety all over the world; while even staid old Connecticut offers a positive reward to connubial infidelity by at once granting a full or absolute divorce upon comparatively slight pretexts, leaving both parties legally free to marry again as their altered fancies may elect.

He who, in New York,

> "Reads the in image act with pride
> And fancies that the law is on his side,"

may soon be taught, to his dismay, that some backwood's court in the West has privately given his artful better-half a divorce, and authorized her to wed at her earlier pleasure with the Lothario whom he—the cast-off husband—had not even begun to suspect of treachery. Or, again the lord and master whose preference has wandered from his lawful wife to some designing female poacher on her rightful domain, may openly give that wife the fullest justification in law for a New York divorce, and, after the petition has been granted, go with his paramour to any State outside the jurisdiction of the State of New York, and there be legally joined to her for whom he has forsworn himself. One might infer from these dangerous and disgraceful possibilities that but few of the married ones who, from whatever cause, were discontented with their domestic relations, would be long restrained by any other than the highest exceptional moral considerations from availing themselves of the relief so variously attainable. It must be borne in mind, however, that an honorable action for divorce, openly and honestly undertaken in any State, involves more or less public exposure with considerable pecuniary outlay. These two considerations, in the present lax tendencies of our divorce laws, constitute the chief bar against a wholesome "popular" adoption of the legal remedy for domestic troubles; while their potency has invoked a class of fraudulent practitioners whose insidious business it is to procure dissolution of marriage for any or no cause, "without publicity," and at a cost suited to the most limited means. In other words, New York has been, and still is, the headquarters of a villainous divorce ring, by the audaciously fraudulent practices of which the solemn marital covenant is made a despised and brittle toy of the law—to be broken and discarded at the will of the vicious and depraved.

Lord Howell, for fifty years a judge of Doctor's Commons, pointedly said: "A knowledge that persons uniting in marriage must continue husbands and wives, often makes them good husbands and wives; for necessity is a powerful master to teach the duties it imposes."

These sinister traders in domestic infamy, secret libel, and suborned perjury announce their business and addresses in advertisements in which "success is guaranteed," "no fee required till divorce is granted," "no publicity," etc., while the decree is warranted to be "good in every State,"—in confirmation of which last assertion the divorce specialist's private circular frequently contains the following extract from Article IV, Section I, of the Constitution of the United States: "Full faith and credit shall be given in each State to the public acts, records and judicial proceedings of every other State."

The question may arise, and it is pertinent, who employ these divorce specialists? We answer: All sorts of people. They may be dissolute actresses, seeking a spurious appearance of law to end an old alliance, and to prepare for a new one. They may be frivolous, extravagant, reckless, misguided wives of poor clerks or hard-working mechanics, infatuatedly following out the first consequences of a matinee at the theatre, and a "personal" in the daily newspaper. They may be the worthless husbands of unsuspecting faithful wives, who, by sickness, or some other unwitting provocation, have turned the unstable husband's mind to dreams of new connubial pastures and the advertising divorcist. They may be the "lovers" of married women, who come to engage fabricated testimony and surreptitious unmarriage for the frail creatures whose virtue is still too cowardly to dare the more honest sin. They are *not* the wronged partners of marriage, who, by the mysterious chastising providence of outraged hearts and homes are compelled, in bitterest agony of soul to invoke justice of the law for the honor based upon right and religion. The manufacture of a case of the contrabandists of divorce is often such a marvel of unscrupulous audacity, that its very lawlessness constitutes in itself a kind of legal security.

Another question naturally arises: What are such divorces worth? We reply that the whole business is unblushing fraud upon the dupes who are entrapped into patronizing the business. Not one of those divorces has ever yet held good when ultimately contested in open court, by the parties against whom they have been secretly obtained. Many of them, however—perhaps thousands!—have served the whole purpose of those purchasing them, because the husbands or wives so cruelly wronged have either lacked the means, or the heart to take public legal measures for exposing the fraud, and setting the divorce aside. How is the poor clerk, or mechanic, the invalid or unfriended wife, to raise hundreds, perhaps thousands, of dollars necessary for such a purpose?

It seldom happens that the so-called divorce specialist applies to any of the courts in the States of New York, Massachusetts, Pennsylvania, Maryland or South Carolina, because in those States the testimony given in divorce proceedings becomes part and parcel of the written court record. The names, residences, and occupations of the witnesses, and all the testimony they offer, is carefully taken down by the referee, and reported upon by him to the court. The judge takes all the papers, and grants the decree or refuses it, upon the report and the testimony, and the record is perpetually on file, and accessible. Consequently when a husband or wife unexpectedly finds that their hymeneal bonds are severed, they have the right and privilege of inspecting the record of the case, in the court archives, and of examining the evidence upon which the decree adverse to them was granted. These are what is termed "dangerous States," in the parlance of the specialists; for there is always a chance of the disbanded mate feeling aggrieved and pugnacious, and of the cat coming with portly stare from the bag with a lively prospect of the perjured witnesses and the specialist having to "scoot" for parts unknown, or run the risk of dignifying the inside of the State prison. Many readers of this page will no doubt remember with what precipitation the notorious Monro Adams made himself "scarce" in January, 1882, upon the discovery of the irregular Chase divorce, and others of the same kind fraudulently procured in Brooklyn.

In the Western and Southwestern States, on the other hand, where the population is sparser, and where no such press of business is before the courts, divorce proceedings are mostly under the immediate control of the court itself. The presiding judge hears the testimony as it is presented, and decides the case on its merits, there and then. There is no necessity for employing a referee, and there are no written records of the case. The decision, the date, and the abstract records appear on the court books, and that is all. And yet, by the section of the Constitution, already quoted, this decree is regarded,—by the court that grants it, at least,—as perfectly legal and operative all over the Union. Although this is not the case, there are almost insuperable obstacles to such a divorce being set aside. For there are no names of witnesses and no records. There is the name of the lawyer; but if a "muss is raised." he is either *non est inventus,* or his memory is paralyzed. He has no recollection of the names of the witnesses, of the date of the hearing, or indeed of the case. No matter what evidence the injured party might be able to produce, he cannot get an iota of satisfaction nor make the least progress until he knows what evidence was presented against him when the decree was granted. Daniel McFarland found this in Indiana, and so have scores of others. These Western and Southwestern States are therefore not unadvisedly deemed "safe," and hence they are very largely patronized.

In Iowa, Indiana, and Rhode Island, again, the court possesses what is termed "discretionary power" in divorce cases. The State Constitution, after specifying the usual prime ground—adultery—goes on to specify: "And for any other cause for which the court shall deem it proper that a divorce should be granted," or "when it shall appear to the satisfaction of the court that the parties can no longer live harmoniously together." It requires no elaborate reasoning to perceive that a decree granted under such conditions remains tolerably secure. For the testimony has been taken *vive voce,* and the decree pronounced in open court, after the judge has been "satisfied" that the complainant "can no longer live harmoniously" with her Johnny or his Jenny.

A case illustrating this point came under our notice some years ago. A wealthy young Frenchman eloped from Bordeaux with the girl-wife of a middle-aged wine exporter. The runaways came to New York, and in a short time, through a specialist, the lady obtained, in an Iowa court, a divorce from her deserted husband. The deferred rite of matrimony was then solemnized between the pair.

About twelve months afterward, business called the happy husband back to France. It was not deemed advisable for his charming wife to accompany him. Neither, as a matter of fact, did she wish to undertake the voyage. But she accompanied him on board the steamer and bade him a touching, emotional and affectionate adieu. Mark what followed! Hardly had he got twenty-four hours beyond Sandy Hook than she proceeded to the same specialist, who had severed her former bonds, and employed him to procure her another divorce. It was applied for, and duly granted by the presiding judge of the Fourth District Court of Iowa. When this decree came to hand, with its flash heading and big red seal, the lady was married to a handsome young dry-goods man.

Meantime the absent husband in Paris kept up a fervent correspondence with his wife, anathematizing his ill-luck in being so long kept from her side. She replied regularly and kindly to these letters until her wedding with the young dry-goods Adonis was consummated, when she abruptly ceased to write. The Frenchman remonstrated, adjured, cursed and cabled, but receiving no response finally hurried across the ocean to find that he was a divorced man, and to be reminded, in the choice phraseology of his supplanter, that "what was sauce for the goose, was sauce for the gander."

With true Gallic impetuosity he sought for VENGEANCE! He employed lawyers and spent considerable money in the expectation not only of setting the divorce aside, but in bringing the lady and her paramour to condign punishment. His efforts, however, proved perfectly impotent. The lawyer, resident at the court, remembered nothing of the evidence, and the court remembered the case only so far as that it was perfectly regular and satisfactory. Thus it will be seen that

> "Domestic happiness,
> That only bliss of Paradise which has survived the fall,"

when once perverted by cunning treachery like this, leaves the betrayed with little chance to cover its poor grave with the ostentatious monument of legal justice.

There are some aspects of this divorce specialist business which would be amusing did they not furnish such a cloak and encouragement to depravity and licentiousness. The following narrative of actual facts illustrates a phase of the kept-mistress ethics, and shows how the Western bogus divorce operates in lowering the tone of society and in sapping the foundations of morality:

A few years since a young stock broker of this city, spent his summer vacation in the sylvan glades of the country surrounding Lake Champlain. He possessed an appreciative eye for feminine beauty, and a soul burning for adventure. Like most men of this type, he was not apt to be disturbed by qualms of conscience where the gratification of his passions was concerned. In an evil hour, he made the acquaintance of a handsome Vermont girl, just merging upon the full meridian of exceptionally voluptuous charms. Without any special claim to mental endowments, Sadie F—— was a superb animal. Her, our frisky broker saw, and wooed. The girl fell madly in love with him, and, before long, ceased to be a virgin of the vale. Lothario was much attached to her, and by his persuasions and ornate representations of city life, backed by aureate promises, she was induced to fly from her once happy rural home and to live with her seducer in this city. He began by treating her well, placing her in handsome apartments in a boarding house on the west side, and for nearly a year the ardor of his attachment knew no abatement. Gradually, however, the affection on his side began to wane. She awoke from her delusive dream to the consciousness that she was alone in a great city without friends, money, or virtue. Whither could she flee? She could not return to her country home to look into the sorrowful depths of her mother's tender eye, or face the stings and sneers of the people of her native village. "A life of pleasure"—as it is sarcastically termed—seemed her only resource. In her terrible extremity, she made a last appeal to her deceiver, and succeeded in touching a tender spot in his heart. Perplexed as to what disposition he could possibly make of the girl who had loved him "not wisely but too well," he consulted an acquaintance notorious for the number and variety of his amours. "Oh, my dear boy, that's easily settled,'" said the friend, "get a Western divorce through one of those advertising fellows." The broker didn't "catch on"—he couldn't see why he should obtain a divorce, and said as much. "But she wants the divorce!" replied the adviser. "Let her be divorced from Frederick Brown, or Augustus Smith, or Maximilian Johnson, and then, you see, her character will be restored, her virtue whitewashed, and she will be corroborated and sustained as a respectable member of society; an object of envy and emulation on the part of her sex, and of interest, admiration and honest courtship by ours." So a decree was duly applied for through one of those "divorce lawyers" wherein the petitioner, Mrs. Sadie Johnson, sought to be severed from the hated yoke of her husband, George Frederick Johnson, who, as the petition set forth, not only treated her with habitual brutality but continually violated the purity of the hymeneal couch, to wit, etc., etc. The papers were duly served upon the defendant, who assumed the name of George Frederick Johnson for the purpose of the suit. At the expiration of the time allowed in such cases for an answer to the petition, no defense had been set up. The lady's lawyer thereupon moved for the appointment of a referee, as well as for counsel fee and alimony. All went smoothly, of course, for the petitioner, and in due course the decree of absolute divorce was granted to this unmarried lady, with permission for her to marry again, while the disreputable

George Frederick Johnson was absolutely debarred from any such privilege.

When the decree was recorded, Sadie returned to her family by the peaceful waters of the lake, and was received with open arms. She was an object of envy to the unsophisticated young ladies of the neighborhood, and of open and unbounded admiration to the young men. She had learned to dress and to put on flash airs, and her experience in vice, gilded over by this divorce sham, rendered her much more attractive metal to matrimonially-disposed Strephons than any quiet, retiring Daphne of the rural district. She soon became the wife of a well-to-do country store-keeper, and made his home a pandemonium, which ended by him employing a regular lawyer to procure a divorce, when the foregoing facts were elicited.

CHAPTER XVIII

BLACK-MAIL

There is a class of crimes prevalent in the metropolis, which, from its secret character and the apparent respectability of those engaged in it, rarely ever sees the light of exposure. Some of these offenses are hushed through the influence or prominence of the operators. In others the facts are never divulged, because the victims prefer to suffer loss rather than have their names dragged into a publicity which, to say the least, would reflect on them discreditably. For these, and other obvious reasons, many kinds of secret crimes flourish and abound in the esoteric life of great cities. In New York, where money is often rapidly acquired, and where little curiosity is manifested as to the mode of its acquisition, there are naturally many facilities for putting black-mailing schemes into successful operation. Scores of persons, apparently respectable, are constantly on the alert to discover compromising facts in connection with persons of wealth. Words dropped from ordinary conversations, hints and allusions overheard, form a clue, which, followed up and reported in a broadly compromising form to the pecunious person concerned, will, in the majority of instances, induce him to imitate the *role* of the coon that preferred to "come down" rather than be shot at.

Experienced New Yorkers need not be told that there has existed among us for years a class of individuals whose only source of revenue is black-mail. Ever on the *qui vive* for real scandal or its counterfeit presentment, these cormorants levy tribute upon both sexes. The high and haughty dame, with a too appreciative and wandering eye; the wealthy banker, with a proclivity for "little French milliners;" the Christian husband, with a feminine peccadillo; the pew-owner at church, with a disposition to apply St. Paul's "holy kiss" a little too literally; and the saintly pastor with a skeleton in his closet, are all alike fish in the tribute net of this insatiable toiler of the turbid sea of scandal.

No uninitiated person can form an idea of the large number of such cases that are yearly silenced by the payment of hush-money in this city. Sometimes the victim and the victimizer meet, the money demanded is paid over, and there the matter ends. More frequently the negotiation is conducted by means of a "go between" with the same pecuniary result. In some cases, again, the trouble receives settlement in the office of a lawyer, when a receipt and full release of past and future claims is taken by the legal gentleman, who thus secures his client immunity from further demands. It is a well-accepted axiom that under like circumstances the same cause produces the same effect. And so the causes which lead to black-mailing in this city are precisely similar to the influences operating in Paris or London to produce the same ignoble crime. A married lady may become too familiar with some gentleman who has not the pleasure of being known to her husband; she may have been tenderly sentimental and gushingly confidential with him, and may even have confided her arduous imaginings to paper, when a rupture occurs—and be sure that a rupture always does occur in such cases—the cavalier may not only threaten to talk and "tell," but refuse to return the amatory correspondence, unless under substantial pecuniary inducements. This is the return she gets for what may be termed her privateering experiences, and there are numbers of creatures, whom it were sacrilege to call men, who make a regular business of becoming acquainted with married women for this special purpose. Instances are on record where a certain stipulated sum of money has been paid for years to a professional black-mailer, who held letters written to him

187

by a lady whose acquaintance was made at a matinee. We were cognizant of a case in which the bird of prey, not content with his own extortions, handed over the lady's letters, on his death-bed, to a confederate, who continued successfully to maintain the payment of hush-money until death removed the weak and persecuted victim.

Ladies have no idea what risks they run when making chance acquaintances, nor how such intimacy may end. They may be successfully fortified against all the arts and blandishments brought to attack their honor, and yet be seriously compromised. The handsome and fashionably dressed street-lounger is very frequently a resourceful rascal. He may invite the lady to take a carriage-ride, and, as has sometimes happened, an accomplice acts in the capacity of hackman. The drive selected is through the principal streets. Some hotel or fashionable restaurant is visited, and if she still successfully resists wine and wiles, it is more than likely that she will be visited the following day by a "detective" who will calmly inform her that he "shadowed" her yesterday. Of course he is after money, and she pays his demand rather than permit him to carry into execution his threat of telling her husband.

Young girls, too, are frequently compromised by the professional "masher." This vile species of the *genus homo* affects the fashionable streets where he saunters in solitary splendor, waiting for an opportunity to make the acquaintance of some young girl on her way to or from school. If her parents happen to be wealthy, the extraction of a neat sum follows this undesirable association; far an exposure in which her name would in any way be associated with the adventurer's, would forever stigmatize her in society. In some instances the immature acquaintance has developed into an elopement, and when parental interference followed, it was discovered that the scalawag husband was not only ready but willing to relinquish his bride when the money agreement was made sufficiently potent. Sometimes, again, a man is sufficiently infatuated to marry a lady with a soiled or shady reputation, and if that circumstance becomes known to the Knight of Black-mail, it is morally certain that potential hush-money will be extorted. In point of fact every kind of "skeleton," social or criminal, if once its whereabouts be discovered and its individuality established, becomes a source of revenue to those unscrupulous pirates of society.

It occasionally happens that black-mailers will systematically weave a web whereby they may entangle a wealthy person. The possession of wealth confers no exemption from the weaknesses and frailties of human nature, and in many instances indeed the unwise use of money only brings the obliquities of its possessor into greater prominence. It is not long since an affluent and well-known elderly merchant of this city, walking in the neighborhood of the Fifth Avenue Hotel, had his attention attracted by a beautiful woman of graceful carriage and voluptuous symmetry of form, who seemed to keep just abreast of him on the inner sidewalk, and maintained this relative position block after block. He was not insensible to the charm of the situation, and, before he exactly knew how, was engaged in conversation with the fair unknown. She was an admirable conversationalist and spoke with that expressive pantomime which gives probability to the blackest lies. Thus conversing, he accompanied her to the residence she had been describing. The "residence" proved to be an assignation house. He entered, unconscious of the character of the house, and, as he had been on his way home, remained within only a few brief moments. Bidding the lady politely "good-day," he took his leave. As he walked rather briskly up the street he was accosted by a gentleman, who brusquely said:

"So, sir! I have got you at last. I have had my suspicions excited for some time past concerning the probity of my wife, but until to-day have failed in discovering proofs of her infidelity. Now, however, I have them! You have just left the house. I saw you and her meet on the street and I followed you."

The respectable elderly gentleman protested with all the

indignation of maligned innocence, and was fluent and resourceful in explanation. He had, he said, simply been doing an act of politeness that any gentleman deserving the name would have as readily discharged, and so forth. His interlocutor didn't see it in that light, and told him so. The following day he was waited upon by the much-injured husband, who informed him that he was about to institute divorce proceedings against his wife. To demonstrate that he was dead in earnest he produced a formally drawn complaint in which the wildly astonished and indignant merchant figured as co-respondent. The result of this cunning maneuver may be foreseen. The old gentleman paid a large sum of money to the "injured" husband on the condition that he would withdraw the legal proceedings against his wife. When the money had been spent, the leech again renewed his black-mailing effort, and with success, although the respectable gentleman had been guilty of no further crime than the indiscretion of accepting the woman's invitation to step inside for a minute or two. With the second payment, however, he obtained a promise from the "husband" that on the receipt of the money he would start for California and importune him no more. It is perhaps needless to state that the scoundrel never left, but soon after made further demands, always holding over the victim threats of exposure in divorce proceedings. This system of extortion continued until as much as eight or nine thousand dollars had been paid. He was then impelled, in sheer self-defense, to consult a lawyer, when further extortion at once ceased and determined. It subsequently transpired that the "lady" and her "husband" were two of the most notorious panel thieves in the city.

The "anonymous letter" dodge is also sometimes successfully operated in levying black-mail. The conspirator becomes acquainted with real or alleged facts, and dispatches an artfully-worded communication for the purpose of frightening the intended quarry. Very frequently silence is obtained by the payment of a lump sum of money, especially where the victim lacks backbone and decision of character.

Another form of black-mail is practiced by women who run fashionable assignation houses and bagnios in this city. Gentlemen well known in public life, fathers of families, and even clergymen, are occasionally found in these gilded palaces of sin. It is a simple matter for the madame of the house to inform "her friend" that Mr. This, or the Reverend Mr. That, has been numbered among her recent visitors. The usual machinery is set in motion forthwith—threats of exposure and importunate demands for money. When the intended victim refuses to be black-mailed, his family—his daughter, perchance—is notified of her father's transgression and informed that the affair will be made public. Under such circumstances she is very likely indeed to pay hush-money rather than have her family's honored name dragged through the dirt of public scandal.

It is not so long ago that a regular business of blackmail was conducted in connection with the leading assignation houses. Ladies, as well as gentlemen, who visited them by appointment were "shadowed" and "spotted"; sometimes followed home and their standing and character in the community carefully determined, preparatory to the application of the financial thumbscrews.

A noted black-mailer of this city at one time maintained his wife in a private house, conveniently within call of a woman who kept a house of ill-fame. The wife promptly responded to any summons from the madame, and when she subsequently made the acquaintance of some wealthy visitor she would inform her husband of the gentleman's name and position. If, as probable, he was a person of ostensible respectability and advanced in years, with everything to lose by exposure, he "came down" promptly and liberally. On other occasions this high-toned husband would procure, through the offices of a mutual friend, an introduction for his wife to some prominent member of the Stock Exchange. The lady, who was a remarkably handsome, fascinating and wily woman, usually entangled the intended victim in the snare. Then the Husband appeared on the scene, boiling with indignation and "breathing threatenings and slaughter" until money was paid. The gentleman so entrapped might afterwards complain to his friend who introduced him to the siren, but he would never dream of associating him in the "crooked" transaction.

We are not alarmists by any means, but simply relate facts as they have come within our personal knowledge. The weakness of human nature, combined with the play of the passions, especially the passion of love, renders the existence of the black-mailer possible and often profitable. In a city like ours, where such freedom is accorded to young wives and demoiselles, it is not surprising that machinations against their virtue and their honor are planned and executed.

The picture has still another side. What does the reader think, for example, of a mother who has three daughters,— bright, beautiful little girls, with long braided hair hanging down their shapely backs, large, lustrous, melting eyes; childish, innocent-looking lambs, aged respectively thirteen, fifteen and seventeen,—and sends them on the street in the afternoons, exquisitely and temptingly dressed, in order to capture susceptible elderly gentlemen? Yet these bewitching little girls have been often seen in the neighborhood of Madison Square, on Broadway, Fifth Avenue, and even down on Wall street. Their mother would follow them at a distance, keeping them in view all the time. When accosted by a gentleman, which happened every day, their mother would follow them, watch the man when he came out of the house or hotel with one of her daughters, and the next day visit him, saying he had destroyed her young and beautiful daughter, and so on, and that she was going to have him arrested. This species of black-mail is not so uncommon as it would seem, even the fathers of young and prepossessing girls are partners in these affairs.

As a fact there is nothing that devilish ingenuity can devise to entice men and women into committing every kind of crime that is not practiced by the blackmailers of this city, and many are the fish that are landed and great the booty that is secured.

CHAPTER XIX

ABOUT DETECTIVES

We are told that "all the world loves a lover," and it is, perhaps, equally true that most people like to read the details of clever detective exploits. The deeds of criminals naturally awaken the emotions of horror, fear, curiosity and awe in proportion to their heinousness and the mystery by which they are enveloped. Consequently the detective officer who pierces the mystery—unravels it thread by thread, and by unerring sagacity penetrates its innermost depths and lays his hand on the criminal—is at once invested, in the popular mind, with qualities approaching the preternatural. The vivid and fertile imagination of the literary romancist magnifies the illusion. The detective of the successful novel resembles the Deity in his attributes of ubiquity and omniscience. In whatever city his functions are exercised we may be sure that he knows every man-Jack of the criminal classes, their past and present history, their occupation and their residence. He knows all their names, their aliases and their soubriquets, just as Julius Cæsar, as tradition tells, knew all the soldiers of his army. Moreover, they are invariably individuals of remarkable personality. While endowed with a strong spice of the world, the flesh and the devil, they are at the same time clothed in a sort of white robe of social immaculacy. They are half lamb and half wolf, if such a paradoxical being were possible.

Take, for instance, the Inspector Javert of Victor Hugo: A tall man, dressed in an iron-grey great coat, armed with a thick cane, and wearing a hat with a turndown brim; grave with an almost menacing gravity, with a trick of folding his arms, shaking his head and raising his upper lip with the lower as high as his nose, in a sort of significant grimace. He had a stub nose with two enormous nostrils, toward which enormous whiskers mounted on his cheeks. His forehead could not be seen, for it was hidden by his hat; his eyes could not be seen because they were lost under his eyebrows; his chin was plunged into his cravat; his hands were covered by his cuffs, and his cane was carried under his coat. But when the opportunity arrived there could be seen suddenly emerging from all this shadow, as from an ambush, an angular, narrow forehead, a fatal glance, a menacing chin, an enormous hand, and a monstrous rattan. When he laughed, which was rare and terrible, his thin lips parted and displayed not only his teeth but his gums, and a savage, flat curl formed round his nose. When serious he was a bulldog, when he laughed he was a tiger. His guiding principles—or perhaps instincts is the more appropriate word—were respect for authority and hatred of rebellion. In his eyes all crimes were only forms of rebellion. Give a human face, writes Hugo, to the dog-son of a she-wolf and we shall have Javert. No wonder that his glance was a gimlet, or that his whole life was divided between watching and overlooking. And, as if all this analytic rodomontade was not enough, we are told in characteristic rhetorical vagueness that he was a pitiless watchman, a marble-hearted spy, a Brutus contained in a Vidocq.

Readers of Dickens will remember that Mr. Bucket appears on the scene in Bleak House in a weird and mysterious way, which suggests that Inspector Byrne, of New York, had been a student of lawyer Tulkinghorn's methods when he undertook to pump Alderman Jaehne. The sly lawyer is plying Snagsby with rare old port in the dim twilight and evolving his story, when suddenly the victim becomes conscious of the presence of "a person with a hat and stick in his hand, who was not there when he himself came in, and has not since entered by either of the

195

windows." This composed and quiet listener is "a stoutly built, steady-looking, sharp-eyed man in black, of about middle age," and he looks at Snagsby "as if he was going to take his portrait." When the poor, hen-pecked wretch, who has thus been drawn into the legal confessional, learns that Mr. Bucket is a detective officer, "there is a strong tendency in the clump of Snagsby's hair to stand on end."

The method of Bucket consists partly of gross flattery and of being "all things to all men," as Saint Paul somewhere advises. "You're a man of the world," he says to Snagsby; "a man of business and a man of sense. That's what you are, and therefore it is unnecessary to tell you to keep QUIET." He flatters the gorgeous flunkey at Chesney Wold by adroitly commending his statuesque proportions, and hinting that he has a friend—a Royal Academy sculptor—who may one of those days make a drawing of his proportions. Further, to elicit the confidence of the vain and empty-headed Jeames, Bucket declares that his own father was successively a page, a footman, a butler, a steward, and an innkeeper. As Bucket moves along London streets, young men, with shining hats and sleek hair, evaporate at the monitory touch of his cane. When there is a big job on the tapis "Bucket and his fat forefinger are much in consultation together. When Mr. Bucket has a matter of this pressing interest under consideration the fat forefinger seems to rise to the dignity of a familiar demon. He puts it to his ears and it whispers information; he puts it to his lips and it enjoins him to secrecy; he rubs it over his nose and it sharpens his scent; he shakes it before a guilty man and it charms him to his destruction. The Augurs of the Detective Temple invariably predict that when Mr. Bucket and that finger are much in conference a terrible avenger will be heard of before long." Furthermore we are told that "Mr. Bucket pervades a vast number of houses and strolls about an infinity of streets, to outward appearance rather languishing for want of an object. He is in the friendliest condition toward his species, and will drink with most of them. He is free with his money, affable in his manners, innocent in his conversation—but through the placid stream of his life there glides an undercurrent of forefinger."

Sergeant Cuff, of The Moonstone of Wilkie Collins, is "a grizzled, elderly man, so miserably lean that he looked as if he had not got an ounce of flesh on his bones. He was dressed in a decent black with a white cravat. His face was sharp as a hatchet, and the skin of it yellow and dry like a withered autumn leaf. His eyes, of a steely, light gray, had a very disconcerting trick, when they encountered your eyes, of looking as if they expected something more from you than you were aware of yourself. His walk was soft, his voice was melancholy, his long, lanky fingers were hooked like claws. He might have been a parson, or an undertaker, or anything else you like, except what he really was." Then as to Cuff's methods: He is introduced to the reader with the usual air of mystery. He makes no allusion whatever to the business he had been hurriedly summoned to investigate, but "he admired the grounds, and remarked that he felt the sea air very brisk and refreshing." To the gardener's astonishment Cuff proved to be quite a mine of learning on the trumpery subject of rose gardens. As in the case of Bucket, the effective armor of Cuff is flattery. "You have got a head on your shoulders and you understand what I mean," is his typical style of address.

It is unnecessary to remind the reader that the detective of the novelist cannot be foiled or turned aside by false scents from the unerring pursuit of his lawful prey. If by *malice prepense* Javert or Cuff is temporarily beguiled, it is simply for the purpose of showing that the writer himself is in reality a very much more ingenious person than even the subtle detective he depicts for the delectation of his readers. These tricks resemble those feints of failure common to professional gymnasts and trapezists, purposely perpetrated with the object of magnifying in the mind of the excited spectator the difficulty or danger of the performance.

In our American literature the most popular detective stories

197

are not composed of the imaginary performances of fictitious characters. We have made a great advance on that unsatisfactory and *effete* style. To satisfy the exacting palate of our reading people, we require a real flesh-and-blood detective, with a popular name and reputation, to pose as the figurehead, while an ingenious scribbler does the romancing. There is something thrilling and realistic in this method, and it carries an air of veracity which is irresistibly attractive and convincing. The French people did something of the same kind for Vidocq and Lecocq; but, as in most everything else, there is a pervading breeziness and expansiveness of horizon about the American product that is totally lacking in the *blazé*, frouzy, over-geometrical, Gallic detective romance.

No doubt the popular conception of the detective has been derived from the flash literature in which the "Old Sleuths" have formed the pervading figure. Concerning them, a clever ex-member of that particular branch of the force recently said:

"Now that I'm out of the business I don't mind telling you what you perhaps already know—that the usual stories of detective work are the veriest bosh. There is not one officer in ten thousand, for instance, who ever disguises himself for any work he may be bent upon. The successful detective is the man who has the largest and most accurate knowledge of a particular class of criminals. For instance, in a counterfeiting case there are one or two United States officers who will look at a bill, and after a scrutiny will say, 'Now, let's see; there are three men in the country who are capable of such work as this. Bad Jack is doing a ten-year stretch in Sing Sing, Clever Charley is in hock at Joliet, and Sweet William is the only one who is at large—it must be William.' So he proceeds to locate William, and when they get him they have the man who did the work."

As to those very interesting newspaper reports about how Detective So-and-So, while strolling down Broadway, saw a suspicious-looking individual whom he "piped" to the east side of the city, and eventually arrested in possession of property supposed to have been the plunder from a certain burglary, they are equally misleading. As the ex-officer, quoted above, said:

"Ninety-nine out of a hundred cases are worked through the squeal of some thief, or ex-thief, who keeps posted on the doings of others of his class in the city. He knows some officer intimately; goes to him and tells him that the night before One-Thumbed Charley turned a trick on Church street, and the stuff is 'planted' at such and such a place. Acting on this information, the officers visit the place indicated, and just sit around and wait till their man shows up. Lots of ability about that, isn't there? Some people have an idea, you know, that after a burglary the detectives visit the house where it occurred, and, after examining certain marks on the window where the man got in, immediately say: 'This is the work of Slippery Sam; he is the only fellow who does this sort of work in this particular style.' Nothing of the kind. It's just as I've told you in ninety-nine cases out of a hundred. In the other cases, some citizen gives the officers information that leads to the capture of the man."

If the foregoing illustrations serve no other purpose, they at least emphasize the point which might have been made at the outset of this chapter, that detectives are a recognized necessity of our civilization. Crime and vice permeate every rank and every profession, and just as surely as crime and vice will always exist, so will detectives be employed to discover wrong-doers and hand them over to justice. Crime and vice are two terms used for the infraction of different kinds of laws—social and moral—and detectives may be conveniently classed in the same way. The detectives who deal with the transgression of social laws, including such crimes as counterfeiting coin and notes, railroad bonds, scrip, etc., forgers, embezzlers, swindlers, and the wide class of criminals generally, are exceedingly useful members of the community when they are inspired by a high sense of duty, and guided by principles of truth and integrity. The other class of detectives who enact the role of Paul Pry on breaches of the moral law, as, for example, the working up of testimony in divorce cases, is mostly a despicable, unreliable, corrupt being, whose methods are villainous, and whose existence is a misfortune.

Concerning our New York detectives, a writer of some note said, as recently as 1879:

"It is claimed that in about eight years the district attorney's office in New York has not known of one conviction of a criminal through the instrumentality of their detective police. And in those years the city has been overwhelmed and startled over and over again by depredations of almost fabulous magnitude. Still, although the scoundrels are known, and their haunts familiar to what are called 'the detectives,' they are never brought to justice unless they stagger up against the representatives of some of the many detective organizations in New York. Instead of surrounding the thieves with a net-work of evidence to convict them, the New York headquarters' detectives furnish them with all the facilities for escape known to modern criminal practice."

No doubt this deplorable condition of affairs was very largely due to the prevailing practice of the victims of robberies compromising with the felons. In this way detectives eagerly seize the opportunity of acting as go-betweens, and hence their relations with the criminal classes are established and maintained. They are thus largely interested, not in the prevention and discovery of crime, but in its perpetration and concealment. By this method they thrive, and their large incomes and accumulated property are no doubt largely attributable to the success of these delicate negotiations.

We are glad to bear testimony to the fact, however, that there is a great improvement in the detective force of this city, noticeable during its present administration. The men now engaged on the local detective force are as a class, those who have kept their eyes open, and have formed a wide acquaintance among criminals in the district, and are therefore able to obtain information from these crooks about the movements of those suspected of having been mixed up in certain criminal work.

For when the reader reflects how easily criminals keep out of the reach of the police in St. Petersburg, Paris and Vienna, where every concierge, every porter, every storekeeper, every housekeeper, is required to report to the police at least once a week all the details of strangers with whom they may have come in contact, it should be no wonder that criminals can elude the police in New York and other American cities.

Concerning the private detective agencies, it has been said by one of their number:

"They are no better than the regular officers so far as skill is concerned. The only real difference is that there is a superior intelligence in the make-up—their disguise—of the agency people. They are first-rate at shadowing a man, but any man with ordinary good sense, who knows how to keep his mouth shut, will make a good shadow. If you will watch the private agency men carefully you will find that they associate largely with the high-toned criminal class. They are solid with one or two leaders and all the gamblers. All thieves of any prominence are gamblers, and as soon as they turn a big trick, they are sure to turn up here or in some other city and 'play the bank' a little. The agency men who are associating with the gamblers hear of this as soon as the crook strikes town, and a little inquiry set on foot will show where the crook came from. If, then, in the course of a few days, a complaint is lodged with the agency people from the town where the suspected party has been that a big confidence game has been played, or that a forged or raised check has been worked on some bank or other institution, it is not very hard to imagine that the thief who was recently so flush is the one who turned the trick."

There are a great many private detective organizations in New York City, some of which are located in elegant and commodious quarters, with a net-work of agencies covering the whole country and extending even to Europe. Between these reliable firms and the guttersnipe operator there are among detectives, as among other professions, every grade of reliability and respectability, some making a handsome living and some earning a bare existence. There are some thousands of them, and they all occasionally find something to do which pays. It may be watching some money-broker's exchange down-town, for the dishonest boy of some establishment clandestinely selling the postage stamps of his firm. It may be shadowing a confidential clerk, whose blood-shot eyes and generally "used-up" air have attracted the notice of his employers, who thereupon desire to learn where and how his evenings are spent. It may be some bank clerk, hitherto enjoying the confidence of the directors, but who now, in consequence of certain rumors, desire to have him watched. Or it may be any of a thousand instances in which an employee ceases to retain the full confidence of his employer, and the convenient private detective's services are at once put in requisition. Undoubtedly it would greatly surprise the army of clerks, cashiers and assistants of this and every great city to learn how many of them are thus under detective espionage. The young fellow may have fallen into the web of the siren. He may be down at Coney Island or at the races enjoying himself; utterly unconscious that a pair of watchful eyes is observing every motion and chronicling every act. Some fatal morning the reckoning comes. He may be a bank teller, and he is requested by the board of directors to show his books and give an account of the situation and prospects of the bank. Despite his proficiency in bookkeeping, he will be unable to figure up and cover the money he has squandered in gambling houses, on the street, or at the race-course. *"Crimine ab uno disce omnes,"* says Virgil. From a single offense you may gather the nature of the whole.

The detective who accepts employment for the purpose of procuring testimony in divorce cases is undoubtedly at the nadir of his profession. No self-respecting member of the private detective organizations will undertake the service even when the pecuniary inducement, as is frequently the case, is large and tempting. For testimony so procured is regarded by the courts with suspicion. The veracity of a person who would crawl into a house, peer through a key-hole or crane his head through a transom window for the purpose of witnessing an act of immorality, can hardly be considered higher than his sense of honor, decency and self-respect. When he stoops to this kind of business he will hardly manifest any remarkable zeal for truth-telling, and he will be quite likely to offer to sell his evidence to the other side—a course which invariably transpires when the other side is willing to pay for the information.

Violations of conjugal faith are, unfortunately, not unknown, but in the majority of cases the intrigue progresses in secure secrecy until some wholly unforeseen accident brings it to sudden and relentless publicity. The recent case of a Brooklyn lady, who was carried into the city-hospital of that city about the beginning of last June, with both legs broken, illustrates this position with singular force and aptness. To quote from the article of the New York *Sun* of June 7, 1886:

"Mrs. Williams is young and pretty. 'She is not bad,' her melancholy husband said of her yesterday, 'only gay like.' She has been married about ten years, and two little children—a boy and a girl—are now longing for a mother's care and tenderness, which she cannot give them perhaps ever again. The faithful husband of the unfortunate woman is a hard-working man, honest if not dashing, devoted to his home, fond of his wife and proud of his children. 'I have been way down,' he says, 'but I am getting good wages now and getting on top again. But Lizzie wasn't content with these things. She was full of life, and I ought to have watched her long ago. Then this wouldn't have happened.'

"What has happened is this: When Lizzie went down on Fulton street on Saturday a week ago, ostensibly to make some purchases, she didn't return that night. Her husband's anxiety was increased when on Sunday he had no tidings of her. Day after day passed without word, and he sent for a young woman friend of Mrs. Williams to come in and look after the children and the household.

"On Thursday a young man from East New York, a friend

of Mrs. Williams and a relative of a certain young lady friend of hers, stuck his head in the basement window of Fainter Williams' house and said:

"'Lizzy is in the City Hospital. She was hurt by a runaway, and both her legs are broken.'

"Mrs. Williams had first sent word to her East New York friend, who had thus taken the first tidings of his wayward wife to her anxious husband. Williams went at once to the hospital and found his Lizzie. She told him she had been driving with a friend in Fulton avenue and had been hurt.

"'Who was he?' Williams asked eagerly, the suspicions which he had been putting away from him for a long time suddenly becoming convictions.

"'None of your business,' said pretty Lizzie, defiantly. This reply was calculated to satisfy her husband that all was not right. In fact, it convinced him that everything was wrong, and in his excitement and pain he upbraided his wife with such vehemence that she called upon the hospital attendants to put him out of the ward unless he quieted down.

"Superintendent of Police Campbell heard of the alleged runaway in Fulton street, and he wanted to know why it had never been reported to him officially. He began an investigation and learned that the mishap had occurred out on the Coney Island boulevard. Mrs. Williams was confronted with this report. She denied its truth vehemently and protested 'before Almighty God' and in the presence of nurses and patients that she was run over and hurt in Fulton street. Nothing could move her from this statement, and when fifty witnesses to her accident sent word to the Police Superintendent of what they had seen, she was not discomfited, but repeated her false statements with determination.

"Mr. Williams says that his wife has for a long time nodded to sportive-looking men as they have passed his Bergen street house, and her absences from home have been irregular and sometimes prolonged indiscreetly into the evening. He has felt that her love of attention and social excitement was leading her beyond the bounds of propriety, but he had no doubt until now of her faithfulness to him and her children.

"Who took Mrs. Williams to drive on this eventful Saturday afternoon a week ago is her secret, shared only by her escort. Where they met is not known by anyone, but they started about four o'clock and drove through Prospect Park to the Coney Island boulevard. The day was fine and many fashionable turnouts and flashy rigs were on the road. Mrs. Williams, in her close-fitting and becoming dark habit, sat beside a young man not over twenty-five years old, in a road wagon of approved style, and behind a well-kept and fleet-footed horse. It was unmistakably a private rig. Her escort was of light hair and complexion, fashionably dressed, and of a style that is called 'giddy.'

"Down the level road they drove at a good pace toward the King's Highway, which crosses the boulevard about two and a half miles from the Park, and just north of John Kelly's hospitable road house. A short distance before this point was reached ex-Alderman Ruggles of Brooklyn came bowling along at a 2.40 gait, and he gave the young man who was driving Mrs. Williams a brush along an open stretch of road. As they were speeding on toward Coney Island a dog-cart suddenly loomed up, coming from the opposite direction, and bore down upon the racers.

"Mrs. Williams and her friend were on the right side of the road and Alderman Ruggles was in the middle. The dog-cart undertook to pass between them, and in doing so struck the wheel of the light road wagon, throwing Mrs. Williams' companion out. He was not hurt, and he held on to the reins just long enough to check his horse's speed and change his course. The spirited animal turned short across the road right in front of Kelly's and the wagon was upset, throwing Mrs. Williams out. She fell under the wagon and her left ankle and right thigh were fractured. A great many people saw the upset and ran to the injured woman's assistance . . .

"When Mr. Williams was told about the accident he said, 'If that's so, I give her up. If she has done that I am through with her. She cannot come back to me. As long as she lies to me, to shield this other fellow, she may go to him. She can't come to me.'"

This giddy Brooklyn woman reckoned too much on her influence over her husband, when she expected to soothe his resentment by holding her tongue. Those women who deceive good, indulgent husbands, frequently discover, to their sorrow, that the most unmerciful and inexorable of men are those who have been deceived by their idolized partners. Yet men of this kind would be far more likely to thrash a private detective, who had possessed himself of the particulars of the amour in a sneaking way, than to recompense him, and properly, while the courts would absolutely refuse to receive such testimony unless abundantly corroborated. For those and other considerations, which will readily occur to the thoughtful reader, the detective who engages to get up testimony in cases of marital unfaithfulness is regarded as quite ghoulish by his fellow-detectives, and looked upon as being entirely unworthy of credence by lawyers and courts.

After all that has been said the press is, on the whole, the best detective—the most reliable and efficient agent against evil-doers. When a crime is committed the daily newspaper, with its Argus eyes, gives such minute and circumstantial details, together with such exhaustive particulars concerning its environment, and the details of its perpetration and supposed authors, that the public at large, so instructed and informed, become detectives. Hence "crooked" and wicked people are really more afraid of the thunderbolt exposure of the newspapers than of the slower and more uncertain action of the law.

CHAPTER XX

GAMBLING AND GAMBLERS

"And there were several offered any bet,
 Or that he would, or that he would not come;
For most men (till by losing rendered sager),
Will back their own opinions with a wager."

—Byron's *Beppo*

Some people are born gamblers, and resemble Jim Smiley, of Mark Twain's "Jumping Frog." Jim was "always betting on anything that turned up, if he could get anybody to bet on the other side; and if he couldn't he'd change sides. Any way that suited the other man would suit *him*—any way just so's he got a bet, *he* was satisfied." If there was a horse-race, we are told, "you'd find him flush or you'd find him busted at the end of it; if there was a dog-fight, he'd bet on it; if there was a cat-fight, he'd bet on it; why, if there was two birds setting on a fence, he would bet you which one would fly first."

Despite all efforts of repressive legislation, games of chance are in vogue all over the country. Gambling is practiced everywhere. Tourists to and from Europe engage in draw-poker and other games of chance, while they make pools and lay wagers on the distance sailed per day, or the length of the voyage, and on the number of the pilot-boat that will first be hailed. Gambling prevails on board those splendid steamers that ply up and down the great rivers of the country, and more than one passenger, driven to distraction by his losses at the gaming-table, has thrown himself overboard. Our legislators occasionally while away the time in traveling between Albany and New York in a poker-game, and they frequently meet each other at their lodgings around the capitol for the same purpose. At picnics in summer, when Nature wears her most enticing garmenture, groups of young men may be discovered separated from the merry-making multitude, jammed into some nook with a pack of cards, cutting, dealing, playing, revoking, scoring and snarling, wholly engrossed in the game.

No game of chance is more extensively played in New York City than policy. Many people are disposed to regard policy as the negro's game exclusively, but this is a great mistake. Policy embraces all classes in its ranks, and the white devotees of the game outnumber the colored five to one. Among the patrons of the policy-shops which, despite police raids and surveillance, still flourish in the district, of which the Post Office may be considered the focus, may be seen lawyers, journalists, advertising agents, book-keepers, mechanics, liquor-dealers, bar-tenders, peddlers, insurance agents, etc. Gamblers, as a class, are very superstitious, and the white policy-player is hardly less so than his colored brother. The latter dreams a good deal, while the former divides his time between trying to guess the lucky numbers and avoiding evil omens. Bad luck walks arm in arm with him beneath every ladder, and below every safe that is being hoisted to a top-floor room. If he forgets anything when he is leaving home in the morning, and has to turn back, he is ruined for the day. If he washes with a piece of hard untractable soap, and it darts from his hand and scoots along the floor, his "luck has dropped" and "slidden" likewise. If he, by some malign fate, meets a cross-eyed person, especially the first thing on Monday morning, he is plunged into despair.

It is estimated by an old policy-player that every dollar a man gets out of the game costs him at least five. To show how slim is the chance of winning, it is only necessary to explain that many men play the numbers 4, 11, 44 every day regularly, and this well-known "gig" only comes out about once a year, or say once in every 600 drawings. This is especially the negro's "gig." He watches for its coming day after day with fond anticipation. He would rather "ketch dat 'ar gig" for five dollars than receive a present of ten.

The lotteries now sold surreptitiously in New York are supposed to be drawn in Kentucky; but years ago numbers were drawn from a wheel on the steps at the old City Hall in the park. When the State Legislature annulled the charter of the lottery company and declared the game illegal, it moved over to New Jersey, where it was drawn as late as 1850.

"It was a standard joke in the old time," said an experienced operator recently, "to find out what numbers a man had played, and then to volunteer to stop at the City Hall and take a copy of the numbers drawn. A false slip was invariably brought back, and when the player examined it, seeing all the numbers he had bought, he generally dropped his work and went to collect the winning. When the lottery was driven from New York, interested persons used to cross over to New Jersey to witness the drawing, and the numbers were taken from the wheel amid the greatest noise and excitement. Some numbers were received with derisive hoots and howls, and others applauded; and all through the drawing certain favorites would be loudly and continually called for, and if they failed to appear curses filled the air. After being driven out of New Jersey, the lottery men found refuge in several other places, notably Delaware, Maryland, and other Southern States. The principal drawings now take place at Covington, Ky., opposite Cincinnati. The numbers from 1 to 78 inclusive are put into glass globes and placed in a wheel. This wheel is turned until the numbers are well mixed, when a trap in the wheel is opened and a boy, with his eyes tightly bandaged and arm bare, draws forth one of the globes, which is unscrewed and the number in it called. From ten to fourteen numbers are thus drawn, according to the size of the lottery. The drawing is immediately telegraphed on to New York in cipher, certain words standing for certain numbers. After the drawing is translated the runners are furnished with a list of the numbers on a 'running slip,' as it is called, which they immediately take to the various policy shops. No 'hits' are paid on the running slips, as some of the numbers are invariably wrong. About an hour or so after the drawings are received in New York, a printed slip is sent to every office, and then all claims are promptly settled. The managers, being in an unlawful business in this State, have the opportunity to swindle as they please. The players have no redress. Ten thousand dollar 'hits' have been made, according to tradition, and 'hits' of from $500 to $1,500 are known of sometimes. Three-number lottery tickets are sold on every drawing, and constitute a very lucrative branch of the business. Prizes are supposed to range from $30,000 down, and any ticket with one draw-number on it entitles the holder to the price originally paid for it. The first three drawn numbers constitute the first prize, and that ticket nobody ever gets."

The most of the money spent in policy is on "gigs" and "combinations." A "gig" is composed of three numbers, and they must all come out of the same lottery to entitle the player to win. Besides "gigs," there are "saddles," "capitals," "horses," "cross-plays," and "station numbers." In fact there are almost as many ways of playing policy as there are numbers in the wheel. As an old gambler explained it:

"You see there are placed in the wheel 78 numbers, from which are drawn 12, 13, 14, or 15, as the case may be. The latter number will not be drawn but once a week. Suppose 13 to be drawn. The rates—that is, the sum the player will receive if he wins—are as follows: For day numbers, 5 for 1; for station or first numbers, 60 for 1; for saddles, 32 for 1; for gigs, 200 for 1; for capital saddles, 500 for 1; for horses, 680 for 1; and for station saddles 800 for 1. Cross plays—the numbers to come in either lottery—may be made at the same rate, subject to a deduction of 20 per cent. You see that some of these offer a remarkable margin for profit. The station saddle, with its 800 for 1, seems to offer unequaled facilities for making a fortune. But since the game was started, no one has ever been known to hit one. To get a station saddle you must not only guess two of the thirteen numbers drawn, but you must also guess the position they will occupy in the slip. The chances of this is so very remote that the policy-player, sanguine as he generally is, very seldom attempts it. The next in order is the capital saddle, with its 500 for 1. A capital is two of the first three numbers drawn. Of course there must be a first, second, and third number, and either two of these three constitute a capital saddle."

The chances of playing a "capital saddle," "gig" or "horse" in policy are easily determined by the following formulæ, well known to all students of the advanced branches of Algebra:

The number of combinations that can be formed of n things, taken two and two together, is

$$n * [(n - 1)/2]$$

For n things, taken three and three together, the number is

$$n * [(n - 1)/2] * [(n - 2)/3]$$

For n things, taken four and four together, the number is

$$n * [(n - 1)/2] * [(n - 2)/3] * [(n - 3)/4]$$

Applying these formulæ to policy, it will be seen that to ascertain the number of "saddles" in any combination you multiply by the next number under and divide by 2; for "gigs," multiply by the next two numbers under and divide by 6; while for "horses" you multiply the next three numbers under and divide by 24. Thus,

$$78 \text{ X } [(78 - 1)/2] = 3,003 \text{ "saddles."}$$

$$78 \times [(78 - 1)/2] \times [(78 - 2)/3] = 76,076 \text{ "gigs."}$$

$$78 \times [(78 - 1)/2] \times [(78 - 2)/3] \times [(78 - 3)/4] = 1,426,425 \text{ "horses."}$$

In other words, there are 3,003 "saddles" in 78 numbers, and it follows that any person playing a capital has two chances in his favor and 3,001 against him.

There is a joke among policy-players that the game is the best in the world, because so many can play it at once. Different players have various ways of picking out the numbers they think will come out. Some go by dreams exclusively, some play chance numbers they run across in the streets, or signs or express wagons, while others make a study of the game and play by fixed rules.

As we have already hinted, the business of policy-playing is insignificant in comparison to what it used to be. Still we are assured that New York City is still spending a good many thousand dollars a day in "policy," two-thirds of which professedly, and really more, goes to the managers and agents. If policy-players would stop awhile and think seriously of their ways, they would cease playing; or if they would keep an account of all the money spent on the game for a month or two, they would discover that they had chosen a wrong road to fortune.

Pool gambling at the various race-courses in the suburbs of New York is now under stern interdict of the law. This feature is greatly deplored by those who are in the habit of patronizing this exciting pastime. Of course the business is carried on *sub rasa* in the city, in a sort of sporadic form. No doubt, if we are to reason from analogy, the pool-fever, emboldened by being "winked at" and tolerated, will, by and by, assume its noisy, epidemic manifestations.

It is hardly necessary to dwell on the familiar auction pool, with its close, stifling, dingy room; its crowd of solemn, stupid, wide-awake gentlemen seated in chairs before a platform, backed with a blackboard, on which are inscribed the names of the horses expected to start; and its alert, chattering auctioneer, gay as a sparrow, and equally active, fishing for bids, with strident voice and reassuring manner. A few words, however, may be spared to touch lightly on what is designated the "Mutuel" system, which was invented by M. Joseph Oller, an ingenious Frenchman, about 1866. Those who had the good fortune to attend Paris in 1867 may remember that M. Oller's indicators were prominent race-course features during the Great Exposition. They are now familiar to all frequenters of our American race-courses, and their mode of operation needs no explanation. The pool-seller's profit is safe as in all big gambling schemes. He subtracts a commission of five per cent., and thus makes a handsome profit when business is at all brisk.

The "Paris Mutuel" would appear to be a pretty square arrangement, but, according to those acquainted with its true inwardness, it has been "easily manipulated by those in control." There are two ways of cheating, according to one authority, and "both are practicable during the last moments of the race, when the horses are coming up the home-stretch. At this time everybody is anxiously intent upon the contest and nothing else, so that it is an easy matter for the operator to see what horse is ahead, and then quietly add five or ten tickets to his record on the indicator; or, on the other hand, if the horse favored by the 'ring' is away behind, he can quietly take off some of his tickets and so save $50 or $100 out of the five. The former, however, is the easier method and can be with difficulty detected, for very few people keep transcripts of the French pools, more particularly that before they are closed everybody is off trying to secure a good place to see the race."

The prohibition placed upon pool selling naturally renders the book-maker's occupation to be at a premium. Book-making is reckoned a "science," and is based upon the principle of the operator betting up to a certain limit, "play or pay," against every horse entered.

Despite all statements, official or otherwise, to the contrary, there are a large number of "hells" or gambling houses in New York city, in which millions of dollars are lost every year by unwary persons. The New York *Herald* of June 14, 1886, contains a synopsis of the experiences of an educated and high-toned young man belonging to a good family, who had descended from gambling to the practices of a sneak thief. According to the story he told Inspector Byrnes, he was in love and at the same time

"became infatuated with the gambling craze. I wanted to make my sweetheart some presents, and hoped to make enough at the gaming table to purchase what I wanted. My game was *rouge el noir*—"red and black"—and the establishments that I visited were on Sixth avenue, between Twenty-eighth and Twenty-ninth streets, and in Thirty-second street, near Jerry McAuley's Mission House. Instead of winning I lost. I bucked the game and it 'bucked' me. Then I was penniless and became desperate. By honest ways I knew it would take a long time to pay my debts, and as I was in desperate straits I determined to steal. As I did not associate with professional thieves I had no reason to fear betrayal, so I became a rogue again."

There is this insuperable difficulty with the born gambler that he is unteachable. The fool who ruins himself at Homburg or Monte Carlo belongs to the same type as the young man above, whose identity was betrayed by a love-letter. Gamblers are always discovering some infallible system of beating the bank. The first word in La Bruyére's famous work—"*Tout est dit*" "Everything has been said,"—is true of gambling against the bank's system, which is to take a positive advantage which must win in the long run. Not only has everything been said, but everything has been done to beat the bank. Every move has been tried, and the result is evident to all but those who are given over to "a reprobate mind" and will not be convinced. "To gamble against the bank," said an eminent authority, "whether recklessly or systematically, is to gamble against a rock."

If the odds are so much against the insane gambler who,

214

secure in an infallible system, hastens to place his foot on the neck of chance in what is called a "square" game, how must he inevitably fare in a "skin" operation. And the stranger who comes within our gates, bent on backing his methods by a wager, is almost sure to be beguiled into the "skin" game; for he is likely to meet, lounging around his hotel, some fashionably dressed young man who spends money freely, and who, by and by, kindly offers to show him around. He has run across a "roper-in," as he is well named, whose business it is to track the footsteps of travelers visiting the metropolis for business or pleasure. It is the engaging mission of those suave and persuasive gentlemen to worm themselves into the confidence of strangers, with or without an infallible system of beating the game, and introduce them to their employers, the gambling-hell proprietors. And when the poor, misguided pigeon is plucked, the adroit "roper-in" receives his commission on the profits realized. This hunting after pecunious strangers is so systematically carried on that it might be dignified by the name of a science. Keepers of gambling-houses are necessarily particularly wide-awake. They take care to be regularly informed of everything transpiring in the city that may be of interest to their business, and their agents and emissaries leave nothing to chance. They are not impetuous. They never hurry up the conclusion of the transaction. When the unwary stranger is in a fit condition for the sacrifice he is led to the gaming-table with as much indifference and *sang froid* as butchers drive sheep to the shambles.

The reader, among other of Gotham's gambling devices, may have heard of what is aptly designated "Skin Faro," but it is altogether unlikely that he may be acquainted with the *modus operandi* of the game. Skin faro is not played at a regular establishment in which the player against the bank is fleeced. The game is liable to drift against the stranger in his journey to New York, or indeed on any railroad or steamboat, and the "point" is to get the unsophisticated countryman to be banker. In this "racket" it is the banker who is to be skinned. According to a recent authority the ordinary process is something like this:

"After the topic has been adroitly introduced and the party worked up to the desire to play, it is proposed that the man with the most money shall act as banker. Now, in an ordinary square game, few would be unwilling to stand in this position, for though the risk is considerable, the profit is generally slow but certain. At this point the question rises as to who has a pack of cards. The question is soon answered; there always is a pack handy, and the swindlers have it; and this pack, if examined, will be found to contain a neat round pin-hole through the center of the pack. The object of this pin-hole is as follows: the player against the bank makes his boldest play on the turn, that is, at the end of the game, when there are only three cards out, tarry; five, nine and all the aces, except spades, can be *guessed* with almost uniform certainty by any one looking on the dealer's hand just before he is about to turn the last two cards (excluding the one left in *hoc*). As the bank pays four for one 'on the turn,' it is a very good thing for the player, and the faro banker, for the nonce the would-be sport, soon finds himself cleaned out."

The people who frequent gambling-houses may be divided into two classes: occasional gamblers and professional gamblers. Among the first may be placed those attracted by curiosity, and those strangers already referred to who are roped in by salaried intermediaries. The second is composed of men who gamble to retrieve their losses, or those who try to deceive and lull their grief through the exciting diversions that pervade these seductive "hells."

CHAPTER XXI

GAMBLING MADE EASY

The following timely article on the newest racket in gambling in the City of New York is from the *Sunday Mercury* of June 20, 1886:

"Since the gambling houses in the upper part of the city, where night games flourished, have been closed and their business almost entirely suspended, a new method of operations has been introduced. A *Mercury* reporter a few days ago was hurrying down Broadway, near Wall street, when he was tapped on the shoulder by a young man not yet of age, whom he recognized as a clerk in a prominent banking house, and whose father is also well known in financial circles. After interchanging the usual courtesies the young clerk pulled a card-case from his pocket, and, asking if the *Mercury* man liked to play poker, presented a neat little piece of white Bristol board which read:

Harry R . . . . n,
First Flat, No. — Sixth Avenue.

"'If you want to play a nice quiet game,' remarked the promising clerk, 'you can take that card and go up there any evening, or come with me to-night and see how the whole thing is done, but whatever you do don't lose that card, for you can't get in without it.'

"Suspecting the nature of this 'quiet little game,' the reporter agreed to meet the banking clerk that evening.

"'You will find a very nice set of fellows in this party,' remarked the clerk. 'There's none of those toughs or men you see in regular gambling houses there, but young men like myself and some of the best business men in this town. Why, I have seen young fellows there whose fathers have got loads of rocks. They lose a good pile once in a while, but don't mind that, because a fellow's no blood who cries just because he drops from ten to fifty dollars of a night.'

"The house was one of a row of French flat buildings, the ground floor of which is occupied by stores. The clerk, on entering the vestibule, gave an electric button a familiar push with the index finger and almost immediately the hall door swung itself open. As soon as the head of the first flight of stairs was reached, a colored man, wearing a white tie, was met standing near a door. To him the clerk gave a card, and the reporter following the example, both were ushered into what happened to be a reception-room. Two heavy and rich Turkish curtains at one end of this room were quickly pushed aside and the front or card parlor was then entered. There were five round and oblong baize-covered tables in different parts of the elegantly furnished apartment. A number of costly oil paintings hung on the frescoed walls and a well-stocked buffet at one side completed the furniture. The adjoining rooms consisted of two sleeping apartments and a rear connecting kitchen, in which a colored cook seemed quite busy.

"At the center table, where a game of draw poker was in full blast, was noticed two celebrated professionals, a couple of race-horse owners and two clerks in a public department office down-town. At a side table were the sons of a prominent Hebrew merchant and property owner, two college students and several young men whose appearance would indicate they were employed in mercantile houses. Another side table was surrounded by a gathering of Broadway statues and gambling house hangers-on, who were engaged in a game called 'hide the heart,' and the last table had a circle of big, heavy-bodied and solid-looking men about it who were putting up on a game known as 'stud-horse poker.' The reporter and the clerk were quickly accommodated with seats at the center table, where 'draw poker' was in operation. The colored attendant with the white tie was at hand, and pulling out a ten-dollar bill the clerk gave it to the negro with the request to get him that amount of chips in return. The reporter followed suit with a crisp five-dollar bill. The colored man went away with the money to the further end of the room, where he passed it over to a clean-shaven and well-dressed young man with a big diamond in his shirt front. This, the clerk informed him, was the proprietor of the place, who sat at a separate table, and, after receiving the cash, handed out to the waiter several stacks of white and red ivory chips, which were then brought back for the money. The play or 'ante' to the game was fifty cents, with no limit. The white chips represented half a dollar each and the red ones just double that sum. In the first two hands of cards the clerk lost his ten dollars, while the reporter made a profit. A short time convinced the reporter the two professionals were hard to beat.

"While an extremely close game was carried on, the house was certainly sure never to lose, as it put up no money and as 'banker' reaped a steady percentage deducted from the chips of all winners who cashed in.

"The clerk was broke in two hours' sitting and confessed he had lost sixty dollars, more than three weeks' salary, and while he wore a gold chain over his vest, he had left his watch in pledge with the game-owner for twenty dollars' worth of chips besides. As the reporter and his guide reached the sidewalk, one of the young men who had been in the place was asked what he thought of the place. Not suspecting the reporter's motive, the player answered glibly: 'Oh, that racket in French flats is getting to be all the go now, and I tell you it's immense. The police can't get on to it, and now as all the faro games are closed or not making expenses, and afraid to open, it is doing well. Then there is such a better class of people that go to these places, people who would not care to be seen or caught in a regular concern.

Now up in Harry's you see how nice it is. There's your parlor to play in. Then if it's an all-night play you can sleep in turns or lay off during the day, and get anything you want to eat right there. 'Get pulled?' Why, there ain't the ghost of a show for that in those flats. In the first place, no one is let in without he is known or has a card; then a 'copper' can 't go in without forcing an entrance or a warrant, and if he does, what evidence can be produced to show the place is a gambling house? Why, gambling in the Fifth Avenue clubs is no better protected. No one in the house up-stairs suspects what's going on. The halls are all carpeted and so are the stairs, and you never can hear any one pass up and down. Then if any raid is made, can't a man swear he was only having a game of cards in his own house with a party of friends?' In society, next to progressive euchre, poker comes the highest.

"'Are there many of these private flat games?' asked the reporter. 'Oh, yes; there's at least half a dozen I know of. There's one on Fifty-ninth street, one on Forty-fifth street, and several more on Sixth Avenue and Broadway, and any quantity now in other private houses run as social club rooms. You see, no games but poker—draw, stud-horse and straight, and hide the heart—are allowed to be run. Now if you never was in Harry's before, and you were seen to be all right, you would be given some cards to pass around to your friends confidentially, which would tell them where to go for play and would get them in without bother."

CHAPTER XXII

SLUMMING

The following from the Cincinnati *Enquirer* tells its own story:
"Slumming in New York always begins with a trip to Billy McGlory's. It is a Hester street dive. What The. Allen was thought to be in the days when he was paraded as 'the wickedest man in New York,' and what Harry Hill was thought to be in the days when the good old deacons from the West used to frequent his dance hall, Billy McGlory is in New York to-day. The. Allen and Harry Hill are both alive, but Billy McGlory bears off the palm of wickedness amid the wickedest of Gotham. If you want to see his place, two things are necessary, a prize-fighter for a protector and a late start. I had both when I went there the other night. My companions were half a dozen Western men, stopping at an up-town hotel, and our guide was a little 'tough' who has fought half a dozen prize fights and would fight at the drop of the hat. We had pooled issues and one man had all the money in the party. Our wallets and watches and jewelry were left behind. It was nearly midnight when we started, and half an hour later when the carriage drove us up in front of a dingy-looking double doorway, from which the light was streaming. The walls around were black; no light anywhere except that which came out of the open door. The entrance was a long hall, with nothing visible at the further end from the outside. It might have served for a picture of Milton's description of the 'Cavernous Entrance to Hell.'

"There was a policeman outside, and down the street a score of shadowy forms flitted in and out of the shadows—prostitutes lying in wait for victims, our guide told us. McGlory's place is a huge dance hall, which is approached by devious ways through a bar-room. There is a balcony fitted up with tables and seats. There are tables and seats under the balcony. There are little boxes partitioned off in the balcony for the best customers—that is the sight-seers—and we got one of them. A piano is being vigorously thumped by a black-haired genius, who is accompanied by a violinist and a cornet player. 'Don't shoot the pianist; he is doing his best,' the motto a Western theater man hung up in his place, would be a good thing here. Yet the pianist of one of these dance halls is by no means to be despised. It was from a position like this that Counselor Disbecker rose within a few years to a legal standing that enabled him to get $70,000 out of Jake Sharpe for lawyer's fees. Transpositions are rapid in New York, and Billy McGlory, who was on the Island a few months ago for selling liquor without license, may be an excise commissioner himself before he dies.

"These side thoughts have crowded in while we are looking around. There are five hundred men in the immense hall. There are a hundred females—it would be mockery to call them women. The first we hear from them is when half a dozen invade our box, plump themselves in our laps, and begin to beg that we put quarters in their stockings for luck. There are some shapely limbs generously and immodestly shown in connection with this invitation. One young woman startles the crowd by announcing that she will dance the cancan for half a dollar. The music starts up just then, and she determines to do the cancan and risk the collection afterward. She seizes her skirts between her limbs with one hand, kicks away a chair or two, and is soon throwing her feet in the air in a way that endangers every hat in the box. The men about the hall are all craning their necks to get a sight of what is going on in the box, as they hear the cries of 'Hoop-la' from the girls there. There is a waltz going on down on the floor. I look over the female faces. There is one little girl, who looks as innocent as a babe. She has a pretty face, and

I remark to a companion that she seems out of place among the other poor wretches—for there is not an honest woman in the hall. Before we leave the place it has been demonstrated that the little girl with the innocent face is one of the most depraved of all the habitues of the place.

"The dance is over, and a song is being sung by a man on crutches with only one leg. 'He is an honest fellow, is the Major,' says one of the girls. 'Poor fellow, he has a wife and six children. He sticks to them like a good fellow and works hard to get a living. He sells pencils in the day-time and works here at night.' A generous shower of coin goes on to the floor when the Major finishes. I begin to notice the atmosphere of tobacco smoke. It is frightfully oppressive. The 'champagne' that it has been necessary to order so as to retain the box has not been drank very freely. The girls have been welcome to it the visitors having discovered that it is bottled cider, with a treatment of whisky to give it a biting tang and taste. It costs three dollars a bottle. It would cost a man more to drink it. There was a young business man of Cincinnati here three or four weeks ago who filled himself up on it at a cost of $300. He had been foolish enough to go to McGlory's alone. He was found on the Bowery at five o'clock the next morning without any hat or overcoat. His pocket-book, watch and jewelry were gone. His only recollection was that he had taken three or four drinks of McGlory's 'champagne.' He went to the hotel where he was a guest and was wise enough to take the advice of the clerk. By paying $100 and no questions asked he got back his watch and jewelry. He also got his pocket-book and papers, but not the $200 that was in the book when he started out on his spree. In the intervals of the dance his story has been told me as a sample of the nightly occurrence.

"What is this that has come out for a song? It has the form of a young man, but the simpering silliness of a school girl. Half idiot, it jabbers out a lot of words that can not be understood, but which are wildly applauded by the crowd on the floor, who 'pat juba' while the creature dances. The girl who has been hanging around me to get a quarter, whispers something like 'Oh, the beast!' in my ear. I hear the other girls uttering similar remarks and epithets. So I look closer at the young man on the floor—for young man it is. He has a long head and smooth face, with a deathly white pallor over it, big mouth and lips as thick as a negro, a conical shaped forehead, and eyes that glitter with excitement like a courtesan's, but from which at times all signs of intelligence have apparently fled. He has a companion whose general appearance is like his own, but whose head is large and round, with a high forehead and full moon face. Who are they? Well, they are part of Billy McGlory's outfit, and that is all I can say about them. There are four more of them in female dress, who have been serving drinks to the customers at the tables, all the while leering at the men and practicing the arts of the basest of women.

"Some of my companions have been drawn into one of the little boxes adjoining ours. They come back now to tell of what depravity was exhibited to them for a fee. 'Great heavens!' exclaims one of them. 'I feel sick. Get me out of this if you can. It is damnable.' No wonder they are sick. The sights they have seen would sicken all humanity. Editor Stead, of London, could find a bonanza every night for a week right here in New-York City at Billy McGlory's Assembly Hall. 'Hist!' says our guide. We look up and find three or four toughs around. They do not allow any adverse criticisms to be passed aloud at Billy's. If you begin to talk aloud what you think, out you go. There have been more round dances. There has been more indifferent singing and some clog dancing. It is getting late. The fumes of tobacco and of stale beer are stifling. Four-fifths of the men have not moved from the tables since we came in. Here and there one is lopped over asleep. But the waiter in female clothing comes along to wake him up and induce him to order more beer. Your glass must always be before you if you want to stay at McGlory's.

"'What are they all waiting for?' I ask. But no one will tell me. Across the balcony a girl is hugging her fellow in a maudlin and hysterical manner. Another girl is hanging with her arms around the neck of one of the creatures I described some time ago. She is pressing her lips to his as if in ecstasy. He takes it all as a matter of course, like an indifferent young husband after the honeymoon is over. His companion joins him—the moon-faced fellow—and they come around to our box and ogle us. They talk in simpering, dudish tones, and bestow the most lackadaisical glances on different members of our party. The girls shrink back as if contamination itself had come among them. 'We are pretty hard,' says one of them, 'but not so hard as they.'

"The piano gives a bang and a crash. The gray light is beginning to stream through the windows. There is a hurrying and a scurrying among the females, and there are a precious lot of young fellows, with low brows and plug-ugly looks gathering on the floor. There are twenty odd women with them, mostly young, none good-looking, all bearing marks of a life that kill. The band strikes up a fantastic air. The whole place is attention at once. The sleepy beer-bummers rouse up. The persons on the balcony hang over the railings. The figures on the floor go reeling off in a mixture of dancing and by-play as fantastic as the music. The pianist seems to get excited and to want to prove himself a Hans von Bulow of rapid execution. The fiddler weaves excitedly over his fiddle. The cornetist toots in a screech like a car-engine whistle. The movements of the dancers grow licentious and more and more rapid. They have begun the Cancan. Feet go up. Legs are exhibited in wild abandon. Hats fly off. There are occasional exhibitions of nature that would put Adam and Eve to shame. The draperies of modern costumes for a time covers the wanton forms, but as the performers grow heated wraps are thrown off. The music assumes a hideous wildness. The hangers-on about the place pat their hands and stamp and shout. The females on the floor are excited to the wildest movements. They no longer make any attempt to conceal their persons. Their action is shameful beyond relation. It is climaxed by the sudden movement of eight or ten of them. As if by concerted arrangement they denude their lower limbs and raising their skirts in their hands above their waists go whirling round and round in a lascivious mixture of bullet and cancan. It is all done in an instant, and with a bang the music stops. Several of the girls have already fallen exhausted on the floor. The lights go out in a twinkling. In the smoky cloud we have just enough daylight to grope our way out. The big policeman stands in the doorway. Billy McGlory himself is at the bar, to the left of the entrance, and we go and take a look at the man. He is a typical New York saloon-keeper—nothing more, and nothing less. A medium-sized man, neither fleshy nor spare; he has black hair and mustache, and a piercing black eye. He shakes hands around as if we were obedient subjects come to pay homage to a king. He evidently enjoys his notoriety.

"I had a chat with an old detective, who says to me about McGlory: 'He is a Fourth-warder by birth. He has a big pull in politics, but takes no direct part himself. He pays his way with the police, and that ends it. I have known him for years, and 'tough' as he is, I would take his word as quick as I would take the note of half the bank presidents of New York. His place is in the heart of a tenement region, where there are a great many unmarried men. Grouped around him are the rooms and haunts of hundreds of prostitutes, with their pimps, thieves and pick-pockets who thrive in such atmosphere. His place is head-quarters for them. These can not be suppressed, and it is part of the police policy to leave a few places like McGlory's where you can lay your hands on a man at any time, rather than scatter them indiscriminately over the city.'

"We go out on Hester street. It is a narrow, dirty, filthy street. It is the early morning—five o'clock. We had spent nearly five hours in the den. The air was reeking with the filthy odors of the night, but it was refreshing compared with the atmosphere we had left.

"We get in our carriage to go home.

"Three or four blocks up-town we pass Cooper Institute and

the old Mercantile Library. A stone's throw from McGlory's are the great thoroughfares of the Bowery and Broadway. You could stand on his house-top and shoot a bullet into the City of Churches. I have not told the half, no, nor the tenth, of what we saw at his place. It can not be told. There is no newspaper would dare print it. There is no writer who could present it in shape for publication. It can only be hinted at. There is beastliness and depravity under his roof compared with which no chapter in the world's history is equal.

"Involuntarily, when I reached my apartment, I turned into the bath-room and bathed my face and hands. It was like getting a breath of heaven after experiencing a foretaste of sheol."

CHAPTER XXIII

OUR WASTE BASKET —
CONTEMPORANEOUS RECORDS AND
MEMORANDA OF INTERESTING CASES

MISS RUFF'S TRIBULATIONS

Miss Louise Ruff was a tall, fair-complexioned young lady of twenty-two, with a handsome form, lovely shoulders, handsome arms and bewitching address. Her family was well known on the east side of the town, and she had received a fairly liberal education. Miss Ruff, two or three years previous to the legal proceedings here chronicled, had the good or bad fortune to form the acquaintance of Mr. Julius Westfall, the well-to do proprietor of a couple of restaurants. Mr. Westfall was a Teutonic "masher" with which any Venus would have been justified in falling in love. He was a brunette with hyacinthine locks and lustrous black eyes, and with hands and feet too pretty, almost, for use. Mr. Julius Westfall fell violently in love with Louise. She had dropped in with a lady friend to drink a cup of coffee. From behind the receipt of custom he took an observation, and then he began to prance round, as one who had suddenly been attacked by a combination of the fire of St. Anthony and the dance of St. Vitus. He skipped around the saloon like a grasshopper on a gravel lot, and smiled, and smiled, and smiled—looking his Fourth-of-July prettiest. Of course Miss Ruff nudged her companion above the fifth rib, and whispered something complimentary to the beaming proprietor; and when the ladies left, he bowed them out with all the grace of a Belgravia footman.

Mr. Westfall began to watch for Louise and to trot after her like a doppelganger. He kept a tub of ice-water in a closet, in which he occasionally bathed his throbbing temples. He was devoured by a consuming passion. When he beheld her at a distance, he smacked his lips like a beautiful leopard. The heart of Miss Ruff was not of adamant. It was not a trap-rock paving stone. She could not resist the young man's loveliness and his innumerable fascinations. They began to walk out together in the evening when the dandelions were being kissed by the setting sun. They strolled into the beer gardens and listened to music's power, while moistening their clay. The Bowery Garden, between Canal and Hester streets, was a favorite resort. So was the Atlantic Garden and the Viennese lady musicians. Thus, for one long twelve-month they loved—after nature's fashion, nor thought of the crime.

Sometime in the latter part of last year—it may have been in October, or November, or December—Mr. Julius Westfall was summoned to the German fatherland. It became necessary to dispose of his business and to bid adieu to Louise. Why he did not marry the young lady doth not appear. He seems to have left suddenly, and probably the idea of matrimony did not occur to him. Mr. Ludwig Nisson became Mr. Westfall's successor in the restaurant business. More than that, he also became the successor of Mr. Westfall in the affections of Miss Ruff. Now, Mr. Ludwig Nisson is a handsome young blonde, with lovely flaxen side-whiskers and a rose-pink complexion. Mr. Nisson's chin and upper lip are shaven clean every morning. He wears the latest Fifth-avenue style of store clothes. An ornamental garden of jewelry adorns his vest. His studs are diamonds; his hay-colored hair exhibits the perfection of the barber's skill. Mr. Nisson's lips are red and pouting. He may be seven or eight and twenty. He is very good-looking, and he knows it. As in the case of Mr. Westfall, Ludwig made superhuman efforts to please

Miss Ruff when she entered his saloon, in which are seats always "reserved for ladies." In the art of soul-floralization, Ludwig was his predecessor's equal. What could Louise do but listen to his blandishments? And when a young lady listens once, the poet tells us, she "will listen twice." Thus it came to pass that before Julius Westfall had been long gone—perhaps before he was even half seas over—Mr. Nisson began to meander around with Miss Ruff, to quaff the foaming lager, and to be on hand in the Bowery Garden when the band began to play.

Some of these affectionate and confidential manifestations did not eventuate amid the glare and blare of the beer garden's, but away up in a sanctum over a drug store and in other "sweet, retired solitudes," where they could listen to the sweet music of their own speech. Early in January of the present year, Louise possessed a secret which she felt she could confide to no ear but Ludwig Nisson's. With reddening cheeks she softly made her confession. The easiest and most economical course under the lamentable circumstances was to offer her some advice. That is just what Ludwig did offer—subsequently, however, backing it with a modest fiduciary bonus. After this Mr. Ludwig Nisson sought no more to commune with Miss Ruff. The poor, indiscreet girl was in a pitiable dilemma. She had no mother in whose heart of hearts she could seek forgiveness and shelter. If her family were made aware of the event impending, she knew the explosion of indignation would be terrific. So she professed to be tired of staying at home, and entered her name in a registry office for servants. Fitfully occupying two or three positions, a victim of anxiety and unrest, she finally consulted an old friend of her family—Mr. Peter Cook, the lawyer, who wrote a letter to Mr. Nisson for his client. In a few days a lawyer called on Mr. Cook on behalf of the restaurateur, and stated that the case would be allowed to go for trial, in which case, Mr. Nisson would defend it. Shortly afterward, or to be more specific, in May last, Mr. Henry E. Von Voss, collector for a down-town business house, called upon Miss Ruff and had a conversation with her in regard to a possible arrangement. Mr. Von Voss was anxious that the conversation should be private, but the lady with whom Louise was residing counseled her to secure the presence of a witness. He advised her to settle the matter amicably, on a pecuniary basis, and thus avoid the scandal of publicity. This counsel was favorably entertained, and in a few days, on the receipt of a small sum of money, she signed what in law is known as "a general release," drawn up by a Second Avenue lawyer, in which she exempted Mr. Nisson from all further claims of any kind whatsoever.

Time passed on, and the money was spent. The tale of the months that would make her a mother were being surely fulfilled. As yet her family knew nothing of her condition. With Disgrace, his gaunt twin brother, Starvation, threatening to assail her, what should she do? Happy thought! There were the Commissioners of Charities and Corrections. There was an asylum for unfortunate girls in her condition. Here would she apply and conceal her trouble.

Before an applicant can be admitted to this humane institution certain preliminary information must be given. Louise refused to reveal Ludwig's name or to make a complaint against him. Thereupon she was taken before his Honor Justice Otterbourg at Essex Market and ordered to reveal the name of her lover, and to make complaint against him. "It is the first case in my practice," said Mr. Cook, "where the girl was compelled to make the complaint." Thereupon the usual order of arrest was issued, and Ludwig was sacrilegiously thumbed by a coarse-handed sheriff. Of course the necessary bail was immediately found, and then he was at liberty to walk down to 89 Centre street and seek legal succor from Messrs. Howe & Hummel.

The hearing came up in the private examination room of Judge Otterbourg on Friday last. Judge, and clerks, and lawyers, and principals, and witnesses were promptly on hand. The Judge smoked a cigar, and his smooth white forehead, beneath his Hyperion curls, looked the picture of judicial impartiality.

Lawyer Cook looked like Charles the Wrestler, waiting for a burly and muscular antagonist. Lawyer Hummel was all brains and diamonds; and when the Judge wanted a light, Mr. Hummel handed him a match-box of solid virgin gold dug from a California mine by Tony Pastor. The fair plaintiff was nervous. Mr. Ludwig Nisson was very handsome but very pale. His counsel fought for him as earnestly as if his client had been arraigned for murder; and when opportunity offered he whispered in his client's ear and bade him keep up his heart. The seven witnesses for the defense sat in the rear. Four of them were former friends of Louise. Miss Ruff took the stand and in reply to Mr. Cook briefly told her experiences. Then Mr. Hummel took her in hand. She answered modestly and straightforwardly, not denying the nature of her intimacy with Mr. Julius Westfall, but stated her inability to remember when that gentleman went to Europe.

Mr. Richard Kloeppel then perched himself gracefully on the witness chair and smiled benignly upon the court and counsel. Mr. Kloeppel is the bartender in the Gilbert House, and in answer to Mr. Hummel declared that he was acquainted with Miss Ruff. He had walked in that portion of Second Avenue known as Love Lane in the company of Miss Ruff, and he had also sweethearted and otherwise mashed other young ladies. Nobody in court—with the possible exceptions of Louise and her lawyer—were surprised when Richard went into particulars about his intimacy with Miss Ruff.

Mr. Rudolph Fuchs was the next occupant of the witness chair; a bewilderingly pretty brunette with coal-black eyes and perfect teeth. During the height of the season Mr. Rudolph Fuchs had been the cynosure of all eyes at Brighton Beach, where, for a pecuniary consideration, he condescended to fill the role of waiter. Last year he was similarly engaged at Cable's. Next year, he will probably be the subject of fierce rivalry among Coney Island caterers. Mr. Fuchs gave his testimony with inimitable grace. Mr. Fuchs had also enjoyed the acquaintance and association of Miss Ruff. He had danced with her; he had listened to the band in her charming society; he had escorted her along the street, and he had accompanied her to an establishment that shall be nameless here.

Then Lawyer Hummel called Joseph Neuthen. He was another exasperatingly pretty young man, with pearl complexion and hazel eyes. He was the fourth of the phenomenally pretty young men who had loved Miss Ruff. Mr. Neuthen rehearsed a soft and scandalous tale. He learned to look upon Louise with love two years since this summer. One evening he had been in a private apartment in West Third street with Miss Ruff.

After this charming witness retired, lawyer Cook lashed himself into a rage. Miss Ruff once more graced the witness stand. She told the incidents connected with Mr. Neuthen's acquaintance in a different, but in an equally interesting way. At the same time she emphatically denied the soft impeachments of Richard Kloeppel and Rudolph Fuchs. She had known them, she swore, as casual acquaintances; but closer relations she positively denied. As to "Joseph," Miss Ruff remembered a certain evening, over two years since, when he brought her tidings that Mr. Westfall wanted to see her. She was gratified by the intelligence, and readily adopted Joseph's suggestion, more especially as Mr. Westfall had charged his messenger with it—to drink a glass of beer, till the restaurateur arrived. Joseph and Louise waited and waited, but Julius failed to appear. Then Joseph said: "Perhaps he has gone home; perchance he slumbereth; let us go after him." They went to Third street, where Julius was accustomed to woo Morpheus. Joseph and Louise entered a room. Soon after he became demonstrative in his attentions. But being comparatively a giantess, she kicked him away, and after he had gone to sleep she put off her outer raiment and went to sleep also.

Mr. Theodore Utz, of Stapleton, L. I., an upholsterer by trade, was the next witness. He had received letters from Miss Ruff, and was familiar with her handwriting. He had seen a letter addressed by her to Mr. Westfall since he left for Europe. The letter was addressed to Mr. Westfall in Hamburg, and he was familiar with its contents.

Counsellor Hummel: "Now state the contents of that letter as near as you can recollect."

Counsellor Cook: "I object."

Judge Otterbourg ruled out the testimony.

"Put this down on the record," said Mr. Hummel. "Counsel for defendant excepts and insists that the question is admissible on the ground that the complainant having sworn that she did not write a letter to Mr. Westfall, charging him with the paternity of the child likely to be born, the defense desires to prove by this witness, who has sworn that he knows the handwriting of, and who has received letters from, the complainant, that the complainant did write a letter to said Westfall charging him with the paternity of said to-be-born child; that it is an impossibility to secure said original letter, or said Julius Westfall, it having been proven in evidence that due effort was made to secure the original letter and Westfall, but Westfall is in Europe and not in the jurisdiction of this court."

Mr. Francis L. Specht, a butcher on the east side, who supplied the restaurants of Mr. Nisson, gave some testimony tending to prove that Miss Ruff sometimes kept late hours. When asked by Mr. Hummel, "Do you known her general character for virtue?" plaintiff's counsel objected, and the objection was sustained. The result of the case, however, was that the proceedings were eventually dismissed, the evidence conclusively establishing the fact that Miss Ruff "loved not wisely but too much."

ASTOUNDING DEGRADATION

Supreme Court.—John Edward Ditmas against Olivia A. Ditmas. Such is the title of an action for divorce instituted by Howe & Hummel, on behalf of an injured husband, against a youthful, educated, accomplished and fascinating wife, who had fallen from woman's high estate, violated her marriage vows, and by her own libidinous conduct and lustful debauchery become one of the many fallen ones of this great metropolis.

Some years previous to the action, at Perinton in this State, John E. Ditmas, a well-to-do young farmer of Gravesend, L. I., was united in the bonds of holy matrimony by the Rev. J. Butler, to the youthful, beauteous defendant, whose maiden name was Olivia A. Mead. And for some time they lived most happily together, but her father, thinking that she was then too young— she being only sixteen years of age—to enter into the marriage state, induced her to leave the husband and temporarily board with him at the corner of Main and Clinton streets, in the city of Rochester, in this State, Her father subsequently succeeded in inducing her to enter a ladies' boarding school at Rochester, but her conduct there in flirting with young gentlemen was so openly improper that the proprietress was compelled to expel her from the establishment.

To the utter astonishment of every one and disclosing an unparalleled revolting case of parental heartlessness, William B. Mead, the father of Olivia, induced his daughter to quit the path of virtue, and to enter a fashionable house of prostitution in Rochester, then kept by Madame Annie Eagan; and, as the beautiful but frail defendant states, the paternal originator of her being told her that as she was inclined to be "gay" she might as well live in a "gay" house as not; and he took her there, making arrangements with the proprietress for her stay, and she became one of the inmates, conforming to the requirements and regulations of the situation.

The plaintiff, hearing this heart-breaking intelligence,

made every effort to induce the defendant to leave her life of debauchery, and portrayed the misery, disease, and prospects of early death consequent upon such a life; but it appeared to be time wasted to talk to her, as she was evidently too far gone to become awakened to any desire for reformation.

Subsequently, learning that her devoted and much injured husband had determined to avail himself of the law to get free from the legal obligation which bound him to one lost past redemption, the defendant addressed to the plaintiff two letters, of which the following are copies, and which but too plainly admit the extent of the degradation and crime into which the unhappy, and lost, abandoned wife had plunged herself:

"Rochester, ...

"MY DEAR HUSBAND,—With a sad and breaking heart I sit down to communicate my thoughts and feelings to you; but oh, if I could tell you how I feel I should be happy, but words can never express or tongue tell. I believe that I am at present one of the most unhappy, as well as unfortunate and miserable beings, that ever existed, but I can only feel to say that it was God's curse upon me, and that I know that I am deserving all, so I do not murmur. But, oh! the tears I have shed for my past follies would make an ocean; and to-night, if I was only laid in my grave, is my wish. John, what shall I say? In the first place, can you ever forgive me? for God alone knows that I am penitent if there ever was one in the world. I can hardly hope to be forgiven, for my sins are almost beyond redemption, but God will forgive at the eleventh hour, and I want to be forgiven and reform. I will reform. I have seen enough, and now I want to settle down and live a virtuous and respectable life the rest of my days and die a happy death, for I have spent many an hour of late in deep thought, and it is not an impulse of the moment, but I have spent hours and days and months, and conclude that this is no life for me to lead. I am cured of my follies and I want to reform. Now, John, I have used you like a dog. I can say nothing for myself only that I am sorry, and have suffered enough, and have had my just dues. But, oh, John, forgive me! I could never do enough for you, and though I should live for years I could never wash out the stain which I have brought upon your name, but I am willing to end my days in your service. I am willing to do anything for you, if you are only willing to forgive me and live with me again, for I am your wife the same as ever, although I never filled that position or deserved the name. I am now willing to steady down and be a wife to you the remainder of my days. I think it was God's will that things should have been as they have; for my part, I know that it has been the making of me. I do not think that I could ever have settled down, and have been a woman and true wife, if I had not passed through what I have, for now I have seen not only the ways of the world, but the follies of my ways, and am cured, and now I am willing to go anywhere, and live with my husband, and be to him a true wife the rest of my days. That I am penitent and want to be forgiven by you and all of the rest, 'though I can never expect that,' and that the words come right from my heart, God alone knows. John, I would have written to you long before, but my pride forbade it, for I thought I would wait and see if you loved or cared anything for me, for I thought if you did that you would write or send for me, but when I saw that you did not, it worried me, too, but still I felt that I would not humble myself enough to write. I thought if you did not care anything for me I would not let you know I cared enough for you to write; but it was pride and pride alone; but it had a fall, and I felt as if I had passed through a fiery furnace and came out cleansed, for I feel like a different person. Everybody says it has been the making of me to pass through what I have. Many and many a time have I repented of the step I took in the month of August, when I left the city of Brooklyn. Many a time I have prayed that I might once again be placed back to that time. Oh! how differently would I act.

Now I can see that I was wholly to blame—alas! when too late, I am afraid. John, you know all, you know everything that has transpired from the time I left you up to the present time, therefore it would be useless to say anything concerning my life for the past six months, only that I am not past reformation, but have steadied down and want to live a virtuous life the rest of my days, and the only one I want to spend them with is my husband, for we are the same to each other as on that October morning when we were pronounced man and wife. Then let us forgive as we hope to be forgiven by that Higher One. Now, John, I know that your mother or any of your family would never speak to me or forgive me, but if my future life will ever be the means of restoring the peace again that once existed between your folks and me, I am willing to do anything, sacrifice everything to live so that they will once more recognize me and term me their daughter and sister. I love them all; but, oh! what hellish spirit ever took possession of me I know not; but, oh! John, forgive me, take me back, and though they discard me, remember I am your wife.

"Now, John, write to me, for God's sake; write for the love you once bore me; write, let me know if you are done with me forever or not, for suspense is killing; but, oh, if you ever hope to be forgiven by God, forgive your wife, and let us once more live together and dwell in harmony and peace.

"Now, John, I send my love to you, and 'Oh, forgive me!' is my prayer.

"John, forgive! But you will have to follow the directions, as no one knows me by any other name. Nevertheless I am your wife. Good-by! From your wife,

"OLIVIA.

"Direct: MAUD COLES, No. 13 Division street, Rochester."

"Rochester, ...

"My dear husband,—I call you so because I have the right to, but, oh, how I have abused that right that I am not worthy of, John. As I sit writing to-day my heart is near breaking and my eyes are filled with tears; and though I have written to you once and heard nothing from you, still I cannot, will not, give you up. Oh, John, I am one of the most miserable and unhappy beings that ever lived. I wish I were dead, and I wish I had died before I ever used you as I did. I do from the bottom of my heart. I shall write just I feel, and as I have felt since I left the path of virtue and abused the only protector and friend, for you were mine for life.' I don't think any one, after doing as I have done, ever has peace of mind. I am sure I do not. I dream of you most every night, and the other night I had a fearful dream, and I will tell you some other time what it was. John, I was talking about you to-day, and I was saying if you would only take me back and live with me, that I would do anything for you. I would beg on my hands and knees. I would do anything to come back and live with you. I would be through life what you would wish me to be. It lays in your power to determine my future end. If you will forgive me and take me back, I will always do right, and you will never have cause to repent it. You say to yourself that I promised once before. This is only the second offense, and if we do not forgive each other on earth for such trivial offense, 'as we may say,' when compared with our wickedness in the eyes of God, how can we ever expect to be forgiven for the manifold sins we commit daily? and, John, I am truly repentant, and what I say is not an impulse of the moment, but I have long thought it over, and God, who alone knows the heart, knows that I want to be forgiven, and that I love you and want to live with you again; and He knows that mine has been a sad and bitter experience, and I am steadied down and profited by it. When I am in trouble and feel unhappy, then it is that I think of you, and all that keeps me up is the

239

cheering thought that at some day you will forgive me and live with me again; but if you should write that I need have no such thought, that you were done with me forever, it would kill me; for, as I have said before, all I care to live for is you, and I do not want to live if you do not forgive me; but, John, you shall never be aught else to me than my husband, and I hope in time to soften your heart towards me, for I want to come back and live with you. I want you to forgive me, for I love you, John, I do; and write to me and say-that I am forgiven. Write, if it is only to say that you are done with me forever, for suspense is killing. I am going to write to Maria and aunt Em to-day, to see how far their influence will go. Oh, John, forgive me! I am your lawful wife, and do not be influenced by any one, for, John, think what I was when you married me—pure and virtuous. I will always be good, and be for the rest of my life a fond and affectionate wife. John, I've got no friends, nobody to love or care for me, but I have got a husband, and it grieves me when I read over my old letters which you wrote to me before we were married, 'as I was to-day,' to think of the words of love and promises, and enjoyment we were to take; but, alas! the devil had possession of me. But now I will throw all things aside but the love and interest of my husband. Oh, John, for my sake, forgive me! for God's sake, forgive me, and I will always be a Christian: if not I will end my days in misery! John, write to me; do write immediately and forgive your erring wife,

"OLIVIA.

"Direct: OLIVIA, 13 Division street, Rochester. N. Y."

To the request contained in the above letters the husband felt he could not comply, as he learned that she was really attached to the immoral life which she was leading; and he was also deeply overcome at finding that her own father, instead of devoting his life to his daughter's redemption, should have actually perpetrated the horrible crime of consigning his own child to a fashionable den of infamy. Detective Rogers, of Rochester, by the directions of Commissioner Hebbard, arrested the defendant in Madame Eagan's house, as being the inmate of a house of prostitution; but she was suffered to escape on her paying a fine of twenty-five dollars, and return to her evil associations.

The plaintiff, coming to the conclusion that his wife was irreclaimable, through Howe & Hummel, sent on process to the sheriff of Monroe County, who served the same on the defendant, whilst she was actually in Madame Eagan's fashionable "Maison de joie," and lost no time ridding himself of the unwholesome partner of his joys. Was ever stranger history of man, wife and father recited?

FALL OF A YOUTHFUL, BEAUTIFUL AND ACCOMPLISHED WIFE

For some time past, Theodore Stuyvesant, one of our most prominent and wealthy lawyers, residing at East Seventh street, in this city, and having a splendid country seat in Queen's County, had cause to suspect the fidelity of his youthful, beautiful and accomplished wife, and, unhappily, these suspicions resulted in sad reality.

It appears that for some time past Mr. Stuyvesant and his wife were in the habit of giving magnificent entertainments to a numerous circle of legal, literary and theatrical acquaintances, at some of which some friends of the gentleman observed indications of undue familiarity on the part of the lady with a repeated and oft-invited guest.

The warnings were from time to time unheeded and disregarded by the too confiding and affectionate husband; but, on the afternoon of Thursday, harrowing facts were whispered

241

n his ear, which induced him to resort to the stratagem which resulted in the detection of his wife in grossly improper conduct.

On the day referred to, Mr. Stuyvesant informed his wife that legal business required his absence from the city, and would detain him, probably, ten or fifteen days; and she parted with him, bestowing so affectionate, and apparently loving farewell, as almost to remove the bitter and heart-rending suspicions which were then racking the breast of the injured husband. But, resolved on carrying out his intent, he simulated departure; but instead of leaving the city he remained at the house of a trusty friend, deliberating upon and maturing plans for the carrying out of that project, which was fated to reveal to him his wife's shame and his own dishonor.

After a lapse of some hours, Mr. Stuyvesant, with two friends, repaired to his residence, and having obtained admission through a rear sub-entrance, proceeded to his bed-chamber, on entering which, on tip-toe, he discovered his guilty wife in the embrace of her betrayer. The dishonored husband stood aghast and petrified—the wife endeavored to conceal herself—while her paramour was summarily ejected through the window by the avenging friends.

The husband, on recovering from the shock which had temporarily paralyzed him, left the house in solemn sadness, and absented himself from the presence of one who had so cruelly dishonored him, and for whom he had always evinced the warmest affection. Fearing lest reason should leave its throne, and he commit an act which would usher the soul of one he fondly loved un-shriven to her last account with all her imperfections on her head, poor Stuyvesant wept and left. His cup of bitterness was full. He repaired to the house of his friend where he passed the remainder of the night. In the morning, depressed and heart-broken, he returned to the home, once so happy and joyous, but now bleak and desolate, for the purpose of winding up domestic affairs, breaking up the house, dismissing the servants, and parting forever from the frail and erring woman, now wife to him but in name.

But the lady, instead of expressing contrition and supplicating for pardon for the irreparable wrong she had inflicted, assailed him with a torrent of vituperative abuse; and on his aged mother remonstrating with the guilty one upon the iniquity of her proceeding, she flew at her with the passion of a tigress, and cruelly beat and maltreated the aged lady, who is now verging on the grave. The neighbors, hearing the disturbance, called in the police, and Mrs. Stuyvesant was arrested and taken before Police Justice Mansfield at Essex Market Police Court, by whom she was committed to the Tombs for trial, in which prison the guilty lady—the lawyer's wife, the leader of fashionable society—was confined, a degraded and fallen woman. Proceedings for a divorce were at once instituted by Mr. Stuyvesant, and the judicial tribunal freed him from his unfortunate alliance. He, however, became heartbroken and shortly after died, the disgrace wrecking his home and nearly driving him insane.

A FRENCH BEAUTY'S TROUBLES

Twelve months before the proceedings in court, at the City of New Orleans, the presiding goddess of the most fashionable milliner's establishment of the place was Mary Blanchette. She was 21 years of age, tall, elegantly moulded, and possessed of a maturity of charms which made her seem three or four years older than she really was—with rich auburn hair, eyes of deep blue, large and rolling, and at times expressing an involuntary tenderness, which gave a voluptuous languor to her beautiful countenance. Her forehead was high and open; she had teeth of pearly whiteness, and possessed all the accomplishments which a French lady of *ion* need desire. It is not surprising, therefore, that Miss Blanchette should have captivated many admirers. Among those who paid homage at the shrine of beauty was a wealthy New York broker named Theodore Raub, who, possessing a handsome person, easy and elegant address, a melodious, yet manly voice, and a fascinating style of conversation, was received by the fair Marie with considerable favor, and he became a daily visitor, and ultimately her acknowledged lover.

Theodore Raub was a thorough man of the world, and deeply versed in all the mysteries and intricacies of the human heart: and especially was he an able anatomist of the female mind, which he could dissect and comprehend in an instant; and on the occasion of one of his visits to the beauteous French girl, after promising her marriage, the emotions which she experienced were not lost upon him. He perceived and deciphered them almost as soon as they had sprung into existence, and he saw in a moment that he had conquered. He had taken her hand, which she had not withdrawn, and when he pressed his burning kisses on her lips, the roseate blushes which suffused her cheeks were indicative of a deep and burning joy, and Raub well knew by the melting voluptuousness which beamed in her eyes that the hour had come when he could secure his victim.

Marie, awakening as it were from a dream, struggled to extricate herself, but he murmured impassioned words and vows and protestations in her ear, and with kisses he stifled the remonstrances and the beseechings which rose to her lips. But suddenly a strong sense of danger flashed into the mind of Marie; aye, and therewith a feeling that all this was wrong, very wrong; so that the virtuous principle which was innate in her woman's nature, asserted its empire that very instant. The immediate consequence was that, recovering all her presence of mind and casting off in a moment the voluptuous languor that had come over her, Marie tore herself from his embrace, exclaiming:

"Oh! Theodore, Theodore, is this your love for me? Would you ruin my body and my soul? Have pity on me. Have pity on me."

"Marie," said Theodore, "you love me not; you will drive me mad," he exclaimed, and he turned abruptly away, as if about to leave the room.

"He says that I love him not!" cried Marie, wildly, as she

sprang to her feet, and in another moment she was again clasped in her lover's arms.

Raub was not less expert in soothing the soul of Marie that was now stricken with remorse, and in quieting the anguished alarms that succeeded the moments of pleasure, and under reiterated promises of marriage, poor Marie retained within her own breast the secret of her ruin, until nature was about, in its own mysterious way, to proclaim her shame itself. As soon as Raub became aware of the fact that Marie was about to become a mother, he absconded from New Orleans, and instead of carrying out his repeated promises to the injured and ruined fair one, he came on to New York, leaving her unconscious and ignorant of his whereabout.

Marie, with that pertinacity which belongs peculiarly to a wronged and neglected woman, tracked him to this city, and demanded of him here the only atonement he could make before man and before God, namely—marriage. To all these entreaties Raub turned a deaf and defiant ear, and, at the suggestion of the French Consulate in this city, Marie retained the services of Howe & Hummel, and proceedings were taken which brought the contumacious Theodore to a satisfactory fiscal arrangement so far as Miss Blanchette was concerned.

LIFE ON THE BOSTON BOATS

Maria Wilson is a beautiful woman, and of that age at which most women are admired by men. She is courteous, affable and lady-like in her manner. So far as appearances go, she is just such a woman as most men would like to have for a wife. But appearances often deceive. Maria has fallen from grace, just as mother Eve did before her.

Her beauty has perhaps to her been her greatest misfortune; without it she might be virtuous; with it she certainly is not. Like many others of her erring sisters, see desires to live like a lady; to dress well; go to the opera in season; go to the theater and, indeed, to every other place where woman is likely to go.

Unfortunately for Miss Wilson, though born pretty, she was not born rich. The good things of this world were not given to her very abundantly. Work, she wouldn't. For some reason or other, certainly not a valid one, work appears degrading to some people. So it appeared to Miss Wilson.

What was she to do then? To steal would be to go to the penitentiary or the State prison. She didn't like to live in either, and yet she had taken the first erring step to go there. She is, in short, a fast woman, yet driven to a gay life in order to eke out a precarious existence, to gratify her love of dress. Fearing that she might get into the hands of the police if she staid in the city, Maria engages a passage on one of the Boston boats every alternate day, for the purpose of affording "noctural accommodation" to gentlemen not having their wives along. A day or two ago Maria, in company with another "lady" of like loose character, went on board one of the boats alluded to, each bent upon securing a state-room, if possible, but one at least was doomed to disappointment.

Miss Wilson's good looks made her a favorite with the officer of the boat, and she succeeded in obtaining a stateroom. Her partner, however, did not, and though unfortunate in this respect, she was well off in another way. She did succeed in "picking up a man," with whom she seemed to become suddenly in love.

After perambulating the boat decks and cabins for some time in flirtation and social chat, Maria's friend asked her if she would be kind enough to allow her the use of her state-room for a short time. Maria being lonely, and not feeling any disposition to retire, consented, when her friend and her company retired. They occupied the room for the best part of the night, and left Maria to do the best she could under the circumstances.

In the morning they left at an early hour, after which Maria feeling sleepy retired to take a "nap." She was not long in the room, however, when her friend tapped at the door and desired an interview. Though fatigued, Maria consented, when she was astonished at being accused of theft by one who seemed but a moment before to place the most unsolicited confidence in her. However, her friend (whose name we have not learned) lost her watch, and said she left it under the pillow, and accused Maria of stealing it. This was ingratitude indeed.

Maria, of course, denied any knowledge of the missing jewel, but her accuser was positive she left the watch under the pillow, and when the boat returned to this city she made the charge of theft against Maria before Justice Dowling, at the Tombs. Maria did not let her indignation run away with her senses, but shrewdly enough kept quiet and employed Counselor Howe to defend her.

When the case came up the attorney explained the whole circumstances to his Honor the Judge, and added that the complainant had also accused the colored waiter on board the boat of the theft. Of course under such a state of things there was but one course left, and Justice Howling, not wishing to prosecute an innocent though erring woman, allowed Maria Wilson to go her way rejoicing.

She left the court in company with her counsel to return to the abode of her sister, where, it is to be hoped, she will abandon her follies, live a life of virtue, and be forever a happy woman.

AN EIGHTY-YEAR-OLD "FENCE"

Before Justice Wandell, Hirsch Lowenthal of this city, was brought up for examination on the charge of being the receiver of $20,000 worth of gold watches and jewelry, burglarized in Baltimore. The case has had the attention of the court for some days, and the premises, briefly stated, are as follows: On the January date the store of Simeon J. Rudberg, of Baltimore, was entered by four men who secured the property in question. For a long time nothing was heard of the goods, but, eventually, they were traced to this city, and, following the same clew, Mr. Rudberg proceeded to Buffalo, where he had the pleasure of confronting two of the thieves, who were held in that lake city on a charge of shop-lifting. He identified them, and saw, moreover, in their company a very handsome woman who had been with them in Baltimore. The whereabouts of the other two burglars are unknown. So is that of the female. She was established, however, as the step-daughter of Hirsch Lowenthal, whose alleged conversation last Wednesday in a Division street beer saloon about the "loot" led to his arrest.

Happy thought! Division street is the place to speak about the partition of spoils.

Bad as it looked for Mr. Lowenthal, who is aged eighty years, he had a *petite* consolation in the fact that he was defended by Mr. Hummel. The prisoner came out of the pen in a tottering way and leaned against the rail. Hirsch Lowenthal is bowed with eighty years that have dashed over him like waves, and he seemed caught in the tangling undertow of death. There was no evidence in his appearance of being a "fence." He looked rather an aged Hebrew who simply wished to go his way. The white semi-circle of whisker under his chin, the trembling hands, the bald head, like a globular map with the veins as rivers, all attested extreme decrepitude. He was dressed in a light suit of fluttering linen that blew about him as if his legs were topmasts and he was a ship running in close-reefed on a stormy coast. He has lived in this city for many years, and has been twice married. The second wife and he did not get along very well, and have abided apart for the last five months. Theresa, who is the central figure in this romance, is the daughter of the second wife by another husband. She is married to a burglar who luxuriates in the euphonious name of "Sheeny Dave." Dave is one of the two men identified in Buffalo, and resides now at Auburn at the expense of the State. When they saw the Baltimore merchant in Buffalo Dave and his companion came sagely to the conclusion that to plead guilty to the local charge and avoid extradition for the burglary would be about the best thing to do. They reckoned without their host. When the New York State term is finished they will be waited upon by Maryland officials. It is sometimes embarrassing to be popular and sought after by everyone.

Perhaps it would be a safe rule in life to avoid drinking beer if you have had anything to do with stolen goods. On last Wednesday evening, Mr. Lowenthal visited a Division street saloon in company with a villainous looking man who had but lately returned from Sing Sing. They ordered the loquacious lager and fell into an easy strain of conversation. After touching upon the weather, crops, trade, etc., Mr. Lowenthal fell to speaking of some goods in his house, the proceeds of a Baltimore burglary in last January. At the next table sat Mr. Rosenberg, who listened. It was Mr. Rosenberg who gave this damaging evidence before Justice Wandell. He was forced to admit, however, that the aged gentleman had not mentioned the name of the Baltimore firm, although he had specified the quality of the goods. Mr. Hummel claimed that as the commodity spoken of was only material in general and had not been identified as Mr. Rudberg's particular property, and that, furthermore, as there was no evidence tracing the stuff to the old man, who had merely chatted pleasantly about some burglarized property to which he had helped himself while occupying a fiduciary position, there was no case and asked for the discharge of his client. The prosecution claimed that the fact of Theresa being the step-daughter of Mr. Lowenthal, and the wife of one of the identified burglars at the same time, taken in connection with the conversation in the beer shop, during which direct allusion was made to a burglary in Baltimore in January, made a good foundation for procedure. Judge Wandell pondered, and then Mr. Hummell pushed his side energetically, using tons of cold sarcasm and barrels of withering scorn. It was the sapling shielding the blasted oak, one of the youngest, and certainly the smallest counselor thundering forth in behalf of the oldest prisoner.

"Oh, by all means, put the gentleman from Sing Sing on the stand," he said, "but let's have him sworn first. It is precisely what I desire. Nothing would charm me half so much."

So they swore the jail-bird, made him confess that he had served his term fully, and then told him to step down and out. His evidence was not needed. Mr. Rosenberg was raked fore and aft, but he stuck to his story. When the diminutive counsellor intimated that he was worse than the prisoner, the witness smiled serenely and winked at the magistrate as if it was a good joke.

"If he talked that way to me I'd punch his head," said the Baltimore man in a whisper.

No one could tell where Theresa was, although weeks had been spent searching for her. And yet she is no ordinary woman. Twenty-three years of age, elegantly formed, dark, lustrous eyes, satiny coils of black hair, olive complexion, seed-pearl teeth, full red lips, small hands and feet, and graceful carriage. She wears diamond drops at her ears and sparkling rings upon her fingers. Her favorite attire, as if life were a perpetual dressing for dinner, is a black-corded silk, fitted close to the figure, made high in the neck, with a trembling edge of lace at the throat clustering about a diamond catch whose brilliancy it veils. This is not a fancy portrait, but word for word from an enthusiastic admirer of Lowenthal's step-daughter. But where is she? It is not known. Where is the John Sherman letter to Anderson? Where is the Boston Belting Company's money? Where is Tom Collins? And where's Emma Collins? An impenetrable gloom shrouds them all.

After a rather protracted lunch on his eye-glasses, Judge Wandell, in reply to Mr. Hummel's motion, rendered his decision to the effect that there was not sufficient evidence to hold aged Mr. Lowenthal. The octogenarian heard it with delight, and came as near skipping like a lamb from the court-room as is possible for one of his age.

SHOPPERS' PERILS

Much of the time of the Court of Special Sessions was absorbed in the trial of a case of some importance to ladies who make purchases. A pleasant-faced looking woman, named Ellen Whalen, was arraigned for petit larceny in having stolen an accordeon from the store of Ehrich's on Eighth Avenue. The main evidence against her was that of Alexander G. Sisson, the detective of that establishment, who testified that the prisoner took the property from one of the counters while he was looking at her, and that he followed her on the street and found it in her possession hid under her shawl.

Mr. A. H. Hummel, who appeared as counsel for the accused, cross-examined the detective at some length and gleaned that there were others in close proximity at the time the property was taken, and among them a Miss Maggie McKenna, a saleslady, who was not, however, in court.

Mrs. Whalen was next called by Counselor Hummel, and deposed that she lived in West Seventeenth street, and went to Ehrich's to purchase the accordeon and showed a marked receipt which she claimed was given to her with her change. That the detective followed her out of the store, treated her roughly on taking her into Custody, and kept her confined fifteen minutes in a cellar before he brought a policeman to arrest her. Mr. Doyle, her landlord, vouched for her general good character, and Mr. Hummel then made a stirring appeal to the court for his client's discharge. He characterized the arrest as a gross outrage, for which the jury would render instant acquittal, and stigmatized the private detective's testimony as unworthy of belief without corroboration, saying that the higher courts had so decided in many cases, as it was clearly evident the desire of such employees to secure convictions for theft in order to retain their place. Mr. Hummel also adverted to the negligence of the real complainants not appearing, and the absence of the saleslady who should have been sent here by them, so that the court might have had a full and ample investigation. With much feeling counsel urged a dismissal of the complaint, and an honorable discharge of the prisoner.

The court remained in consultation for some time and announced a verdict of "not guilty," which was greeted with a round of applause from the assembled multitude. Mrs. Whalen thanked the court and fervently pressed Mr. Hummel's hand in gratitude and left the courtroom, accompanied by her three children and a host of friends.